# CUBA RISING
An American Insider's Perspective

BY

JONATHAN SHOWE

GLOBAL INSIGHTS PRESS

# CUBA RISING

Published by Global Insights Press
316 Mid Valley Center, Suite 105
Carmel, CA 93923
www.CubaRising.net

First Edition
January 2010

Printed in Canada on 100% post-consumer waste, recycled paper

Book and cover design by The History Company

Library of Congress Control Number: 2009912061

ISBN: 978-0-615-32361-9

# CUBA RISING

## DEDICATION

*To the people of good will in the United States and Cuba who have worked so hard to end a half-century of irascible fumbling between our governments, and who will succeed in bringing about a mutually beneficial normalization of relations between our countries and their people.*

# CUBA RISING

# CUBA RISING

# CONTENTS

# CUBA RISING

## ACKNOWLEDGEMENTS

For the past 12 years, I have been accumulating the observations, insights and interviews that are reflected in the following pages. Imagine a video of an explosion of information, slowly played *backwards,* until it coalesced into a reasonably coherent whole. Hundreds of friends, acquaintances and complete strangers have contributed importantly, far more than I could name individually, and to all of them I am deeply grateful.

Many stand out, nevertheless. Among the Cuban people who have shared so much, whose first names only am I comfortable revealing, are Ileana, Adela, Norberto, Turcios, Sylvia, Dionis, Susel, Orestes, Manuel, Carlos, Rafael, and Delio. And in the States, playing key roles ranging from wordsmithing to rousing encouragement have been Elena Kornetchuk, Bill Daniels, Jan Wingad, Mona Espy, Mark Baer, Kitty Koenig, Lynne Boyd, Michael Hemp's excellent book design and counsel, David Wechsler, Louise Wechsler, Lewis Leader's fine editing, and Miguel.

For those Cuba aficionados who might offer additional information or arrive at different conclusions, let me emphasize that all sins of omission and commission are mine alone.

# CUBA RISING

## INTRODUCTION

Cuba is amber-colored rum with a like smoothness. Cuba is rhythmic salsa music so pervasive that hips sway slightly on every street corner. Cuba is tendrils of aromatic cigar smoke curling upwards in the parks where old men under frayed Panama hats gather. Cuba is an architectural wonderment with continuous allusions to the countries that seduced her starting half a thousand years ago.

Indeed, being Cuba is as much a mental state as a nation state. How else can I explain how a country that barely registers by most national measuring sticks seems perennially to have a leading role on the world stage? Cuba is six-tenths of one percent of the size of the world's largest country; her population is fewer than one-tenth of one percent of the world's most populous country, and the size of her military force ranks 74th in the world, at two-tenths of one percent of the world's largest, China.

Yet Cuba has brought the world to the brink of nuclear extinction, she is a leader among nations in many categories of the health and education of her people, and she has stood toe-to-toe, eyeball-to-eyeball, with the world's greatest superpower for 50 years and not retreated an inch.

In the words of Robert Redford in the classic film *Butch Cassidy and the Sundance Kid,* "Who are those guys?" and what is this place?

I am bombarded with sights and sounds and information that my mind races to synthesize. The result is not tidy; it's more of a kaleidoscope of impressions. For much about Cuba is confusing, contradictory, ironic, enigmatic or opaque. World-class modern biotechnology research centers abut lush farm fields that continue to be plowed by lumbering oxen. Bustling modern brass and glass tourist hotels are served by jostling throngs of battered half-century-old taxis. From one of the world's most sleek airport terminals, I can see the domestic fleet that includes World War II vintage DC-3's and biplanes that are older than all but their most venerable passengers.

Cuba can be described as being a state of mind in a more literal sense as well. Although it is a sovereign state in the community of nations, it is small and woefully lacking in natural resources; its economy is in massive default; its industrial capacity ranks low, and its economic system has been consigned to the dustbin of history.

Yet Cuba stands quite tall among nations. To Americans, at least, Cuba has seemed to be practically omnipresent on the world stage – certainly since 1959. How? Why? Precisely because of its dearth of physical assets, Cuba has proven to be remarkably adept and agile by resourceful use of its collective brainpower and ideological passion under the half-century long reign of the irrepressible Fidel Castro. It could be reasonably described as a state propelled by mental power. Being Cuba is largely a state of mind.

In reality, Cuba is a state of mind in both respects. It is sensory overload and it is a nation driven by mental assets more so than by its tangible assets. What is surprising about Cuba is not that it has experienced profound difficulties in recent years but that it has functioned as well as it has.

Sure, I can go online and read page after dry page of (questionable) statistics about the Cuban economy, geography and annual rainfall – courtesy of the CIA or creative Cuban bureaucrats. Or I can visit a bookstore and find a dozen or more excellent tourist guidebooks about Cuba, all of which will describe in exquisite detail the hundreds of hotels, restaurants and obscure watering holes that I could never visit in a lifetime. And there have been some fine novels and feature films about Cuba, Che

Guevara, the Revolution and other snapshots of poignant moments in Cuba's remarkable history.

But I have found, and here I want to share, a different genre. A narrative painting, if you will, of the perspective of a frequent visitor to this unique island. This canvas with pages is neither realism nor abstraction. It blends the visual, audible, aromatic, verbal, intellectual and countless other impacts, impressions and yarns of an eager and serious student of Cuba. It is my muse.

Cuba's palette is a rainbow of ever-changing colors. It can dazzle and it can drone, uplift and depress, as it continuously bombards me with new insights. It amazes, confounds and seems surreal. But it is never static, always in motion offering new images. Regrettably, mere facts seldom illuminate much about Cuba. How deficient, for example, would be a clinical description of about 11 million people whose genes have been scrambled for 500 years with native Indian, Spanish, African, Chinese and fragments of a host of other ethnicities? How can a percentage describe what is a flowing spectrum of fascinating skin tones to the eye? Only by analogy, only by an impression.

In the renowned cigar factories of Cuba, there are a very few seasoned experts in discerning color who sort thousands of cigars daily to ensure that *only* those of identical hues recline comfortably together in a box of *Habanos*. Incredibly, I am told their long-trained eyes can distinguish *over 70 shades of brown!* I suppose I should have asked one of those old gentlemen to craft the pages describing the racial mix in Cuba. For there is no better way to visualize today's blend than as a rainbow of browns, just like in the sorting room of the Cohiba factory.

My goal is to make it perfectly clear that *nothing* about Cuba is perfectly clear. For the first-time traveler, let this raise your comfort level a little and prepare you to return baffled, with more questions than answers about the country. To the veteran traveler, you may find the cacophony to be all too familiar. And for the merely curious, rest assured that Cuba is as far from the demonized versions of its critics as it is from the rapturous praise of its enthusiasts.

While you will find this book reflects no particular political agenda, it cannot help but to be subtly influenced by the values and filters that any observer applies. I have traveled to Cuba some 75 times, sometimes "under the radar" and sometimes with the burdensome documentation required by the U.S. government of its citizens who choose to travel to this "forbidden" land. Those many visits are a *lot* for an American. In fact, one of Cuba's cabinet ministers recently asked a mutual friend, "How the hell does this guy Showe keep getting to Cuba?"

I have spent thousands of hours with an enormous variety of Cubans, from humble farmers to heads of enterprises, from dissidents to top government officials. My own filters include a graduate degree in international relations, years involved in international issues at highest levels of the U.S. government, and still more years dealing with global commerce in the private sector. I've been registered as a Republican, as a Democrat and as an Independent. I don't believe that I carry much political baggage, and my skills as an observer in the international realm have been honed by travel to over 60 countries. In the end, my observations are little more than a basis for you to hone yours.

In my opinion, the political system of Cuba is not *so* diabolical that it has no redeeming features, and the socialist economy is certainly not *so* good that it has given rise to legions of imitators. Cuba is a distinctive blend. It spawns highs and lows, good and wicked, the authentic as well as cheap reproductions. At the risk of mixing metaphors, it is a stew, much like a Cuban *ajiaco*. It has been stirred by (far too) many chefs, both foreign and domestic. And the outcome has been splendidly unpredictable. Come dine with me…

# CUBA RISING

# CUBA RISING

CHAPTER 1

## CUBA'S MILIEU

Being in Cuba is a marvel. I step onto a crumbling sidewalk in Havana and I'm immediately enveloped in an array of impressions that draw a smile on my face. As a 1953 Packard chugs by belching fumes and smoke, I notice the brilliance of the sunlight and the pastels adorning the colonial architecture and the soft salsa rhythms and aromas of cigars. It is the gentlest sort of embrace that does not command my attention but rather creates a soft context for all I see and do. It is the essence of the personality of Cuba, and it could no more be duplicated elsewhere than Don Quixote could topple a windmill.

Why? Because Cuba is the sum of countless disparate parts, much like a mosaic: historical, environmental, topographic, cultural, political, religious and many more. They are ever changing and evolving, not lending themselves to academic typecasting but rather creating a hybrid unique in the hemisphere, indeed, unique in the world.

Above all, the country is its people. Over the centuries racial and ethnic groups have mixed and mingled and created a bewildering and beautiful array of skin hues and deeper personal characteristics. Nowhere is this more evident than in beaming smiles and proud bearing. As will become more evident as you read on, Cubans may have considerable to be proud of but far less to smile about – yet their contagious joy is something that does soften the heart of even the most hardened visitor to the island.

A particularly memorable experience comes to mind. One fine summer day I was flying from Havana to the Isla de la Juventud, a short hop off the south coast. We were bumping along in a vintage DC-3, a twin-propeller airplane whose heyday was 60 years earlier. My advice: Be wary of flying in planes older than you are, especially if you have reached middle age. We had a routine approach, a soft landing, and were cruising along the runway when the right landing gear crumpled like an old tin can. The plane swerved, spun crazily around and stopped abruptly in the swaying green grass alongside the runway. We disembarked in a hurry, no injuries, no fire, and terra firma never felt quite so good to me.

What did I do after a crash landing once my adrenalin had run its course? Taking a photo seemed to be still within my capability, so I backpedaled far enough to frame this giant ruptured duck in a snapshot. However, as I was focusing the shot, I noticed the pilot and copilot racing across the field toward me, arms waving and legs churning. Looks bad for the memoirs, I thought. Likely they want no photographic record of this scandalous incident that *Yanquis* probably would publicize to slander the hallowed regime in Cuba! I was prepared for the worst when they suddenly stopped about 10 strides before reaching me. As if they were appearing on stage to an encore of thunderous applause, they threw their arms over each other's shoulders and beamed their broadest smiles while posing for a photo with their disabled plane in the background! I am convinced that only in Cuba could the pilots reach back and be joyful after a crash landing.

Let us assume that my impression is correct, that perhaps among Cubans there is a special gene for joy. In part this happiness flows from both a real and an imagined sense of family. All appear to revel in time spent with family members. Nothing is too precious to share nor too mundane to discuss, no amount of time together can be too much. Family gatherings are frequent and invariably seem to range from fawned-over infants to scrubbed and scrambling children, proud parents and the elderly matriarchs and patriarchs so happy to be holding court.

What is perceived, to foreigners and Cubans alike, is an extended sense of family that encompasses practically everyone on the block, in the neighborhood, in the city, province and country. While I may be a typical gregarious American, I confess to having little more in common with my fellow countrymen in Montana than a shared wariness of cold winters. And I will forgive them if they feel a similar lack of camaraderie for me and my West Coast peculiarities.

But Cubans? Well, I have seen the pain etched on their faces when they learned a neighbor had fallen ill, people in a distant region had been victimized by crop failures, or another unknown rafter had perished in the Florida Straits. And I have witnessed their joy when some scarce dollars found their way to a friend, a corrupt official got his due, or a hurricane's path spared a faraway part of the island. It gave new meaning to the concept of an extended family. Nowhere is this better embodied than in the perennial popularity of the melodic Cuban song *Guantanamera*. A lovely ballad of the heartbreak of a peasant woman from the eastern province of Guantanamo, it practically brings tears to the eyes of Cubans everywhere, not just to those from remote Guantanamo.

Perhaps living on an island contributes to a sense of fellowship. Especially when that island has been under various forms of assault from outside forces for the last five centuries. From pirates, colonial powers, disease, hurricanes, and worse. I am confident that an aspiring Ph.D. candidate will explain this phenomenon more fully some day. Meanwhile, I am keenly aware that family is a source of strength and inspiration on the island. Thus, *divided* families, a harsh reality of the Revolution and its aftermath, have been one of the most tragic, debilitating and painful realities among Cubans for three generations.

No trip to Cuba could pass without facing the omnipresence of sports. They seem to be on everyone's mind and are by no means limited to men. Are Cubans absolutely wild about sports? (Is a bullfrog waterproof?) Can you drive a thousand yards without seeing a baseball field? (Not likely). Have you found the special corner of Central Park that is devoted solely to spontaneous noisy public debate about baseball? (Don't miss it – passions run high with animated, stomp-on-your-hat enthusiasm.) Are you aware that in the quadrennial Olympics Cuba has a record of winning more medals than all of Latin America put together? (True.) That Cuba, in the 2008 Beijing Olympics, won medals equivalent to one per 465,000 population while the USA lagged far behind with only one per 2.7 million? (Also true).

Cubans verifiably excel in both team and individual sports, with a long history of world champions such as Olympic heavyweight boxers Teofilio Stevenson and Felix Savon. Athletes like these are heroes known to all, sought out by kids with scruffy scraps of paper in search of an autograph, which seem always to be graciously given and accompanied by a broad smile and a pat on a young shoulder. The popularity of sports in Cuba relates to many quirks. It is a small country, and *everybody* knows *somebody* who knows a famous athlete. The jocks are humble, would not stand out in a crowd (but for some of them being super-sized), and it is known that they are not "apart," not celebrities as opposed to mere mortals. Indeed, every competitive athlete in Cuba remains on the employment roles at whatever position they occupied before: a plumber, a farmer, a factory worker. And their salary is the *same* as that of their early job description. No special pay grade for super jocks; nope, the same $17 per month they would otherwise be earning as a carpenter or truck driver. It is true that leading athletes do enjoy some special perks not commonly available, such as permission to buy an automobile or assignment to favorable housing. Those small privileges are applauded, even by those who are denied them.

This egalitarian feature of sports was etched in my memory on a sadly revealing occasion a few years ago. I was fortunate to have been enjoying cocktails and hors d'oeuvres on a splendid yacht moored in Marina Hemingway. Several of the country's best-known athletes were aboard and were enormously enjoying this rare glamorous moment. When the time came to go our separate ways, a friend and athlete whose name was known to every Cuban approached me shyly. He was the Cuban equivalent of a Babe Ruth or a Muhammad Ali, and he tugged my sleeve and humbly asked if he could take home to his family a scraggly bunch of green grapes left over on a platter. Seventeen bucks a month just doesn't go as far as it used to, I suppose.

Perhaps because their athletes have an impressive record in international competitions, Cubans applaud the universality of sports and have largely succeeded in insulating it from the political realm. It helps that Fidel is a huge sports fan, especially of baseball. I recall one fine day when I was among a group of Americans scheduled to meet with a dozen of Cuba's finest athletes. Until, that is, Fidel summoned virtually all of the country's leading sports stars to a lunch he decided to host on short notice!

Politics, unfortunately, recently sometimes rears its head in sports. From time to time, nationally acclaimed athletes have defected while competing abroad. And starting in 2006, the too politically correct Ministry of Sports has refused permission for groups of Americans to either meet with athletes or engage in informal sports events. In 2007, I requested that a little group of visiting Americans could play a baseball game with a Cuban factory team. That I had to make a formal request at all struck me as bizarre. That we were *denied* permission struck me as outrageous. It was a regrettable sign of the times when the acclaimed universality of sports was sacrificed on the alter of political bickering. As the pendulum swung back in 2008, permission was granted for baseball games between school kids from Cuba and the United States.

On an island where natural beauty may abound but natural resources are scarce, it is understandable that two crops for which Cuba is known worldwide are embedded in the national consciousness: sugar and tobacco.

Sugar, in particular, is associated both with some of the country's greatest prosperity and some of her most conspicuous commercial failures.

The vast expanses of red soil across Cuba, in combination with her tropical climate, have proven to be friendly to few crops, but sugar cane has flourished. For centuries the fields of green spiked leaves, which can tower over a man and run to the horizon, have dominated the rural landscape. Great green undulating waves of plants rustle in balmy breezes. But today the crop has fallen from grace, if not from the national psyche. Mostly what remains is a spiderweb network of idle and rusting narrow-gauge railways that once hauled millions of tons of cane from the fields to the sugar mills. What happened?

Starting in the early colonial era and booming by the early 19th century, vast plantations prospered on the backs of slaves. But even today in Cuba rural labor may cost only 75 cents a day – not exactly what I would term prohibitive. What happened was more efficient competitors elsewhere and sugar beets. That crop results in an identical product to spoon into your morning coffee, can be produced in a wide range of climates, lends itself to mechanized efficiencies, and yields considerably more per acre than sugar from cane.

The inevitable decline of sugar as a profitable crop in Cuba was postponed for a century by politically motivated foreign import quota allocations with subsidized prices being paid to Cuba, first by the Americans and for another 30 years by the Soviets.

Oh, the Cuban effort was indeed heroic in search of the perennially elusive 10 million ton crop. Tens of thousands of inexperienced "volunteer" city dwellers were dispatched to the fields to help with the harvest. Urban students were relocated to the countryside so they could spend part of each day working the fields. Zealous *Fidelistas* from abroad came to toil and sweat alongside their comrades. Scarce resources from other important sectors of the economy were diverted and left those neglected areas in chaos. And enterprising executives found ways to monetize virtually every bit of the harvest by converting residuals to wallboard for furniture, and extractions for chemical and pharmaceutical purposes. All to naught.

In 2005, the government threw in the proverbial towel and closed almost two-thirds of the country's sugar mills and idled a proportionate amount of land. The crop was allowed to muddle along at a record annual low of 1.1 million tons, just enough to meet domestic demand and satisfy essential export commitments. Hundreds of thousands of workers, who had the unprecedented good fortune to have their wages continued, although unemployed, were retrained or redeployed to grow alternative crops. Only seldom now am I able to enjoy the sweet evocative aroma of the harvested cane fields being burned before replanting. Although sugar always will remain poignantly in the minds of Cubans, one of its derivatives may be more enduring – Cuban rum.

Who among us could fail to associate rum with Cuba and salsa and balmy tropical evenings? Bacardi may be better known in some circles than Cuba itself. Now amigos, true rum devotees are not talking about those pastel tropical drinks with a pink paper umbrella stabbed through a chunk of pineapple and a splash of belly wash for good measure. No, I am talking about some of the planet's most exquisite rum, either light or dark, and aged to your preference – three years, seven years, how about *15* years? So smooth that it truly glides across your palate on its mission to offer a warm sensation that perfectly dovetails with mild Caribbean evenings. Unfortunately for Cuba, Bacardi has prevailed in a decades-long legal battle over rights to its name. Not surprisingly, Bacardi has been found to own its name, although it exited Cuba after the Revolution in 1959. So the Cuban brand and label have been changed to Havana Club. But please trust me on this: The special contents of those distinctive bottles are still so fine.

For many folks, a glass of rum in one hand seems to be more finely balanced if there is a cigar in the other. And what of Cuba's milieu is more evocative than the tantalizing words "Cuban cigar"? In reality, it could be a single four-syllable word. It is said that the Spanish *conquistadores* discovered the native Indians inhaling smoke from these leaves – and they probably had big grins on their faces, as well. Before long, smoking tobacco had become an upper-class indulgence in Europe.

Fast forward several centuries, and Cuban cigars continue to enjoy a cachet unlike any others. To true aficionados they are simply known as *Habanos*. Certainly, there are fine hand-rolled cigars created with carefully nurtured tobacco leaves in other countries. You are challenged, however, to name one that elicits the same magic and nostalgia and remarkable smoking experience as does the premier Cohiba. Perhaps it is true that Cuba's unique combination of soil and climate and expertise, found especially in the western province of Pinar del Rio, lends itself to an inimitable cigar smoking experience.

So now I am imagining myself in Havana, relaxed and comfortably seated at a sidewalk café with a glass of rum (I recommend it "neat," or straight) in one hand and a fine cigar in the other. What more could I possibly desire? Little more. Because the pleasing rhythms of salsa surround me. Music is simply everywhere in Cuba. As I stroll from block to block, I stroll from salsa to son to bolero to jazz. Live bands, CDs, the radio. Rhythmic tunes seem to emerge from doorways and windows so often that it becomes the occasional quiet moment that I notice, not the music. During those rare times when the traffic noise bars the melodies, just watch the gals waiting to cross the street. Hips that sway gently from the music in their minds are merely the epicenter as the entire body is in motion. As a result of countless personal observations, I can confirm that the *least* coordinated Cuban (male *or* female) between the age of 3 and 97 indeed has more natural rhythm in their pinky finger than I will ever have in my entire body.

In an attempt to overcome that genetic handicap, some years ago I attempted to engage some salsa instructors for my amigos and me, so we wouldn't make complete fools of ourselves when we ventured forth onto the dance floor at our intended salsa club. To assure that I would not be accused of subterfuge or engaging in some prohibited form of creeping capitalism, I directed my request through an official travel agency. The response that I expected in a minute, then in an hour, then in a day, was not forthcoming. So I gently pressed on. In response I got a stern look and a terse comment, "That will not be possible." Although I have learned never to accept the first couple of *impossibles* from Cuban officials, I could discern real problems from his frown. Much later I was advised that the hierarchy in the chain of decision-making had concluded that I was *really* trying to engage a gaggle of hookers, and they wanted no part of my nefarious scheme. Such can be the level of mistrust and misunderstanding that sometimes resides just beneath the surface in a land that can be fraught with "political correctness" despite, or perhaps because of, the many temptations and considerable beauty of the country.

As I sit in my "virtual" sidewalk café, immensely enjoying my cigar, rum and salsa music, my eyes carry me to an amazing streetscape. Assume I am planted in Habana Vieja (the center of the original city), certainly among the most interesting places for the casual observer. Before me rumble vintage American cars likely to be older than I. It is as if the city has been transformed into a living automobile museum. There goes a '48 Packard. Wow, isn't that an Edsel? How come that '53 Chevy has Caddy tail fins? It's an absolute hoot to see and never fails to bring a smile to my face! For the Cubans, however, it is called transportation. You see, since the Revolution the national inventory of cars, for private citizens, has been frozen. How do they manage to keep them running? Well, I suppose automobiles were simpler a half-century ago. Nevertheless, I bet Cuba would be the hands-down winner of the automobile mechanics Olympics.

Not long ago I was waiting to meet a friend in front of a hotel in Havana. Along came what I was told was a 1919 Ford pickup truck, in mint condition with a flawless cherry red paint job. The driver parked it near the front door, and I drew closer for a look at what I assumed to be the first arrival for an antique car show. It was magnificent, impeccable, like new. Ten minutes later the driver reappeared with another fellow, and between them they were wrestling with a big old mattress. Which they heaved into the back of the pickup truck. And then they drove away. I was dumbfounded, speechless. They had an incomparably rare pickup truck more than 85 years old and they were using it *to lug stuff* around!

Beyond the challenges of an automobile fleet frozen in time, the owners take immense pride both in keeping them rolling and in their appearance. I recall one fine Sunday morning when I opened the curtains of my hotel room to behold seven, yes *seven*, pristine Edsels parked on display! Shortly afterwards I went to meet a friend who drove over in his 1960s vintage Soviet Lada. To be charitable, it was an exception to the "pristine" rule. Hopelessly dented, shredded fabrics inside, holes in the floorboards revealing the street below, and apparently held together mainly by the rust. I noticed that he handed a boy a coin as he walked over to greet me. Ever curious, I asked why. With a straight face, he replied, "He'll keep an eye on it and make sure nothing happens to my car." Leapin' lizards, I thought. Surely, everything and anything cruel and unusual that could possibly befall a car already has happened to that one.

Not only cars but also motorcycles can be astonishing in Cuba. To my surprise I discovered a Harley-Davidson club (unsanctioned) in Havana. No, they haven't much of an agenda, but they do have an old garage where they rebuild vintage Harleys from bits and pieces found in the countryside and where they can exchange tales and dream motorcycle dreams as bikers everywhere are prone to do. But not just *any* Harley nuts, and certainly not the wealthy middle-age dilettantes found in the States with bikes that easily cost the equivalent of 200 years of wages for a typical Cuban. No, Harley riders in Cuba are expected to have just leapt from the frames of a James Dean movie. The scruffier the better, leather jacket required, no helmet permitted, and long hair to be tousled in the wind.

Perhaps my oddest encounter with a motorcycle in Cuba really falls into that notorious category of "the best photos I never took." While driving along the Malecon, that splendid undulating ribbon of concrete that winds along the seafront, a motorcycle with a sidecar approached. Actually, that is not uncommon in Havana. What was mightily uncommon was that the two occupants had flame red long curly hair, large red rubber bulbs for noses and colorful clown costumes everywhere else! Can you imagine – two circus clowns on their way to a party, chugging along the Malecon in a 60-year-old motorcycle and sidecar. Hands down, that was the best picture I never took!

The streetscape, from which I have digressed, includes much more than vintage autos, crowded buses and throngs of people. It is framed with wonderful examples of architecture dating as far back as the 16th century and the colonial era. Happily, there is a substantial effort underway by the Office of the Historian of Havana to preserve and reconstruct large numbers of the historic buildings. Unhappily, it is a race against time (and Cuba is losing *this* race as the ravages of nature continue), and it is chronically short of funds. I see fine examples of other classic architectural styles, such as art deco, art nouveau, eclectic, the not-so-remarkable Bauhaus Soviet style, and even a few modern buildings. Havana itself could be cited as an architectural museum perhaps for two reasons. First, a series of Cuban governments apparently lacked either the money or the inclination, or both, to knock down and replace old buildings, and, second, the city has been built out in somewhat concentric circles. The old city is in the center and subsequent styles and centuries are reflected as one moves outward from the original center (Plaza de Armas).

Not so visible to the eye, but still swirling in the mindset of the Cuban people, are a host of other ponderables. How keenly in their consciousness, for example, is the memory and lingering presence of author Ernest Hemingway. For over 20 years (from 1939 until 1960) he resided mainly in Havana and crafted there some of his most famous works, including the exquisite portrait of a niche of Cuban life in *The Old Man and the Sea* and the acclaimed *For Whom the Bell Tolls*.

As legend has it, Hemingway and the local fisherman of Cojimar, still a quaint coastal village east of Havana, where he moored his boat *Pilar*, had a powerful bond. After a long day on the sparkling Caribbean, often they would retire together for beer and *mojitos* – the distinctive Cuban drink that features white rum, sugar, lime, sparkling water and mint – and to spin fishermen's yarns at their favorite watering hole in Cojimar, the wood-paneled bar La Terraza. And when Hemingway's fame resulted in the filming of *The Old Man and the Sea* in Cuba, in Cojimar, he insisted that his humble fishermen friends work with Spencer Tracey and play *themselves* in the film, rather than by professional extras.

So firm and enduring was the bond between them that, upon learning of his death, the Cubans were determined to memorialize him with a small open-air rotunda surrounding a bust of their famous friend. A sculptor was commissioned, and he traveled to Cojimar to meet with his "patrons" and secure funds for the project. Sadly, the fishermen had no money for such an ambitious venture. The sculptor, sensing the depth of their affection, volunteered to create the bust of Hemingway at no charge – provided the fisherman would at least provide to him the necessary materials. This, too, would seem to have been out of reach. Instead of abandoning their dream, however, each went back to his modest fishing boat and brought to the sculptor his reserve propeller. These were melted down and cast into the bronze memorial for their friend, which stands today in Cojimar by the sea he loved so much. Could there be any more wonderful testimony to the timeless bond among these old men of the sea?

Ironically, two of Cuba's true icons of the 20th century, Fidel Castro and Ernest Hemingway, met only once. Castro came into power in 1959, and Hemingway left Cuba in 1960, as his mental and physical health declined. The only time the men crossed paths was when Castro was invited by Hemingway to present trophies to the winners of the Tenth Annual Ernest Hemingway Billfish Tournament in 1960. To everyone's surprise, Castro landed the biggest catch and rightfully kept the largest trophy for himself.

Another key element of the Cuban milieu is the unobtrusive but undeniable presence of religion. It is not at all like places where Buddhism or Islam have prevailed for thousands of years. No, like so much else in Cuba, religion has wound a circuitous path and only subtly pervades the society today. Of course, the Spanish *conquistadores* brought with them a determination to spread Catholicism among the "heathen" natives. Over time, however, they introduced to the island hundreds of thousands of slaves from Africa, especially Nigeria, who held a variety of nature-based beliefs. Rather than reject the determined proselytizers and be subjected to harsh penalties, the blacks found a clever course of less resistance. They provided for Catholicism to become an overlay of their own beliefs commonly known as Santeria. When told to revere a supreme god, for example, perhaps they reasoned, "Well, let it be the god we call Olofi, who is our supreme god and father of all creation. When they urge us to pray to Saint Peter, let us think of him as Oggun, our father of the forest. St. Francis may be a kindred spirit to Orula, protector of all animals, and let us think of Agayu-Olla, our protector of travelers, when we are told to honor St. Christopher."

The domain of a good friend, an Afro-Cuban Catholic priest in Havana named Father Elpidio, was the largest and poorest parish in teeming Old Havana. Always with a broad and impish smile, he struggled on behalf of his people and radiated appreciation for the smallest assistance. Over a demitasse of Cuban coffee I asked him, "What is the percentage of the Catholic population in Cuba today?" and he responded, "Ninety per cent." And then Elpidio coached me. "And now ask what percentage of those professing to be Catholics are, in addition or instead, practicing Santeria – and again the answer will be ninety per cent!"

So in this way the religions introduced from Europe and from Africa have been able to coexist and not foster division and violence as is all too evident elsewhere in the world today. In synthesis they have found harmony. Elpidio, like so many of his countrymen, was torn between his love for his people and homeland and his family across the Florida Straits. He eventually left Cuba for Miami, just one more statistic beneath which rests yet another tale of heart-wrenching decisions and divisions that confront so many Cubanos.

Another ever-present facet of the milieu in Cuba is the nasty reality of hostile political relations between the governments of the United States and Cuba since 1959. It takes an emotional toll, inflames politics and suppresses the standard of living. Cuba's political officials and Communist Party leaders frequently and enthusiastically recite a litany of real and imagined misdeeds by the United States, no one more single-mindedly than

Fidel Castro. And how likely was I to encounter one of those true believers and be subjected to a diatribe? It is more likely that a rogue asteroid will destroy our planet during one of my visits. So what *can* I expect in the political realm? *Virtually nothing!* The Cuban people radiate affection for visitors from the States. They seem sensibly able to differentiate between personal relationships and the irascible fumbling between our officials. Perhaps Cubanos privately harbor some grievances against the U.S. government – and certainly the U.S. economic embargo of the island (or *bloquero*, as the Cubans call it) has contributed to real hardships. But nowhere among the scores of countries worldwide where I have roamed have I been greeted with more genuine warmth, friendliness and generous hospitality.

And to what extent, I might reasonably ask, is this lovely milieu of Cuba being jaded by the growth of tourism? Rather little, it seems. Yes, in a tourist area now I can find an occasional raggedy panhandler and sometimes a native strangely attired to attract a photo op and a dollar. But these are so vastly apart from the norm, the sweet authenticity, that I cannot imagine any erosion of the essence of Cuba that is so wonderfully evident.

Such is the enveloping milieu I found in Cuba: diverse, pervasive and pleasing – even seductive. The seemingly superficial often is deeply rooted in Cuban history, culture and in the minds of its people. Being aware of these many threads of the country's fabric enables me to better understand and share so much that might otherwise be dismissed as illogical or simply bizarre.

Chapter 2

THE SHAPE OF HISTORY

In view of Cuba's colorful and robust history since the Revolution, I almost was lulled into an illusion that the country somehow sprang from the bushy brow of Fidel Castro. While he has propelled Cuba to prominence and controversy, the eventful centuries before he took his first breath created both the man and the country.

Many sources have chronicled in detail the countless events that have shaped modern Cuba. Here let me simply cruise through the highlights of a rich tapestry more than five centuries in the making, for familiarity with the background helps to understand this enigmatic country today and, more importantly, tomorrow.

Before the age of discovery, the island we know as Cuba was a thriving land of an estimated 200,000 indigenous Siboney, Guanajatabey and Tainos people. They fished and farmed and, to the surprise of the Spanish *conquistadores*, they also inhaled smoke from burning tobacco leaves.

# CUBA RISING

Along came Christopher Columbus in 1492, who "discovered" Cuba, although the natives actually had done so some 10,000 years earlier. With all due respect to Queen Isabella's Admiral of the Ocean Seas, Columbus mistakenly thought he had reached Japan or China. That error, on a scale that spanned about half the planet, was soon corrected. By early in the 16th century, the Spanish conquest of the island was in full swing. The fabled search for gold soon ran its course, but tobacco farming and cattle raising thrived and enriched the colonizers, enabled by West African slave workers starting in 1522.

Soon Havana, with one of the world's finest and best-protected natural harbors, became pivotal to Spain as it ravaged Mexico and South America in its successful quest for gold on the mainland. Havana was astride the sailing routes of the *conquistadores*. It became the rendezvous point for both the mighty gold fleets and those returning laden with riches from China and the Far East. Twice each year fleets, so large that their luffing sails blocked the view of the sea from the land, sailed in heavily armed convoys back to Spain. This proved to be an irresistible attraction to notorious pirates who proliferated in the Caribbean, longing for their share of vast riches. Buccaneers, such as Frenchman Jacques de Sores and Englishmen Francis Drake and Henry Morgan, roamed the nearby seas, captured ships carrying unimaginable fortunes and rampaged through Havana and other well-endowed cities as well.

To defend against pirates, the original city of Havana was surrounded by a massive wall and heavy fortifications. The Spanish deployed tens of thousands of workers for 25 years to ensure their Havana would stand. Today only a few fragments of this great wall remain, a reminder of the city's relentless expansion. Many of the fortresses have been restored and add noticeably to the ambiance of Habana Vieja today.

To protect the city at night, gates were closed and a massive chain was raised at the harbor entrance to prevent vessels of ill will from entering. To this day, a colorful ceremony with soldiers in colonial era military garb takes place nightly at La Cabaña fortress overlooking the harbor entrance. It concludes with a cannon blast that was the signal to shutter the city each night by their colonial masters. While tourists are present in abundance at this nightly reenactment, they are far outnumbered by enthusiastic Cubans, perched on every overlooking wall and ledge, who never seem to tire of the spectacle. Pity the lonely fisherman I saw rowing past in a tiny skiff one night when the cannon was fired. His wooden boat rocked and spun, and he strained at the oars. Unless my eyes failed me, I would guess that he is still genuflecting to this day.

Spanish colonial rulers enthusiastically exploited the people and resources of Cuba. Sugar, coffee, tobacco and precious woods fed the growing appetites of old Europe and hugely enriched Spain. Never ones to miss out on a ripe colonial opportunity, the British eagerly sought to open the island to commerce, from which Spain had excluded them. In 1762, the British fleet attacked Havana, and troops landed at nearby Cojimar and approached from the east. The massive iron cannons of the Spanish were aimed in the opposite direction, toward the harbor entry. After two and a half centuries, Spain was forced to relinquish control of Cuba to England. That turn of events lasted only one year, as the colonial chess game resulted in Cuba being traded back to Spain in exchange for tantalizing Florida. What an extraordinary era when entire nations, with millions upon millions of people, could be slid back and forth like in a game of shuffleboard. (Come to think of it, I know more than a few people who wouldn't mind trading Florida for Cuba *today!*)

By the end of the 18th century, Cuba's native people were largely decimated by a combination of disease, neglect, abuse and overwork. The importing of slaves satisfied the compelling need for a growing workforce. At its terrible peak in the mid-19th century, slaves comprised almost half of the entire population of the island. Slavery in Cuba totaled an estimated

850,000 souls during three and a half centuries of its savagery in Cuba, before it was belatedly abolished in 1886, more than 20 years after the end of the Civil War in the United States.

During the 19th century, the pulse of a national movement for independence in Cuba began to quicken. Uprisings escalated into battles and then into wars. All were suppressed. The intellectual force behind the later movements has been attributed to Jose Marti, a gifted writer, patriot and freedom fighter who devoted his life to independence for Cuba, although he wasn't there much. He spent most of his years in exile, having been forced out of Cuba (twice), Guatemala, Spain and Venezuela by inhospitable regimes. Marti lived more than a decade in New York City, writing, painting and seeking funds for the independence movement in Cuba. Shortly after returning to Cuba, Marti died during a battle for independence in 1895 at the age of 42. Unwisely, he had chosen to ride into battle atop a huge white stallion. That might have looked good in his memoirs, but as a military tactic it was deeply flawed. He proved to be an irresistible and easy target to Spanish sharpshooters.

To this day, an impressive statue of Marti sits in New York City's Central Park, and another is in the green expanse of a park with the same name in Havana. Countless small white marble busts of Marti are found in manicured schoolyards and vast public squares and along roadsides throughout Cuba; billboards show his smiling face and balding dome, and his inspiring words are routinely quoted by officials in their speeches and propaganda. Indeed, only Fidel rivals Marti as a native hero.

Marti's writings are critical of all forms of colonialism and express deep concern about longstanding American designs on Cuba. In what strikes me as ironic, his writings extol the virtues of individual freedom, justice, tolerance and human rights – the absence of which in Cuba today has aroused the ire of critics of the Castro regime. How does today's government evade this quandary? As a Cuban educator explained to me, "The printed collections of the works of Jose Marti that are available in Cuba have deleted the sections of his writing that could be offensive to the current regime."

A rising chorus of voices from the United States, echoing the wishes dating as far back as President Thomas Jefferson in 1805, proclaimed the "destiny" of Cuba to come under U.S. control. Those sentiments emerged again in 1829 when President Andrew Jackson ordered the U.S. Navy to suppress piracy against American vessels off the coast of Cuba. Another crescendo was heard in the years prior to the Civil War when southern states savored the idea of Cuba joining the Confederacy.

But the Spanish-American War in 1898 provided the perfect opportunity. While the U.S. battleship Maine was visiting Cuba, it exploded and sank in Havana Harbor, under suspicious circumstances, with the loss of 278 American sailors. Investigations at the time concluded it had been sabotaged by an underwater mine. Recent scientific studies, however, have given strong credence to the explosion having been caused by spontaneous ignition in the gunpowder magazines, rather than sabotage. In the United States, the "yellow press," captained by William Randolph Hearst and Joseph Pulitzer, inflamed the highly charged political atmosphere of the times. America promptly declared war on Spain, sent Teddy Roosevelt and his Rough Riders to Cuba, and rapidly was victorious. Along with the Philippines and Puerto Rico, Cuba came under American administrative control (a "colony" for all practical purposes) as the spoils of victory under the Treaty of Paris of 1898. So ended all but fragments of the Spanish Empire, but her rich legacy lived on.

Independence was granted to Cuba in 1902, with the exception of a U.S. naval base leased at Guantanamo Bay, at the eastern tip of Cuba. The base, known in slang as "Gitmo," occupies 45 square miles of arid land that adjoin an impressive natural harbor. For decades after the Revolution, Castro seldom failed to mention its continuing presence as an intolerable outrage during his frequent diatribes against the United States.

For nearly five decades following independence, economic ties bound the two countries ever more closely together, and the infamous Platt Amendment allowed for U.S. military intervention in Cuba virtually at will. A series of elected (but marginally effective) governments ruled Cuba. Consistently, however, they were responsive to the powerful political and economic interests of the United States in Cuba. Indeed, much of the nation's economy was owned and operated by U.S. firms, such as United Fruit, International Telephone and Telegraph, and even the King family (famous for its huge ranch in Texas) with its massive land holdings. The U.S. and Cuban economies were so intertwined, my friend Rafael recalled, "I ordered a new Chevy one morning, and it arrived on the afternoon ferry from Key West."

Rampant poverty and government corruption were the rule, not the exception. In 1952, Fulgencio Batista, who himself headed one of the failed governments of the 1940s, staged a second coup and installed himself as the president of Cuba.

The beauty of the island, its close proximity to the United States, and the rowdy reputation of Havana drew great numbers of American tourists, who indulged not only in sun and sea but also in gambling, drugs and prostitution. Increasingly, hotels and tourism came under the control of the notorious American Mafia. Corrupt government officials continued to be more than accommodating. Taking liberties with the words of Somerset Maugham, Havana became "a sunny place for shady people." Meyer Lansky, Lucky Luciano, Santo Trafficante and George Raft , and a host of characters resembling the gangsters played by Raft in films of the 1930s, enjoyed a fast growing empire, thanks in part to the extraordinary wealth careening around Havana and compliant governments that profited from being America's playground. Precious little of the vast sums accumulated by the Mafia found its way to the Cuban people.

One slight but contrary example was described to me by an elderly Cuban friend. "My father was dead and my family was in poverty," he said. "Out of desperation, one day my mother found her way to Meyer Lansky and pleaded for 100 pesos. He pulled out of his pocket a fat roll of bills and handed her a hundred pesos, which enabled us to survive and me to go to school." (It was the equivalent of $100.)

The monstrously unfair distribution of wealth and widespread abuses of the government, as well as by foreigners, gave rise to increasing dissent in the 1950s. Among the grievances was the unruly behavior of the U.S. Marines stationed there. A Cuban friend who was a youngster at the time recounted, "Often the Marines were rude and drunk and they peed in our little front yard."

One of the most outspoken critics was a young firebrand lawyer named Fidel Castro Ruz. Driven by frustration and ambition, on July 26, 1953, he led a hopelessly ill-planned, disorganized and poorly executed attack on Cuba's Moncada military barracks at the eastern end of the island, near Santiago, where he had been born. Some skeptics say that it was mainly a publicity effort by the ambitious Castro, more than a carefully planned military operation, to secure a national reputation for himself. More than half of the revolutionaries were killed or captured. Many were later executed. Castro and his brother Raul were among those who were taken prisoner and jailed. Despite the debacle as a military venture, Castro succeeded beyond (or in accord with) his wildest dreams to establish himself as a household name in Cuba, and his revolution became a credible emerging cause celebre.

Imprisoned on the Isle of Pines, Fidel and Raul were freed in a general amnesty for political prisoners in 1955. (General Batista was soon to seriously regret that kind gesture.) Fearing for their safety, the brothers Castro fled to a more accommodating Mexico just months later. There they continued with their plans to rid Cuba of the despotic Batista regime.

And there Raul introduced Fidel to another energized young man with radical political change on his mind – an Argentine physician named Ernesto "Che" Guevara.

Late in 1956, Fidel, Che and 80 other revolutionaries secretly sailed a rickety old yacht named Granma from Mexico to eastern Cuba. Seas were rough, the navigation was befuddled, and the landing was late and 15 miles distant from waiting collaborators. Talk about rotten luck, a guide betrayed them to Batista's soldiers, and after three days only 12 of the men survived. Fidel, Raul, Che and their fellow survivors trekked into the rugged Sierra Maestra mountains. There they endured terrible hardships and frequent attacks by the army, but there they also attracted more followers. During the next several months their fighting ability grew, their attacks became bolder, and their movement gained popular support and momentum.

The guerilla movement in the mountains was not in a vacuum. It was sustained by many sympathizers throughout the island, especially the politically disenchanted in urban areas. A friend of mine recounted her personal revelation about the breadth of support for the movement. "Our family dentist in Havana was a handsome young man, very prosperous and devoted to his medical practice. He always showed a personal interest in me as well as providing fine treatment. After the Revolution I went for an appointment and noticed he was wearing military pants under his white coat. He explained that he had long been a member of The 26th of July Movement, as Fidel's band of revolutionaries was known at the time. He said he had arranged for many supplies and a lot of money for the rebels at enormous personal risk. Many Cubans were tortured and executed by Batista's police for less. Evidently, he had been so effective that he was given the rank of captain. Also, he explained that he was tempted to recruit me into the underground, as he did with many others."

In 1958, the rebels moved out of the mountains and won a skirmish led by Che near Santa Clara. The Batista forces, underpaid and debilitated, virtually collapsed from within as they were attacked. No major battles, just a regime change that ended with a whimper and not a bang after only 22 months. Batista fled (allegedly with $300 million in cash and 180 pals) on New Year's Eve of 1958. His first stop was the Dominican Republic, where he was welcomed by that country's notorious dictator, Rafael Trujillo, who is said to have enjoyed a $6 million gratuity from Batista for his hospitality.

Fidel conducted a leisurely victory march into Havana, arriving on January 8, 1959. At the time, Dwight Eisenhower was president of the United States, it would be another two years before the Soviets launched the first man into space, and a computer as powerful as a modern laptop was the size of several buses. Fidel Castro and his *barbudos* (bearded ones) initially settled into the Havana Hilton, soon to be nationalized and renamed the Habana Libre. There he held court for Cubans and tourists alike, as the victors quickly consolidated power. During his first speech to his countrymen, an auspicious moment occurred, perhaps unsurpassed in recorded history. A white dove flew from the sky to the rostrum and landed on Castro's shoulder. In the Santerian religion, practiced by most Cubans, the dove is regarded as the messenger of Oshun, a powerful deity. It was a seemingly miraculous sign that Fidel had become the anointed one, a confirmation of the man and his mission that lay ahead.

In one of history's supreme ironies, the United States, with Eisenhower then president, was the first country to recognize, and thus legitimize, the new Castro government. Many of the Cuban people were not so sanguine. Thousands of her best and brightest already had fled the island, and many more were to follow. Fidel wasted no time in dismantling the old regime and installing his own.

The Mafia was unceremoniously thrown out of Cuba, despite the fact that they had hedged their bets by sending large sums of money and many weapons to the rebels at the same time they were reportedly skimming 20 percent of their casino profits and passing them along to dictator Batista. While Lansky and Luciano fled, Trafficante stayed in hopes of preserving the Mafia's holdings in Cuba. No doubt to his surprise, Castro arrested and jailed him, but he was released after making a $500,000 bribe.

Businesspeople bailed as their companies were expropriated, and many counter-revolutionaries were jailed or executed. Landholders of massive tracts saw their holdings taken by the government and parceled out to landless peasants. In the cities, the elaborate villas of those who fled were turned into tenements for dozens of families, and in at least one case, a beautiful villa in Miramar became the property of the previous owners' black maid. Homes of the politically correct remained their private property.

Most Cubans had completely lost confidence in Batista's government and held high hopes for the new Castro regime. Over 1,500 new laws were enacted during the government's first year in power, many launching desperately needed reforms and reversing the gross inequities of the past. "My generation fell in love with Fidel," said a woman who was, at the time, a student from a prosperous upper-class family. But when Castro nationalized not only foreign businesses but also Cuban ones and froze all bank accounts, most Cubans with assets lost everything in a moment. Free elections were promised, and then postponed. For many hope turned to fear, optimism to pessimism, as it began to appear that one despot had replaced another. In the words of one of those victims, a member of the middle class, Eduardo Machado, "The savior had become the tyrant, Fidel was now the source of all suffering for my family, more than Batista ever was."

A downward spiral of relations between the United States and Cuba followed, as is more fully detailed later. In summary, the U.S. economic embargo was initiated under Eisenhower in 1960, amplifying Cuba's isolation and driving the country into the open arms of the eager Soviet Union. The United States broke diplomatic relations with Cuba in January 1961, shortly before John F. Kennedy took office as president, and the calamitous invasion at the Bay of Pigs followed in April. In October of 1962 came the Cuban missile crisis, when the Cold War heated up to the brink of a nuclear World War III.

Cuba's policies and revolutionary zeal were importantly shaped by Fidel's comrade Che Guevara. No one, not even Raul, was closer to Fidel, nor had greater impact on his transition from a disgruntled outcast to a head of state. Che's acolytes proclaim him as one of the world's most influential transforming figures, certainly in league with Gandhi and Mao. His critics profess that Che was a disorganized and mindless revolutionary with a lot of blood on his hands and a lengthy string of failures on his resume. Probably the only common ground between the two historical views would be that his iconic image, based on a 1958 photograph by Cuba's most famous photographer, Alberto Korda, is among the most recognized images among our planet's 6 billion residents.

As the Revolution became solidly entrenched in Cuba, and its dependence on the Soviet Union grew, Che Guevara left Cuba in 1966 to promote revolutions in the Belgian Congo and then throughout Latin America. Why did he leave after his wonderfully successful partnership with Fidel? Speculation is rampant. Was the island too small for two such "alpha male" leaders? Was Che disillusioned by Cuba's huge and growing dependence on the Soviet Union? Did Che and Fidel have a flap? Was Fidel jealous of the attention lavished on Che and unwilling to share the spotlight? Had Che grown restless of being a politician and administrator and wanted to resume the path of slogging through the wilderness and triggering revolutions? It is unlikely that we will ever know, but it may well have been because Che was a pure revolutionary spirit looking for new possibilities.

Often at the behest of the Soviet Union, Cuba became active in supporting revolutions around the world on a scale as if it were a superpower: Ethiopia, Angola, Nicaragua, the Congo and many more. Over 500,000 Cuban soldiers and advisors were dispatched overseas during a period of about 20 years. Most of these ventures fared badly, but none worse than its 15-year quagmire in Angola, virtually an interminable slow motion train wreck for Cuba.

Castro went so far in expressing his appreciation to the Soviet Union for its generous support as to back its invasion of Czechoslovakia in 1968. Although this tarnished his reputation among Third World governments, he later became a leader of the Non-Aligned Movement and seemed to thrive in bedeviling the United States at every opportunity. Under a communist political system and a socialist economic framework, Cuba muddled along for decades with massive Soviet subsidies. Estimated to be between $5 billion and $6 billion per year, they helped to offset some of the shortages that arose from the impact of the U.S. economic embargo and inherent shortcomings of the Cuban economy. Such was the reward for being a dependable Cold War ally of the Soviet Union. To this day many Cubans look back wistfully at that 30-year alliance as fairly good economic times. "We did not have prosperity, but neither did we have food shortages or power blackouts when the Soviets were our patrons," one father of four said to me.

And then came the collapse of the Soviet Union in 1990. Practically overnight the Soviets abandoned Cuba, and the country's economy went into a tailspin. Was Cuba prepared? Well, that's like asking when is the best time for your car to run out of gas. There is no good time, only a cosmically miserable time, to have a country's domestic and international economy disemboweled. After nearly total economic reliance on the Soviet Union for three decades, the economy of Cuba was set adrift on very stormy seas.

Her exports, which had primarily gone to the Soviet Union and Comecon – a multilateral organization of communist nations – were, almost overnight, cut by 80 percent. The annual loss of 13 million tons of oil provided by the Union of Soviet Socialist Republics caused a calamity beyond measure. Mere inconveniences grew into hardships, which quickly escalated into widespread deprivation. There weren't enough jobs or food or fuel or almost anything. Austerity ruled. This Special Period, as Fidel termed it, lasted well beyond the 1990s and gave new and harsh meaning to the words self-reliance.

Cuba turned to foreign investment and tourism to rebuild the economy, with some success. Swallowing a bitter pill in 1993, Castro permitted the U.S. dollar, the currency of his archenemy, to be used and freely exchanged in Cuba . The Cuban peso was just funny money, and hard currency was in desperately short supply. The country became a land of bicycles, as there was virtually no fuel. Those bicycles often were stolen, along with just about anything else that wasn't nailed down, as folks were unemployed, hungry and broke.

Although national deprivation lasted over a decade, Cuba proved to be resilient. It slowly emerged and began to benefit from new friends abroad. The enthusiastic support of Hugo Chavez, the left-wing president of nearby Venezuela and a Castro wannabe, resulted in a boost to Cuba's economy. Most importantly, Uncle Hugo provided for Cuba's petroleum needs on subsidized and deeply concessional terms. Soon thereafter along came an infusion of political interest and cash from the People's Republic of China and, to a smaller extent, from Vietnam. As the first decade of the 21st century rolled along, Cuba rebounded economically and continued to lead the jeering section in opposition to the "capitalist and imperialist" American ways.

Having been crushed in the 1960s, when the United States disappeared off Cuba's financial radar scope, and again in the 1990s, when the Soviets did likewise, it might be logical to assume that Cuba would be reluctant to again become dependent on the good will of a foreign government. And what could appear to be stranger than bonding between little crippled Cuba and massive thriving China, half a world away? It is rooted in China's worldwide search for natural resources to sustain her rapidly growing economy, as well as her quest for greater political recognition as a world power.

The seriously declining health of Fidel Castro and his passing the baton of the presidency to his brother Raul in August 2006 draws into question whither Cuba goest. As seems to characterize all mental gymnastics about Cuba, opinions vary widely.

So who is Raul? Is he a tough guy who, with the backing of the military, will continue on Fidel's path? Or is he a sweet old fellow who wants to see Cuba become more mainstream politically and economically? Or is he merely a transitional figure who will give way to the generation that followed, but was not among, the revolutionaries in the Sierra Maestra mountains?

Raul is an enigma, despite being at his brother's side and holding great power since the inception of the Revolution. Those who have seen him in action recount times of ruthlessness, including the ordering of executions and the imprisonment of dissidents, rivals and counter-revolutionaries. He has commanded an army of 150,000 soldiers that has engaged in revolutionary struggles abroad, and which has now morphed into a catalyst for economic development at home – especially in agriculture, industry and tourism. Military service is mainly a discretionary labor force for the government and a pool of administrative talent. Perhaps he has mellowed. Some say he longs for the calm life of retirement to enjoy friends and family, maybe more so in view of the passing of his wife and national heroine, Vilma Respin, in June of 2007.

As this brief recounting of Cuba's history suggests, it has been a colorful and wild ride. It is safe to say that the people of

Cuba long for less adrenalin and more serenity and prosperity. I believe that is likely to be forthcoming based upon the players and policies, at home and abroad, that will be shaping her future, as described in the coming chapters. But first I would like to meander through the streets of Havana with you, for it is that remarkable city that has shaped the people and the outlook that have charted Cuba's course.

CHAPTER 3

## WELCOME TO HAVANA

Havana is a remarkable and seductive place where I found much of what is the best about Cuba, and some of the worst. To have been there and say that I know Cuba would be no more credible than for me to visit only New York City and claim that I know the United States. But it is necessary to have been to Havana to enable me to understand this baffling island. My emphasis is on the word "necessary," however, and it's a pity and practically a breach of faith to miss the great city where almost a quarter of all Cubans live, despite the many temptations of Cuba's crystalline beaches and lush countryside.

My personal preferences are not entirely in sync with the policies of the leaders of Cuba. In fact, the government appears to have made a purposeful and successful effort for the maximum number of tourists to miss Havana entirely! How can this be, to skip the kaleidoscope of Havana and confine one's understanding to only the dry pages of a guidebook? One explanation came from a deputy minister of Tourism who said to me, "At great expense we have built modern international airports to serve each of the major tourist regions. This way the many charter flights can go directly to the tourism developments near the beaches or other cities." Indeed, I've seen jumbo jets full of pale-faced Canadians being disgorged at seemingly obscure destinations, such as Caya Coco, Caya Largo and Santiago. And a week later, the same hundreds of visitors, sunburned, rum-logged and exhausted from late nights of salsa dancing, shuffled back onto their planes for the direct flight home. Havana, for them, would be no more than an asterisk in their memory bank.

I can commend the visionaries in the Ministry of Tourism for dispersing airports around the island. Indeed, it is convenient for visitors, saves fuel as well as time in moving folks about, and avoids the prospect of massive congestion in Havana's airport and logistical nightmares throughout the city. But I believe that another less charitable explanation is credible.

It is far from secret that *El Comandante* has long been devoted to ideological purity on the island. All that is good is attributed to the revolutionary and socialist zeal of the people and their leaders. And all that is wicked is attributed to the degenerate political practices of the impure – the capitalists and imperialists, which include just about everyone that declines to subscribe to Castro's beliefs and goals. Presumably, that could include most of the millions of tourists. Because the "ideologically challenged" are assumed to be among the throngs of visitors, why take a chance that they would disrupt the calm and compliant political atmosphere in the capital city? Such possible ne'er-do-wells cannot be forced to wear blinders or muzzles after all. But the risk of political pollution can be reduced by ensconcing them in beautiful resorts far from the seat of power, far from the magnificent city of Havana.

Those who have established the practice of keeping many hundreds of thousands of tourists away from Havana are those who are keenly aware that just a handful of people, in times of frustration and dissatisfaction, can overthrow an entire government. Recall 1959. I am mindful that the decisions to build remote resorts and their airports were made in the early 1990s, the years immediately after the Soviet Union abandoned Cuba and sent her former ally into economic ruin, precisely when unprecedented political discontent and widespread economic deprivation spanned the entire country.

Havana is in no way diminished by the absence of hundreds of thousands of additional visitors. In fact, for those who do spend time there, it is much the better for it. Even in the peak seasons for tourism, the city is not packed with camera-toting, gum-snapping, Bermuda shorts-wearing throngs. Despite its sprawling size, there are limits in terms of hotel space and other tourism infrastructure that seem to keep a lid on. Sure, some of the highlight destinations will find rows of parked tour buses and clusters of tourists trailing their multilingual guides. But they remain not only predictable and proportionate, they also fail to measurably detract from the city's abundance of monumental and miniscule attractions.

Havana is so much more than mere bricks and mortar. At varying times it has been at the epicenter of drama and turmoil within the country, its region, the hemisphere and, indeed, the world. It is countless stories ranging from tenderness to murder, soft rhythms to violent explosions, swooning beauty to horrible depravity. Volumes of stories of tough guys and vulnerable people interacting against a backdrop of exquisite carved stone and cobalt blue waters. It has been all these and more.

Approaching Havana by air, I have seen it clearly, as if it were a child's toy model, before looping south to the nearby airport. In fact, Havana *does* exist as a toy model *twice*, for I have found detailed *maquetas*, or scale models, in both Havana and in nearby Miramar. Those miniatures serve well for orientation, but Havana can truly be known only by foot through its meandering byways, by vehicle along its expansive tree-lined boulevards, and above all, by knowing its inhabitants and experiencing its many wonderments. Descending to the airport on the flights from Miami, I've seen great expanses of red soil dotted with occasional farmhouses and lush green foliage. Closer still are runways and buildings surrounded by open spaces that end at a formidable barbed wire fence line. Yes, there is comfort in knowing that a wayward cow is unlikely to be found on my runway. And there is discomfort in recalling earlier times when desperate people would furtively gain the airport grounds in attempts to hide in airplane wheel wells as a means to escape the island. Most died trying.

Wheels touch runway in Havana and the passengers erupt in raucous applause and laughter, for the vast majority are Cuban-Americans who are returning to visit family and friends after fleeing the island during difficult times, years or decades ago. "Born in Cuba, always Cuban" goes the saying. The plane taxis past the beautiful international arrivals building, a gift of Canada and the welcoming port for flights from everywhere except Miami. At the gates are planes flaunting the logos of Aeroflot, Mexicana, Air France and many more, which remind me of the global role of Cuba. In the distance is the domestic terminal, a mere shadow of the days when Pan Am Clipper flights were greeted with salsa bands and great gaiety. Now the terminal is home to aging Russian passenger planes, even biplanes, which comprise the domestic fleet. Onward to the downright ugly Terminal 2 of Jose Marti International Airport. It is a sterile, high-ceilinged, warehouse-looking building, populated with numerous green-uniformed "soldiers" of the Ministry of the Interior. It offers a cool reception, a passive welcome to Cuba despite the strains of Latin rhythms leaking through thin metal walls, and the faint aroma of cigar smoke. A long overdue facelift in 2009 signaled expectation of greater numbers of visitors from the United States.

Although these flights usually comprise fewer than 60 passengers, slow-moving lines snake through the arrivals area as I inch toward the immigration booths. Slow because of the many arriving planes? No, there are usually are just several inbound flights each day. Slow because of the detailed interrogation of each visitor? No, just a couple of perfunctory questions are asked. Why then, slow? Slow because, in my opinion, we are far more than arriving visitors from the United States. We are a form of entertainment! We are a moment of activity that punctuates a day of otherwise excruciating boredom. Our presence is to be savored, our passports are to be fondled, our faces are to be stared at, for when we are long gone more hours of waiting and boredom and shifting from foot to foot lay ahead.

A modest sense of excitement courses through me as I approach the spartan immigration booth bathed in harsh fluorescent light, looking forward again to being with Cubans on Cuban soil. Then I am met with the dour, accusing stare of a uniformed officer, who simply says, "Passport." No doubt there is a special course for immigration officers worldwide, who must pass "Dour 101" in order to graduate. But I had hoped for "Glad you have overcome all the obstacles to visit Cuba," or at least "Welcome." It doesn't happen that way. Eventually, I'm buzzed through a locked door to a security scanner that I believe never worked properly, and then into a cavernous baggage claim area where I wait interminably. Evidently, all baggage is x-rayed before it emerges onto a frayed conveyor belt.

If the contents of my bag are suspicious, a discreet mark is placed on my luggage tag and I am pulled aside for an extensive baggage search before I head for the exit doors. The emphasis is on *extensive*. Each bit of clothing is raised skyward and shaken loose. Books and papers are scrutinized and sometimes photocopied. Possible gifts and medicines are closely examined and sometimes taxed right there or confiscated. Uniformed officials come and go, frowning, furrowing brows, asking questions and causing further unexplained delays. Eventually, the crumpled heap that formerly was the neatly packed contents of my suitcase is returned to me. I cram it all back into my bag, which invariably seems to have shrunk. After being subjected to such searches several times, I learned of the secret mark on the bag tag that placed me under suspicion. So the next time I simply removed the tag and its telltale forecast of woe, and aimed myself toward the way out. Not so easy, I learned. For the same fate awaits anyone who has either the marked tag, *or no tag at all!*

Should this be your destiny, be forewarned that a Cuban airport bag search can be more thorough than one at the exit of an African diamond mine. Why so? Because there are many items whose importation into Cuba is illegal and many others that can be brought in only limited quantities without being subject to a heavy tax. No satellite phones, no devices for copying, no laptops for gifts, no Playboy magazines, no more than a miserly amount of medicine, toys, or gifts for friends and relatives. And this, it turns out, may be the real reason for the flights from Miami being segregated from other international arrivals. It enables, conveniently and out of public view, the Ministry of the Interior inspectors to intimidate, confiscate, or heavily tax those – especially returning émigrés – who would otherwise be sharing their bounty with their friends and relatives in Cuba. Officialdom in Cuba does not look kindly on those who fled tough times for the good life in Miami.

On one occasion I was with an American woman who never even got as far as these hassles. As soon as her bag appeared, it was approached by a decrepit old cocker spaniel whose mission was bomb sniffing. The canine corps at the airport is mostly a sad looking bunch of half-breeds who long ago should have been basking in a doggy retirement home. Sniffer the dog moaned, nuzzled, slobbered and created quite a stir before he hobbled away and was replaced by a half-dozen uniformed experts in bomb detection and disposal. An hour came and went as the huddlers gazed and pointed and occasionally exclaimed a few words. Eventually, a fancy electronic device appeared, but no one seemed to know how to make it work. Another hour came and went, with more gazing, pointing and exclaiming. Our pleas and protests were ignored, as our inspectors seemed to experience a memory lapse of spoken English. The bag was finally carefully opened and thoroughly searched, to no avail. No bombs, nothing threatening, just female stuff. We were waved off without a word of explanation, as if we were a couple of annoying mosquitoes. As we finally headed to the exit, my friend turned to me and said, "You don't suppose all of that had anything to do with the fact that my kitty slept on my suitcase last night?" I doubled over with laughter. Oh, well, at least Sniffer the bedraggled old dog still had some working parts!

Emerging from the bleakness of the terminal and the less than hearty "Welcome to Cuba" in the 1990s, the first powerful irony of this struggling socialist economy was finding a bullpen full of sleek black air-conditioned Mercedes Benz taxis waiting with their meters calibrated in U.S. dollars. Whoa! Have I traveled through space and time? Hardly. This simply reflected the government's surging efforts to promote tourism and the desperately needed cash it provided.

Gentlemen, start your engines! My driver, Emilio, did so and we launched the 20-minute career to downtown. Along the way came the first glimpse of vintage American cars clambering along the highway. Some were in mint condition, some appeared to have just emerged from a demolition derby, and others were barely recognizable because they had been hybridized with parts from many models, such as a lemon yellow Chevy with Cadillac tail fins and a Nash grill and others beyond recognition to anyone but an antique car buff.

Those not fortunate enough to have a vintage family car were buzzing about in government-owned Soviet era Ladas and Moskvas. With a broad smile, Emilio asked, "Do you know why those old Ladas have heating systems in the back?" Sensing my bafflement he followed up, "So you can keep your hands warm when you are pushing it!" I came to realize that the Cubans' sense of humor is as enduring as their resilience. That which you cannot cry about, you may as well laugh about.

Soon I learned how to distinguish the owners, if not the operators, of most vehicles. The key to this mystery rests with the color of the license plates. My driver was pleased to enlighten me with TMI (too much information): "Yellow ones for private cars; brown for enterprises; green for military; orange for foreigners; red for tourist rental cars; black for diplomats; blue for government officials, and white for the 'Intelligence Ministry.' A virtual rainbow of information awaits anyone who simply gazes out the window in Havana's careening traffic.

One friend whose license plate suspiciously disappeared one dark night explained the baffling process of replacing it. No, he did not simply go to the Ministry of License Plates and apply for a new one. That would be way too easy and logical. First, he had to go to some obscure office and file a lengthy application for a *temporary replacement* plate. In due course that arrived, and its number provided the basis for the application for the permanent replacement plate, which finally arrived some months later. And why wouldn't he have been able to apply directly for a replacement plate? Here I had an "Aha" moment as I began to understand the workings of an economy proud to boast of its full employment statistics.

Meanwhile, back on the highway, we bobbed and weaved through rambling wrecks, shiny government vehicles, motorcycles – many with sidecars – and the giant mass transit vehicle affectionately dubbed *cameo*, the camel. Although it has to be seen to be believed, it consists of your basic giant tractor pulling behind it a two-humped motorless bus. A reasonable estimate of its capacity would be 150 cramped folks. In reality, which gets pretty ugly on a hot humid day, up to 400 miserable souls are crammed into this nightmare on wheels. It makes a rush hour subway ride in Tokyo seem like a picnic. Cubans joke that riding *cameos* can be compared to an X-rated American film: a lot of bad language and more than a little body contact!

In one of my *least* politically correct moves in Cuba, I once asked permission to lease one of these mass transit monsters for a party on wheels. Nice idea, I thought. A few dozen friends, a little salsa band, some snacks and *cervezas* – something that would give new meaning to the term "a moveable feast." Well, after very little deliberation I was turned down flat. Emphatically. In no uncertain terms I was told that it would be insulting to the people of Cuba to cruise the city having a bash in a vehicle that had come to symbolize the dire deprivations of the 1990s, after the Soviets bailed, and which caused people the discomfort and embarrassment of commuting in such pathetic style. To no one's dismay, time marches on, and the miserable fleet of camel buses was replaced with new buses, courtesy of Cuba's new friend, the People's Republic of China. No official seemed inclined to reveal to me the destination of the old *cameos*, but I suspect they'll be found in Cuba's distant cities and towns for many years to come.

As we cruised toward downtown, we passed through a sparsely developed area dotted with little patches of vegetable gardens. Interspersed among them were stately royal palm trees, Cuban hallmarks reaching skyward with the voluptuous curve of a woman's back. The roadside vista soon evolved from rural to light industrial. There was a cement plant, then an ice cream factory, and an apparently abandoned industrial building with so many smashed windows that it looked as if it had been transplanted from old Brooklyn, N.Y. A shiny new practice facility for Cuba's fine Olympic volleyball team was soon followed by a huge aging sports complex with competition courts, arenas, pools and stadiums.

As I tried to absorb this unfolding panorama, Emilio emoted in reasonably good English about his relatives in Miami and how surprised he was to see an American visitor. He, and all others in the tourist trade, only needed to glance into their empty wallets to be reminded of the reduction of Americans on the island during the course of the George W. Bush presidency. Cubans truly miss the *Yanquis*, as they are affectionately known, for they are genuinely fond of Americans as well as their free-spending ways. Meanwhile, the streetscape continued to unfold: more noisy traffic, more jam-packed buses, more sandlot baseball diamonds and some high-rise apartment blocks which, from their appearance, could only have been souvenirs of the era when Soviet-style architecture was preferable to none at all.

The tall apartment buildings, each housing hundreds of families, were Cuba's minimal response to the country's glaring housing shortage. They appeared to be functional but sad, although their little balconies were enlivened with colorful paint, breaking the monotony of otherwise dreary canyons of concrete. Among the first signs that I really was getting to the heart of town were various institutional lumps of buildings that turned out to be a cluster of government ministries surrounding Revolution Square. Quickly the monumental white marble statue of Jose Marti came into sight, with a soaring tower behind it and the offices of the President of Cuba adjoining. The driver explained, "This is where Fidel has given many of his speeches, often to crowds of a million people, often under the hot sun." And this is where, in 1998, Pope John Paul II celebrated mass to another million adoring Cubans.

We cruised across the square, catching a quick look at the building that houses the Ministry of the Interior, home of the grumpy greeters at the airport. Its huge steel silhouette of Che Guevara covered the façade, and the roof sprouted antennae like a fertile field bears weeds in the springtime. A mental note was made to return here for a snapshot. Then down lovely Paseo, a beautiful boulevard adorned with a park-like median that boasts delicately sculptured trees and flowering shrubs. It runs downhill to the white-capped sea, past block after block of early 20th century villas, each huge, distinctive and beautifully restored – or at least sporting a coat of fresh paint.

At the end of Paseo I found an early surprise, the ultra-modern high-rise, Spanish-built Melia Cohiba Hotel. (If you happen to be a president of a country and plan to visit Cuba, this may well be where you would prefer to stay.) Across the street are a contemporary multi-level shopping mall, a jazz club and the somewhat dog-eared Riviera hotel, formerly one of the American Mafia's finest in Havana. The brightly painted one-time casino, now a cavernous restaurant, sits like the dome of a giant mushroom beside the hotel and the famous seaside boulevard the Malecon.

We were in the heart of Vedado, an area connecting the Old City with the modern, further west fashionable neighborhood of Miramar. My chatty driver explained, "Vedado first was a forbidden zone for housing, to keep the common people and possible disease from the wealthy residents whose villas were in the Old City." Today it appears to be chock-full of dwellings that transition to an unremarkable business district a few miles closer to town.

We zoomed onto the Malecon, a wondrous seven-mile long thoroughfare that parallels the oceanfront. Past impressive new apartment buildings, past a soccer stadium that has seen far better days, and past miles of beautiful villas. During earlier visits to Cuba in the 1990s, I was saddened to see so many once-lovely dwellings that had become dilapidated and apparently abandoned. Until one evening I drove by and noticed little lights inside. Only then did I realize that these many candidates for demolition were actually still inhabited. During the intervening decade, most had been restored, although too many have started to crumble once again.

The vista was punctuated with great statues of heroic cavalrymen on huge bronze horses. "So many revolutions and so many heroes," Emilio volunteered. Evidently, interpreting my moment of silence as an entrée for more, he added, "Do you know that if the horse has both legs in the air, then the rider died in battle? And if only one horse leg is in the air, then the rider died later from wounds in the battle. And if the horse has all four legs on the ground, the rider died of natural causes." I was in awe of his mastery of the obscure, which signaled some informative days ahead. But I couldn't help chuckling to myself about some of the other variations: What if the horse had no feet on the ground? What if the horse was lying on the ground with all four feet up in the air? Well, this deteriorating digression quickly gave way to the unfolding beauty of the Malecon. In the prosperous decades of the 20th century, it must have rivaled the magnificent avenues of seafront cities, such as Monte Carlo.

The wind off the Florida Straits was high, and huge frothing waves crashed over the seawall, soaking passersby. It seemed as if we were driving through the surf. We were undeterred, unwilling to detour away from this grand promenade.

Into view came a tall modern building with green-tinted glass and a cordon of police surrounding it. My best guess was confirmed by Emilio: "Here is your embassy, although today it is called something else."

I was aware of the countless controversies surrounding and emanating from this place, the U.S. Embassy since 1953 and later dubbed the U.S. Interests Section after diplomatic relations crumbled. In recent years, the American officials whose offices were found there have orchestrated the continuing game of political cat and mouse that has characterized Cuban-American relations for decades. The directives came straight from Washington, D.C., for absolutely no margin was left for on site creativity or innovation. From here emerged a variety of carefully calibrated provocative acts. Thousands of transistor radios have been distributed, for example, so Cubans could listen to the politically slanted transmissions of the U.S.-funded Radio Marti. The Christmas tree in the yard was decorated with dissident-related items during one recent season, and a huge red electronic news crawler, displaying news and commentary, was placed across the upper stories of the facade of the building so Cubans could read "objective" news. In response to the latter, the Cuban government consumed the building's parking lot and erected 126 flagpoles with waving black flags symbolizing Cuban martyrs in the perennial fight against America. Conveniently, the flags perfectly blocked the view of the news crawler!

Another response from *El Comandante* was the erection of huge billboards across the street from the building, ripe with slogans of political invective and images portraying America as a terrorist nation. Although the images are mainly cartoon characters, that in no way diminishes the stern underlying message and it may, in fact, amplify it for the intended audience of common folks in Havana. Further along we zipped by the Elian Gonzalez protest plaza – dubbed Dignity Plaza – occupying prime waterfront real estate next to the U.S. Embassy building. It was used as a destination for more than a few million-man (and grandma) marches during the bilateral flap over the little rafter who floated his way in 1999 to controversy in Miami and was returned to Cuba the following year

Moving swiftly along, we saw the majestic towers of the grand dame of Havana, the Nacional Hotel. Her gilded and glorious public spaces belie the somewhat threadbare condition of the guestrooms, but there is no better panorama of the Malecon gently curving along Havana's waterfront than from the lush gardens of the hotel. My driver alerted me to another obscure but interesting landmark along the way to Habana Vieja. Off to the right stood a huge personality-less building that Emilio noted was a hospital. With his continuing wondrous grasp of historic detail, he volunteered, "This was constructed to be the headquarters of the Central Bank of Cuba, so in the basement are huge vaults that were to hold currency and gold bullion. I think it is the only hospital in the world with bank vaults." Well, I thought, perhaps they'd make great isolation wards, for surely Cuba has no need to store vast quantities of bullion in light of its struggling economy.

My pulse began to quicken as we left behind buildings of the 20th century, then passed the 19th century as if being transported through a time machine and then came upon structures clearly from the colonial era.

A sharp right turn along the harbor entrance brought us to a stoplight that we blithely ignored, and past the ornate facade of the Embassy of Spain. In quick order came the elaborate architecture of the (former) Presidential Palace, from which Dictator Batista escaped into exile on the last night of 1958, then a tree-shrouded park with amusement rides for children and a sea of colorful umbrellas extending for blocks and providing shade and shelter to a massive handicrafts market for tourists. Suddenly a turn to the right brought us to an abrupt halt at historic Plaza de Armas, Havana's oldest site, and the location of my finely restored Santa Isabel Hotel.

As no vehicles were permitted in the square, I bid farewell to Emilio. Only then it became clear to me why he had turned off the taxi meter some miles earlier. What I thought was an extraordinary act of hospitality turned out to be an ominous sign of the times in Havana. The actual fare was about double what the digits on the meter read. Said Emilio, "Half for Fidel and half for me. It's only fair, isn't it?" I smiled at this first brush with the human face of Cuba's economic plight and strolled the short distance to the hotel.

After scores of visits to Havana I have come to realize that the Santa Isabel Hotel is quintessentially Cuban. Not because it is rated five stars, not because it sits on Havana's most important historical plaza, and certainly not because its meticulous restoration (in anticipation of Jimmy Carter's visit there in 2002) is typical of the city's ageing structures. In those respects it is quite uncommon. What makes it evocative of Cuba is its staff.

I was greeted by smiling doormen, bellmen and security guards, all of whom seemed genuinely happy to have not just another guest, but especially an *American* guest. As the 1990s waned, deteriorating political relations between Cuba and the United States resulted in American visitors declining from infrequent to rare. In the hospitality industry, Americans are regarded as somewhat less demanding and more generous with gratuities than most others. But there is much more afoot. Cubans have a deep affection for U.S. visitors, regardless of the political turmoil between the governments. They are, after all, Americans themselves. And in many cases we share divided families.

Upon entering I was struck by the design of the building, formerly the villa of a wealthy merchant family. The marble reception area led into an open courtyard, so typical of early villas: breezy and lovely except during the occasional rainstorm. An archaic elevator with gleaming brass grillwork invited me upstairs to rooms overlooking the early morning serenity and later the buzz of activity of Plaza de Armas. The spacious rooms are mellowed by low lighting and dramatized by sunlight streaming through stained glass window transoms.

It was an amazing introduction to Havana. Distinctive sights and sounds, so many smiles, so much that was baffling to me, and so much more ahead.

CHAPTER 4

HAVANA'S EMBRACE

Without delay I ventured forth to the awesome discoveries that awaited. On the cobblestones surrounding the plaza I was greeted by one of Havana's leading architects, Orestes del Castillo, who had agreed to act as guide on an architectural walking tour of Habana Vieja. He was an elf-like fellow with a wide smile and sparkling eyes. He had designed many of the restored buildings in the Old City and is a virtual library of knowledge not only of restoration but also of the history and styles of the incredible structures that adorn this old neighborhood.

We passed the early 20th century Embassy of the United States, which has been transformed into a modest museum of natural history, while looming ahead was the former Palace of the Spanish Captain Generals, the colonial rulers of Cuba. It occupies an entire block with elaborate limestone facades and now serves as a museum of the city's history with impressive displays of colonial era furniture. As we stumbled along the cobblestones toward the soaring entrance, we noticed that our footing suddenly seemed more secure. It was apparent that the street surface had changed. "Why" I asked, "in just this one block is the surface different?" The response came with a chuckle. "Look closely and you will see that this section is a street made of hardwood," my host told me. "The Spanish governor was annoyed that his siestas were being interrupted by the clanging of metal carriage wheels on cobblestones, so he had it rebuilt to be quiet for him!"

Adjacent was a comparable building housing the Deputies of the Captain Generals. And next to it was a beautifully restored fortress, built in the 16th century. To one side was a fine statue of the erudite-looking King Fernando VII of Spain holding a scroll extending from his lowered arm. Amusingly, the statue was moved from a more prominent location nearby as a result of certain sensitivities about its appearance, especially during a rain. You see, the water runs down the arm, down the scroll and streams forth . . . well, let your imagination run wild.

Lining the entire perimeter of the lush park in the center of the plaza were dozens of stalls of purveyors of antique books. There I found wealthy Europeans buying leather bound volumes by the *foot* instead of by the title! The repertoire of the vendors had expanded to include a great diversity of antiquities, including maps, stock certificates, postage stamps and more. The "more" included contemporary items the source of which I would rather not know, and I had the good sense not to ask. And if you happen to be in search of an item that is not to be found, simply ask for it. More than a few times I have sought a book on an obscure subject, or multiple copies of an out-of-print book about Cuba. And within an hour those always have appeared. I have no doubt that your request for a left-handed monkey wrench would be filled in short order. And no doubt in whose pocket the profit resides – black marketers.

Moving along a side street we passed a gaggle of restaurants and shops, including one dispensing small ice cream cones and another with a modest selection of meat. A vendor passed by, hawking little white paper cones of roasted peanuts, a perennial favorite snack of Cubanos. Most of the buildings, formerly villas of prosperous families, sported stucco surfaces with fresh coats of soothing pastel colors. Many had windows and doors adorned with decorative iron grillwork, and a few had the original lathe-turned wood instead. Most were laid out, as was the custom in centuries past, with a grand carriage entryway into an open courtyard. Street-level spaces were generally for horses and storage while the second floor always included impressive rooms for reception, dining and entertaining. The third floor included the bedrooms and family quarters, as it was high enough to capture the cooling breezes off the nearby ocean. A stark reminder of the centuries of slavery in Cuba was to be found in the low ceiling spaces between the ground floor and the second floor, which housed the slaves.

Then we were distracted by a most startling encounter. A rising cacophony of drumbeats and horn toots drew our gaze further ahead. Into sight came a scraggly band of jesters and stilt walkers in colorful costumes. "Another surprise," explained Orestes, "A diversion provided by the Office of the Historian for the amusement of our visitors." They danced and hobbled by, trailed by laughing children. Surprised tourists snapped photos and happily dropped coins into the orange and green high hat of a jester.

As we continued along it became evident that these byways of the Old City were for pedestrians only. Access at intersections was blocked by massive old cannons embedded into the streets, sometimes with cannonballs the size of basketballs or larger Noticing my curiosity, evidenced by my photographing these splendid alternatives to concrete barriers or bright orange plastic cones, Orestes volunteered, "Cuba has a huge supply of old cannons and cannonballs from the pirate and Spanish sailing fleets and we've put them to good use, don't you think?"

# CUBA RISING

Suddenly we emerged onto expansive Plaza San Francisco, across from warehouse buildings serving the harbor and Havana's lone cruise ship terminal. The harsh terms of the U.S. embargo prevent all but a handful of cruise ships from visiting Havana. "You'll need a lot more than one berth here when American tourists can add Havana to their Caribbean cruise itinerary," I commented. Glancing back, I noticed a towering building that once served as Havana's stock exchange, presiding over one side of the plaza. It faces, across the plaza now populated with horse-drawn carriages for tourists, the impressive cathedral and convent of San Francisco, which date back to the 16th century and are now a museum. Inside the cathedral I found beautiful sculptures and paintings and a notice posted for baroque music concerts. Although this sacred ground no longer serves a religious mission, its majestic heights, lovely courtyards and glorious architecture make it worthy of a moment for reflection.

A small storefront to one side appeared to be a post office, although the lobby was filled with display cases not only of stamps but also of a diversity of little tourist tchotchkes, including souvenir coffee mugs, salt and pepper shakers, postcards and music CDs. With tourists close at hand, no sense missing an opportunity to help them share their wealth, I supposed. Being in the post office reminded me to jot off a few postcards – but not necessarily because I expected them to arrive in the United States. Why then? Because, despite the absence of a postal agreement between Cuba and the United States, somehow the mail does get through from time to time. The operative word here being *time*. When I have done this before, some of the cards have been delivered after four to six weeks, some never. I was told that mail to the United States ends up in a barrel somewhere and then is shipped off to Mexico on a space-available basis. From there it may be passed along to the addressee, but not always. And it doesn't seem to matter much if I put a stamp on it or not. Thus, I am never surprised when a complete stranger comes up to me on the street and asks if I would carry out and then stamp and mail a letter to a friend or relative in the United States.

Nestled off one corner is a small park dedicated to the late Princess Diana. "The first such park in the world," said Orestes. The Cubans are so proud they cannot resist any opportunity to cite their "first, best or biggest" of anything Cuban! It was a small green space, beautifully landscaped and marked only with a simple plaque. Havana reveals its treasures, large and small, only gradually and ever so gently.

Then Orestes led me across the expanse to a fanciful bronze statue of a man who used to roam the byways of Old Havana, telling tales and amusing the children. This homeless beggar was dubbed El Caballero de Paris. He evidently lost his mind while imprisoned, and he emerged believing that he was a French nobleman. It is said to bring good luck to stroke his flowing bronze beard and, judging from its shininess, that legend has many believers.

Moving along past several impressive art galleries, we found ourselves facing a neighborhood restaurant, with most likely Havana's only popcorn machine. Then the local barbershop, where indigenous folks pay about a dime for a haircut, and we were offered the same for three dollars. It dawned on me that a two-tier economy, one for locals and one for visitors with hard currency, was the norm. Not that it is unusual in Third World countries, but in Cuba it is *very* pronounced. It is perfectly reasonable that a Cuban earning perhaps $17 per month would not be expected to pay 20 percent of his monthly wage for a trim.

Our eyes shifted quickly to a young man ahead who was attired in the flowing brown robes of a monk. Could this be another facet of surprising Cuba? Well, yes and no. I quizzed Orestes and learned that we had stumbled upon a tiny hotel named Los Frailles, where all the employees were clad in the simple traditional garb of a monastery – which is exactly what the building had been before its conversion to a petite hotel. The theme was thoughtfully carried throughout the restoration, with only one conspicuous drawback. Just two of the rooms had windows, as the remainder were authentically restored cells formerly occupied by the resident monks.

Meandering through pedestrian-filled cobblestone streets under repair, we found ourselves gazing through the window of a perfume shop, which was full of attractive ladies. So we dove in, trying to act like we were on familiar turf. Far from it. With the help of a friendly saleswoman, I learned that the rows of glass tubes full of colored liquids were actually various perfumes that could be blended to suit the client. Conveniently, silver necklaces were also for sale, each with a tiny vial dangling from it. Turns out the lucky recipient of these items is to pour some of item one into item two and never be caught without her perfume again. Selecting a fragrance blend struck me as beyond my rank and pay grade, so I settled for a little woven bag of aromatic potpourri for a dollar.

Only a moment further along we found ourselves in Market Square, a lovely open expanse that had transitioned from a slave market to a commercial market, to the site of an underground parking garage during the Batista era. Now it was resurfaced with cobblestones, and the centerpiece was a magnificent carved stone fountain. This plaza was clearly a work in progress. Orestes proudly pointed to a remodeled office building that reminded me of a seven-tiered wedding cake, rich in white icing and gold trim. It was one of his many architectural achievements.

While other structures nearby also had been wonderfully restored, including shops, residences, a school and a micro-brewery, some remained in tumbledown condition. The vista reminded me of a broad smile, with unsightly gaps where major orthodontics remained ahead. Though there is a certain beauty to century-old facades with crumbling stucco and colorful laundry waving like celebratory flags from the wrought iron balconies, improving the quality of such tenements continues to be an urgent need. Someday this square again will become a thriving public marketplace as well as the heart of the neighborhood. For now it remains simply an oasis within Havana's most densely populated area. Among its attractions are a bird market on Sundays, where I have found a virtual aviary of species, including special breeds of pigeons, parrots and colorful songbirds for sale.

Our journey through history and architecture continued along a street lined on both sides with restored buildings painted in a rainbow of pastel colors. Past a small restaurant that served *tappas*, plates overflowing with bite-size samples of a variety of Spanish favorites. Adjoining was a small hotel that gave new meaning to the words "small hotel." It comprised a grand total of four rooms. How this can be economically viable may be one of the best-kept secrets in Cuba, and it certainly is unknown to the familiar chains with buildings of mind-boggling capacities one finds spreading across the globe. In reality, it is a charming use for a small restored space.

Glances down the busy side streets offered a new glimpse into the habitat of your everyday Cuban. Narrow streets sorely in need of repair, puddles where cobblestones used to rest, crowded buildings, electrical wires running hither and yon both overhead and attached to crumbling facades, open windows beyond which families were watching television, faded signs, laundry waving, noisy children playing stickball, apparently abandoned cars straddling the sidewalks and people laughing and jostling along with scraggly dogs jumping and barking in between. A far cry from your basic Norman Rockwell scene. In the distance I saw the soaring dome of the Capitolio, a clone of the U.S. Capitol Building in Washington. Cubans are quick to point out that theirs is actually six inches taller than its inspiration. And up close was a particularly poignant sight, a fading white-painted scrawl on a crumbling gray stucco-faced building reading simply, "Viva Fidel."

Although I already was on sensory overload from our sojourn, we continued onward toward the fourth of Habana Vieja's remarkable public plazas. My curiosity was whetted but not yet satisfied. We passed another open-air cantina, with a salsa band drawing Cubans and tourists alike off the streets and into the ambience of an afternoon *mojito* – a potent cocktail that Ernest Hemingway favored – to complement the music. Past more little houses with the living rooms converted into *mercados* (markets) overflowing with souvenirs. Small paintings of landscapes with palm trees, wood carvings both modern and traditional, the ever-present bongo drums and castanets, and children's toys made of colorful hammered soft drink cans. Along the way we passed an elementary school, full of jostling, chattering little children dressed in their immaculate blue-and-white uniforms. In the small front courtyard was a huge stone carved bust of Lenin. Overgrown with green lichen, surely it actually had to be the world's largest Chia pet!

Then the *piece de resistance*, Cathedral Square, suddenly appeared before us. Looking more like a Hollywood movie set than reality, it is an open plaza surrounded by wondrous colonial era architecture. Overwhelming the sights and senses was San Cristobal Cathedral itself, a baroque design that combines elaborate carvings as well as two simple bell towers. Its beauty, described by Cuban author Alejo Carpentier as "music turned to stone," resulted in its status being promoted from church to cathedral during the late 18th century. Inside were magnificently carved altars and exquisite frescoes. Yes, it does offer religious services on a continuing basis. Around the square were finely restored villas dating back to the 17th and 18th centuries. In one building is, in my opinion, Havana's finest art gallery, with paintings, sculpture and jewelry to suit discerning tastes and bulging wallets. Just off the square was a unique *taller* (a print-making studio), where I always find artists crafting and printing (and selling) fine works of art on paper. Also of high importance to us was a fine restaurant with patio tables in the square itself, where a cool drink amid these evocative historic surroundings was savored.

In this remarkable venue, Pope John Paul II gave a mass to thousands of adoring Cubans during his 1998 visit to Cuba. On more light-hearted occasions in recent years, Cathedral Square has hosted gala parties on New Year's Eve. I will long remember my marvelous New Year's Eve there, with a night-long celebration that included a cornucopia of food and drink and non-stop entertainment. Swirling dancers, melodic singers, even a pair of soaring gymnasts. An abundance of confetti and noisemakers for the stroke of midnight. Perhaps a thousand revelers experienced the party of a lifetime.

Cathedral Square may be the premier tourist destination in Old Havana. As such it attracts not only visitors but also an assortment of Cubans who reinvent themselves as photo ops for rent. They customarily are given a coin in exchange for a click or two of the shutter. And what do you get for your investment? Often I have found there a young man who has laboriously and, presumably, painfully adorned his face with body piercing. Not just earrings, lip rings and nose buttons, mind you. But perhaps a hundred or more silvery decorations that practically obscure his face. This one is not for the faint of heart, and I surely wouldn't want to be responsible to get him through an airport metal detector.

More amusing and less gruesome are several elderly gals attired in colorful flowing dresses, usually holding a small dog or cat wearing a silly hat, and always with a huge stub of a cigar drooping from their brightly painted red lips. And sometime I have found there the owner of the doggy mascot of the Havana *Industriales* baseball team, with his little half-breed mostly beagle pup in the wire basket of his bicycle. The puppy seems to thrive on the attention he earns with his little wristwatch, mini-uniform and baseball cap. All of this beauty and gaiety succeeds well in attracting tourists. And they serve as a magnet for the rare but inevitable panhandler, pickpocket, purveyor of fake cigars, *Granma* huckster and peanut vendor.

Just around the corner from Cathedral Square is one of Havana's most prominent, if not most excellent, restaurants: La Bodeguita del Medio. Formerly a neighborhood market, it was converted to a bar and restaurant that became known as a hangout for one of its most famous regulars, Ernest Hemingway. As legend has it, at the small bar of La Bodeguita, Ernest consumed enough *mojitos* to float a boat. Adjoining the bar, as well as up a narrow winding staircase, are tables from which I've ordered many of Cuba's most well-known dishes. Particularly tempting ones include varieties of chicken, roasted pork and shredded beef, always served with mouth-watering fried plantains and mountainous heaps of steaming rice and black beans.

During the time of his frequent visits, Hemingway was residing in the nearby Ambos Mundos Hotel, allowing for a short, if somewhat wobbly, trip home. For anyone who passes through Havana's many arts and crafts markets, paintings of the facade of La Bodeguita, invariably with a vintage car parked in front, will abound.

Another block off the square Orestes proudly showed me one of the Historian's Office's most formidable achievements. On a square block that had formerly housed an impressive colonial building that was part of the University of Havana, at the orders of President Batista, that magnificent structure was demolished. In its place was built a modern office building, completely incompatible with the historic neighborhood, and with a heliport on the roof to attract gamblers from Key West and Miami. "Now we have designed and built a new education facility in keeping with the historic importance of the community," said my friend, the architect. It has modern features, such as reflective glass facades, but its distinctive bell tower and many architectural details are historically correct and a splendid asset in the neighborhood.

# CUBA RISING

With weary feet and my mind awash with the flood of information provided by my expert guide, I decided to recess for the day and resume the following morning to explore the highlights of Havana by car. For it is a sprawling, low-rise city with historical and architectural surprises spread across its hills and boulevards and byways.

An interlude followed, where the heat of the day gave way to cool marble floors and columns of my hotel. Even unpacking provided a brief respite from the splendid bombardment of my senses with new sights and sounds and understanding. I entered my room to find colonial-style furniture and wooden louvers over tall windows overlooking the still bustling square. Streaming light through stained glass cast a rainbow of colors onto the bedcover, which the housekeeper had carefully decorated. Covering the bed and its lumpy mattress and creaking springs was a sprinkling of ruby red hibiscus flowers surrounding white swans created by origami-like folded towels. And a nice effort at a welcoming note was nearby, that read, "You welcome I hope touristics be enjoyed."

I flipped on the television expecting to see the bearded visage of *El Comandante* offering proud rhetoric. Instead I found the setting on a channel for lively music videos, no doubt the preference of the housekeeper, which made me long for a harangue by Castro. Changing the station I found myself tuned to America's news station, CNN. I was aware that CNN had a bureau in Havana, but I continued to be surprised to find it on the air. It is accessible in the tourist hotels, but not elsewhere – at least not legally. But how does a government prevent its people from siphoning an electronic signal out of the air? Not easily, I discovered later.

The phone rang and I was summoned to the lobby by a friend to launch an evening of exploring. He was another American intrigued by Cuba and being in Havana at the same time afforded us a welcome opportunity to share new adventures. A pleasant walk along Obispo Street, crowded with Cubans shopping and strolling, led us to the famous watering hole El Floridita. It is yet another bar made famous by Hemingway's earnest efforts to quench his thirst. While it offers a fancy French restaurant, it is the long mahogany bar that made it a required stop for foreign visitors. It was crowded with boisterous tourists and an occasional Cubano. The drink *du jour*, every *jour*, is the daiquiri. Blenders whir, sugar and rum flow freely, and a bronze statue of Papa, placed where his favorite barstool used to stand, gazes over the happy throng. The inevitable T-shirt vendor passed by, a platter of banana chips appeared on our small bistro table, and a salsa band worked its magic from the corner. Too soon our appointed rounds drew us back onto the street, where Havana's early evening hustle and bustle was gaining momentum.

Before us stood a novel transportation mode that we *had* to experience again, the inimitable cocomobile. Banana yellow in color, half a clamshell in shape, three small wheels, we squirmed into this tiny device for the ride to dinner. Our enthusiasm was slightly tempered when we noticed the driver was wearing a crash helmet. None for us. The young woman at the wheel, with a beaming smile, tried to comprehend where we wanted to go. Being in no hurry, we signaled with looping arm motions, and she grasped our goal of cruising the area first. The "cruising" part got lost in translation. If you can imagine something like a rocket-propelled golf cart, that was us as we accelerated like a missile into a swirling jumble of cars, buses, trucks and pedestrians. "Are we using jet fuel or merely propane?" my amigo asked through gritted teeth. We tilted around corners and darted back and forth to avoid potholes while the driver's glee increased in direct proportion to our rising terror. So we abbreviated the side tour and aimed our projectile toward La Guarida, one of Havana's finest *paladares*, which is a permitted small private restaurant.

Our dinner destination was located in a residential area of central Havana which, to be charitable, can be described as untouched by restoration. We bobbed and weaved through various secondary streets brightened only rarely by a dim streetlight, with folks on the cratered sidewalks chatting, kids tossing baseballs and dogs acting amorously. We stopped in front of a dilapidated building, leaped joyfully from our coco and rewarded the driver with a generous reflection of our gratitude for having survived the ride. Our delight was subdued only by our vista, which resembled London after the blitz. A small sign over massive carved wooden doors confirmed we had reached our destination. A huge Afro-Cuban Habanero (resident of Havana), the greeter and security guard, smiled broadly and swung open the doors, which, in a bygone era, had allowed for horse-drawn carriages to enter what was once the great villa of a prominent family. And now it housed 40 families.

The crumbling stucco walls were adorned with a faded painted flag and some Spanish words, probably an inspirational script by a revolutionary hero. Before us was a winding marble staircase leading upwards into the dark, to the second level high above. There we found what may once have been a grand ballroom with still visible remnants of elaborate moldings and statues, now crumbling. From nearby windows and doors, flickering light suggested the resident families were following their dinners with television. The white marble path drew us upwards to another landing, where little children were scurrying about and asking for ballpoint pens. An unmarked door with a buzzer dangling from a loose wire proved to be the *paladar*, a small restaurant run by a family. We were admitted, feeling like we had been granted rare access to Hernando's Hideaway. The foyer was decorated with photos of fashion shoots that had been posed here, the sleek cutting edge models juxtaposed with the disintegrating structure. Fading movie posters of the film *Fresa y Chocolate (Strawberry and Chocolate)*, some scenes of which had been filmed here, added to the ambiance.

As required by Cuban law, the *paladar* was located on the premises of the owner. Somewhat divergent from law, it appeared to have many more than the permitted number of 12 seats, and it appeared doubtful that all of the staff was, in fact, members of the owner's family. How does Havana's most famous *paladar* get reviewed in the *New York Times* and continue to thrive in open violation of the law? That is yet another of the bafflements quintessentially Cuban.

The décor, perhaps to be dubbed neo-colonial crumbly, was enhanced by wonderful modern artworks, flickering candles in antique candelabra, and old artifacts adorning practically every space that did not have a chair with a pleased visitor on it. The menu was diverse, the food was excellent, and the dessert *de rigueur* is, of course, strawberry and chocolate ice cream. We learned only later that selecting the strawberry flavor often evoked a wink and a smile, as it was an allusion to being gay in the film. Adding to the surreal setting was our awareness that from a kitchen not much larger than a closet somehow emerged a hundred or more fine meals each evening.

Although hours had passed like minutes, we had miles to go before we slept. So down the spiral staircase we stumbled, rather gingerly in light of the *mojitos* and *Cuba libres* (rum, Coke and a lime wedge) we had enjoyed, and back to Havana after dark.

As we were only blocks from one of the city's premier salsa clubs, Casa de Musica, we walked along a lively street to enjoy yet another of Havana's signature delights. It was not hard to find. The rhythmic music drew us closer, "independent" taxi drivers and their ramshackle vintage cars crowded in front, hustlers waved us over, and a group of gals awaiting entry beckoned as we came near. That night, at least, the women were in the majority, and evidently it was required that they could enter only if accompanied by a fellow.

And who were these women? Let me explain, for "working girls" are not uncommon in Havana. Understanding the realities of this facet of life in a poor country is important. Prostitution was illegal after the Revolution, and the law was enforced. Inevitably, it crept back onto the social scene as tourism expanded and the economy teetered on the verge of collapse. In the early 1990s it simply got out of hand. Food was scarce, jobs were hard to find, and even if one were earning a customary salary of $17 a month, how did that stack up against earning a multiple of that sum in a few hours? Tourists had to plow through a cordon of prostitutes around each hotel and restaurant. Those excesses provoked stronger enforcement and, in anticipation of the papal visit in 1998, the gals were swept from the streets and often were penalized or "re-educated." As the pendulum later swung back, and enforcement gave way to higher priorities, they began to reappear – sometimes on the streets but predictably in abundance in the salsa clubs. There seems to have evolved a tacit understanding that "out of sight, off the streets," was marginally acceptable.

Despite allegations to the contrary, it appears to me that Cuba has *not* become a destination for "sexcapades," except for perhaps a very few visitors. Yes, prostitution does exist in Cuba, and it is a sad reality of the times and sadder still for the young women who follow this path.

As mentioned, the gals must enter the salsa club accompanied by a guy. So some clamor erupts as potential male companions arrive on the scene. On one indelibly memorable occasion, I arrived at a salsa club in a minivan with a half-dozen fellows. (Yes, most visitors go to the clubs solely to enjoy the music and dancing.) As had been the case in the past, a gathering of about 20 attractive young women in colorful spandex stood just beside the entrance. When we drove up and the van parked, this gaggle of gals, en masse, raced the 50 feet to our arrival. They surrounded the van, singing, smiling, waving, and gently rocking the van. My bewildered friends, who had neither seen nor even imagined such a reception, were rendered speechless, and all were sporting very quizzical looks. They weren't sure if they were about to be slain or if they had already died and gone to Heaven! Such brave fellows were not deterred and leaped from the van into the waiting clutches of new amigas who were in high spirits for this opportunity to get into the club, and maybe even have their cover charges paid for them.

So into the haven of salsa we cruised, soon thankful that the music was likely to be more memorable than the décor. In better days this dancehall had been a grand movie theatre, but when we arrived it looked like a deteriorated bingo parlor, and we were thankful that the lighting was dim.

The penalty for being early was that the population was mostly male and that recorded music, not live, was blaring. After an hour of nursing *Cuba libres*, a magical transition swept through the building. Lights dimmed and scores of pretty gals streamed in – perhaps a Cuban version of certain species that migrate in response to the changing amount of moonlight. Some gathered in murmuring little huddles while others cruised through in search of an empty chair or a single fellow. All showed their excitement in anticipation of a live salsa performance and their opportunity to sway to sensuous Latin rhythms.

The musicians finally emerged on stage about an hour after their scheduled time. You see, in Cuba, carefully choreographed nonchalance is in evidence. The higher your celebrity status, the later you may start without fear of reprisal. In fact, tardiness tends to confirm your elevated status. One memorable evening I was drawn to a club where Cuba's premier salsa group Los Van Van was to play. I arrived at about 11 p.m., assuming that I'd be an hour early, but determined not to miss this acclaimed band. Eleven o'clock turned to midnight, and the *mojitos* kept flowing. Twelve turned to 1 and then to 2 o'clock. Weary of recorded music and saturated with *mojitos*, but knowing the band would appear at any moment, I held my ground. Finally, hugely disappointed that my watch read 3 o'clock in the morning and I hadn't heard a note of live music yet, I bailed. But that was another night.

Soon the brass blared, the drums pounded and the salsa began. No, this was not your basic tourism rendition of the all-too-familiar *Guantanamera* (however lovely), nor the melodic *Ode to Che Guevara*. This was ear-piercing, table-tapping, hip-swinging, 20 magical musicians exulting a uniquely Cuban performance. Watching the dance floor there could be little doubt about which of the dancers were Cuban and which were not. The Cuban men were graceful partners, always beautifully in motion with the music, perhaps a little deferential to their gals. The rhythm of the women was nothing short of poetic. They were in the zone, the syncopated sounds seeming to capture their souls as well as their bodies. Even the women who were not on the dance floor were swaying by their tables and in the aisles, unable and not wanting to disconnect the sounds of salsa from their hips and arms and legs.

We assumed the spectacle went on until dawn, but quietly withdrew to ponder the day and capture a few hours of sleep in anticipation of the next one. We left the club to find a beehive of activity outside. Latecomers were arriving, gals continued to await their prospective escorts, and enthusiastic drivers of (illegal) taxis were waving to catch our attention. In the wee hours, the likelihood of finding a customary taxi were slim, so we dove into the throng of drivers until we found the proprietor of an ancient Packard that would meet the need, or so we thought. We piled in and negotiated a small fare for the short ride back to the hotel.

Then another splendidly Havanan experience unfolded. A young fellow, evidently the son of the car's owner, popped open the hood and connected a plastic tube somewhere in the engine. Then he crammed himself into the tiny remaining space in the front seat, holding a plastic bottle at the other end of the tube. My amigo and I exchanged bewildered glances, and we soon discovered that the bottle held a quart of gasoline and was a clever improvisation to overcome what was apparently a disconnect between the lumbering antique's gas tank and its carburetor! Our eyeballs rolled and *nobody* lit a cigar! Away we chugged, for half a block anyway. The engine sputtered, died like an old mule, and we drifted a short way. Frantic hand waving by the driver left no doubt that his plan was to steer while the rest of us got out and pushed. We joked about our AAA cards, then pushed. The engine sprang to life as our trusty steed lurched into gear. Having overcome gravity, the driver was not inclined to stop. So we trotted alongside and leaped into the rolling car, with the son continuing to manage the fuel department. Finally, we reached the hotel, probably long after we could have walked the distance, and we parted friends with a generous tip. The surprising adventures Havana has to offer seemed to start when my eyes opened and did not cease until they closed for a brief respite.

A quick shower with water that swayed between scalding and chilly, failing to elicit lather from a soap bar about the size of a pack of matches, water flowing toward a drain that did not want to release its latest catch. It felt good anyway, as I grabbed for the towel that felt like a loofah and should long ago have been retired. No problem. After all, I was in Havana to escape from conventional places and their too many amenities. And that escape had many more miles to cover.

Chapter 5

## AN EXPANSIVE METROPOLIS

What seemed like minutes passed, but actually a grand three hours of sleep expired with the roar of a motor outside the window on the square. No sirens, but a continuous rumble that finally drew me to the louvered doors that led out to a small balcony. There, in the predawn darkness was a behemoth battered water tanker truck, disgorging its potable water into the hotel's tanks. Not so conducive to a good night's rest, but better than some of the alternatives that came to mind. Back to bed, out like a light. Until the next rumbling outside that sounded like a brigade of tanks was approaching over the cobblestones. Up again, now well past dawn, back to the balcony to see a constant stream of older men pushing and pulling battered carts with metal wheels, laden with treasure troves of antique books to be displayed and sold at the plaza.

Fate had conspired against me, so I flipped on CNN, still amazed to be in the loop of news in this seemingly faraway place. Curious to see the streetscape before the meandering dogs and pigeons were supplanted by throngs of tourists, I dressed and inched my way downstairs on the elevator, whose age was far beyond mine. The clatter of opening the sliding gate awoke the barman, bellman and security guard who likely had passed their graveyard shift snoozing. Quickly the lights came on, the clunking of cabinet doors suggested that *café Cubano*, a hearty aromatic espresso customarily doused with sugar, was soon to be available. After precisely such a brew, double in my case, to jolt me awake and compensate for lack of sleep, I drifted into the plaza. Several elderly ladies were swatting at the dust and few leaves that had appeared overnight with brooms so raggedy that it is a generous stretch to describe them as such. More like a stick with some ruffles of straw at one end. Well, every little bit helps when the government statisticians strive to achieve their much-publicized "full-employment economy." As the square came to life I returned to the hotel to prepare for an outing to revisit some of the highlights of Havana.

With driver, guide, camera and amigo in tow, we clambered into another vintage taxi, a sky blue Buick convertible that had rolled off the assembly line in Detroit over a half-century earlier. The engine coughed, a plume of blue smoke puffed out of the exhaust pipe, and we headed west following the expansion of Havana from the colonial area around the harbor toward progressively later construction and architectural styles. As we had seen much of the Malecon, we decided to drive through the back streets to Central Park and the Capitolio. This continues to be a thriving commercial area and the streets were lined with battered vehicles that serve as taxis for the locals. Under Cuban law they are available *only* to Cubans, not to tourists, who pay in Cuban pesos – the native currency that would be of virtually no use to foreigners. First we came upon Fraternity Park, dotted with magnificent royal palms and home to a fine sculptured bust of Abraham Lincoln, clearly revered in far more than one country. The streetscape transitioned to Central Park, lined with many of Havana's fine old hotels, the splendid new Saratoga Hotel and beautiful buildings, such as a grand theatre that is home to the National Ballet of Cuba. Dominating the neighborhood is the towering 300-foot-high dome of the gleaming white Capitolio. It is now home to the Ministry of Science, Technology and the Environment, as the People's Assembly meets in more humble quarters several miles away. It's a pity, as the former legislative chambers are formidable, beautiful and rich in history.

Weaving past pedestrians, crammed buses, pedicabs, horse-drawn carts and an assortment of other wheeled anomalies, we drove a short way to the University of Havana. Founded in 1728, it is the oldest university in the Western Hemisphere and maintains an impressive reputation. Its fine old buildings sprawl across many blocks, but most impressive is the wide expanse of steps leading up to the campus. At the entry rests a beautiful sculpture of Alma Mater. It was on these steps, walked frequently by Fidel Castro and generations of student activists, where troops of dictator Batista fired upon and killed protestors during his brutal regime in the 1950s.

Shifting gears, literally and figuratively, the huge Colon Cemetery was not far and certainly ranks among Havana's most distinctive landmarks. Approaching, I was impressed by the massive stone archway that invites us in to this place that so many have made only a one-way trip. Similar to the famous St. Louis necropolis in New Orleans, the tombs are mainly above ground and range from sadly simple to majestic, even flamboyant. We were drawn to the largest monument, which turned out to be for a group of firefighters who perished in the line of duty. Certainly, the most famous tomb is the Milagrosa, commemorating a woman who died in childbirth, and the stillborn child was placed at her feet in the tomb. When opened years later, legend has it that the remains of the child were found miraculously to be at her mother's breast. The tomb is always adorned with fresh flowers, and many Cubans come here to pray for children. However fascinating, we were drawn away by less somber possibilities.

# CUBA RISING

Maneuvering through traffic, we found ourselves approaching the towering Habana Libre Hotel, formerly the Havana Hilton. You can be certain the Hilton folks would love to have that property back in their possession, but it seems unlikely in the extreme. Hope springs eternal, at least, that someday the company could be compensated for its expropriation after the Revolution. The hotel's vast lobby was where the newly victorious Fidel Castro held court among foreign tourists and local admirers after his return to Havana in 1959, when his charisma and enthusiasm won the grudging admiration of many a skeptic. In fact, it served as a temporary headquarters for his key people. Quickly our attention was drawn to another green expanse across the intersection from the hotel.

In the center of this park sat a structure that resembled a spaceship, actually one of the most popular destinations in all of Havana, the Coppelia ice cream parlor. This sweet place is known not only for the mouth-watering excellence of its only fare, various flavors of delicious ice cream, but also for the long lines that snake around the building, through the park, and along the sidewalks. One sees not only children but also adults, by the hundreds, chatting and socializing with whomever is nearby. It has become an institution, a ritual, and a pleasing way to pass several hours waiting in line to spend a few pennies on a delicious ice cream cone. It is not just the price nor the fabulous taste of the ice cream that draws these throngs. It has become a social event, and no one complains about waiting in these long lines. Those who persevere are eventually wonderfully rewarded with not only a social highlight of their day or week but also with what may be the planet's most mouth-watering ice cream. No artificial flavors, no artificial preservatives, just smooth, rich ice cream with a butterfat content that must be sky high.

We could not resist. Our enthusiasm for a morning dessert break was amplified by knowing that we, as foreigners, could go directly to a small kiosk to be served without waiting in line. Presuming we had hard currency to spend, that is. Of course, we missed the socializing, we did not miss hours that we had dedicated to sightseeing, and we did pay enormously more for our cones than the Cubans. Passing it by was unthinkable!

Back to the Malecon and out its undulating broad expanses. At its end the roadway dipped into a tunnel under a river marking the dividing line between Vedado and fashionable Miramar. As if someone had flicked a switch, the road widened and a broad median planted with lush green shrubs and manicured trees appeared. On each side of Fifth Avenue were fabulous villas, dating back to the early 20th century. Each in a different style, a variety of pastel colors, and wonderfully restored and maintained. Many housed foreign embassies and chancelleries, each flying the flag of its native land. Some of the fine villas had been converted to use by various Cuban government agencies, while others had been leased as offices for foreign companies. The fabulous blocks were interrupted only by occasional green open spaces and parks, including one with a fine statue of Beatle John Lennon seated pensively on a park bench. Elderly residents of the neighborhood watch over the statue to ensure that Lennon's eyeglasses no longer disappear into the pockets of enthusiastic admirers.

Our meander down Fifth Avenue, through synchronized traffic signals, soon led us to an architectural encounter of the worst kind. Alongside us was a huge walled compound with a tall windowless monstrosity that looked like a failed effort of a child and its Lego blocks. It was totally out of harmony with the neighborhood. It was the former Embassy of the Soviet Union, and it now housed the diplomatic corps of Russia. With a lurch and a sigh we left it behind as a series of large, ornate oceanside buildings loomed ahead.

"Those were the private clubs of the rich people before the Revolution," we were told, "and today they are social clubs for different groups of workers." The condition of those buildings, mere shadows of their former selves, might not be impressive. But for a factory worker to be able to relax seaside in Havana did seem to be a nice perk, as well as a very long way from the days when only wealthy foreign folks used Cuba as their playground.

Cruising further along Fifth Avenue we were surprised to find an elaborate carnival site for children. Gigantic plastic cartoon characters, little roller coasters, colorful buildings that had yet to reveal their intentions and lots of merriment in the offing. In a country that is flat-out crazy about its kids, this has become a welcome addition to a city that offers precious few amusements to its inhabitants.

Well past the villas and embassy row we came across a huge development of modern office buildings. It was being built out over several phases, and about one-third of the office towers were completed and occupied, the finest first-class office space in Havana, with rental prices reportedly in the stratosphere. Interestingly, this was a joint venture between the Cuban government and an Israeli firm. Those two countries have had an acrimonious relationship in recent decades, Israel being one of the handful of nations that routinely supports the U.S. economic embargo of Cuba. But those political policies clearly are no obstacle to thriving bilateral business partnerships on the island.

Nearing the westernmost point on our explorations away from the city center, we arrived at a beautifully landscaped development called Club Habana. Before the Revolution it was the elegant Biltmore Habana Yacht and Country Club. As legend has it, membership was denied to President Batista because he was mulatto and not white-skinned. Recently, modern condominiums for foreign businesspeople and diplomats have been added, but the focal point remains the club's exquisite beachfront villa itself. Inside it offers finely decorated ballrooms and dining rooms, bars, covered verandas and meeting rooms.

But it is the outside that is so special. It sits on the only sandy beach in Havana, punctuated with colorful umbrellas and chaises. A vast swimming pool is tempting, the beach volleyball court is vibrating with laughter and grunts, the jet skis are flying by with their watery rooster tails, and the oceanside bar has attracted a crowd. Time kept us from exploring the fitness center, but an earlier visit there was surprising.

I was in town with some friends, one of whom owned a company that manufactured exercise equipment. Like any good businessman he was curious to see the products of his competitors, whose ability to export to Cuba was not limited by their governments, nor by the U.S. economic embargo. So into the fitness center we went, past a fresh juice bar, past a tiny shop selling western sportswear, and into the expansive room full of treadmills, step climbers and an assortment of other body-punishing devices. My friend stopped dead in his tracks, eyes wide open. "What's up?" I asked, "You look like you just saw a ghost." "Not a ghost," he said, "just a room full of equipment that was manufactured by *my* company!" He walked through the facility, checking serial numbers, gently touching each piece as if they had arrived through divine intervention. That, however, was not to be the explanation. "It's a leaky economic blockade." I chuckled. "Your items could have been transshipped to Havana from any of dozens of foreign countries." We all sported wide smiles and, as for my friend, he had received the best imaginable souvenir of Cuba.

Ever onward for the intrepid visitors to Havana, for we were approaching the turnaround point of our day's adventure. We chugged past Marina Hemingway, which was a fine place for visiting yachts to be moored. Often I have been surprised to find vessels there proudly flying an American flag. And it continues to host an annual billfish tournament in honor of the famed author's passion for sport fishing. An interesting historical footnote is the fact that Hemingway and Fidel Castro met nearby, for the *only* time, when Castro presented the victory cups to the winning fishermen after the first tournament in 1960. Shortly thereafter Hemingway left the island for the final time, and he died the following year at his home in Idaho.

Our final visit during our westbound adventure was to the small village of Jaimanitas. It is a sleepy little town full of modest homes within an easy commute of Havana. And it is home to one of Cuba's most remarkable and certainly most unconventional artists, Jose Fuster, a world-renowned painter in oils who also excels in watercolors and ceramics, aptly described as a very Cuban Picasso. Fuster has exhibited worldwide, including in the United States, and his artworks are available in prices ranging from modest to tens of thousands of dollars.

We approached to find colorful, playful ceramic mosaics embedded in the stucco walls surrounding the neighboring homes. And then, as if arriving at the gateway to a wonderland, his home and studio came into view. I was overwhelmed by the elaborate and detailed mosaics of people and animals and designs, all of which are in some way evocative of Cuba. There is the sprawling crocodile, reminiscent of the shape of Cuba; the white rooster with a brilliant red comb, representing *machismo* on the island; towering royal palm trees that are a symbol of Cuba's rich flora; a voluptuous caricature of a woman reminding us of the island's beautiful females; and a *bracero* in a cowboy hat, a traditional worker. Some tower overhead, others are on the walls, and still others are embedded in benches, chairs and even the small swimming pool. It was a surprising welcome.

Through the portal and into the small yard we went, eyes swaying from side to side to try to absorb the fabulous array of color and characters. Out of the doorway emerged a beaming Jose, arms outstretched in anticipation of a bear hug known as an *abrazo*. "Mister Jonathan," he beckoned. "It is wonderful to have you visit again!" The pleasure, of course, was ours. Recovering from our shock and amazement at the spectacle we had seen already, Jose waved us toward the studios, which occupy all three floors of the house, and also the house next door that had been merged into his own.

A glance at the colorful oil paintings in the first floor studio confirmed the fanciful excellence of his work. Floating cartoon-like Cubanos around a table sharing a small fish, apparently a parody of the Last Supper; pleasantly distorted *Habaneros* in front of a scene reminiscent of Havana's skyline, and a woman in rich hues of blue and brown with a snow white rooster, an allusion to the sexuality that is so characteristic of the country. Up the narrow staircase, with an arrow pointing to a low-hanging beam taped with foam, to the ceramics studio Jose shares with his ceramic artist son, Alex. Brightly enameled plates and tiles and sculptures of bizarre characters cover the table surfaces and hang precariously from the walls. In the corner sits an electric kiln used to fire the ceramics. It occurred to me, but I was too politically correct to ask, how can such a siphon of electricity be permitted when many simple kitchen appliances were banned to conserve power? Up another staircase, past a relic of a sewing machine mounted on a pedestal to the third floor studio and a splendid large balcony with a panoramic view of the low-rise pastel town and the blue sea beyond.

Jose scurried about, pointing enthusiastically to this and that creation, all the while jabbering at incomprehensible speed in Spanish. Once again my brain registered sensory overload. We bought a couple of small artworks, my new acquisition soon to join more than a dozen already adorning walls in my California home. The artists, father and son, were busy preparing for their upcoming exhibit in Madrid, which they would stage and attend. As the adrenalin subsided, we bid farewell and bon voyage to our dear friends whose talent and creativity seemed to know no bounds. I chuckled on the way to the car, pondering the saying "Money can't buy happiness." That soul, whose name is lost to history, may have been able to turn a phrase but surely had never been to the studio of the artist known as Fuster of Cuba. For he is a wonderment, a national treasure who has not only bought happiness for his community by transforming it into a fantasyland of decorative art but also has provided it to visitors – one cherished artwork at a time.

We sped back to the Old City, savoring the sights and sounds of the morning and ready to replenish our camera batteries as well as ourselves. Past more lovely embassy buildings, lush parks with giant drooping banyan trees and past the small road that led secretively to Fidel Castro's compound. Soon after we emerged from Miramar and back onto the Malecon, its entire length came into sight as it gently curved along the waterfront, all the way to the harbor entrance with El Morro's lighthouse blinking a friendly welcome. On a slope above the highway we passed the huge Nacional Hotel, a landmark that continues to exceed all other Cuban hotels in the beauty of its public spaces, the lush grounds with strolling peacocks, waterfalls and the encyclopedic array of photos of the world's most famous people who have stayed there.

As we were in the vicinity of a good friend, we used our guide's surprisingly reliable cell phone to call and learn if she were home and if we could stop by for a brief visit. To my delight, she said we would be welcome. Our driver maneuvered through cratered side streets and came upon her family home. She maintained possession after the Revolution because it was private property before and she was entitled to keep it. Cuban law provides for the continuance of private ownership, and it is a legal concept with strong foundations. In fact, in the case of this woman, a government ministry has been asking her for years if they could purchase the home from her so they could expand nearby offices onto her site. She responded, "I will not sell my home to you, but if you can provide me a comparable dwelling in a neighborhood that I like, I would move." Time after time the officials approached her with alternative homes, and each time they were rebuffed. So did the Cuban government confiscate her property? No, absolutely not. They fully respected her property rights and there she remains.

# CUBA RISING

We were welcomed at the gate by my friend Maria and her two beautifully groomed little white corgis, each with a pink ribbon on its bobbing head. Although one sees a few stray dogs on the streets of Havana, it always amazes me, in view of financial limitations, to see how many Cubans have pets and how wonderfully they are cared for. We entered her patio, overflowing with tropical plants surrounding a little pond. Then into an enclosed porch, where wicker rocking chairs surrounded by more plants gave the impression of a lush oasis. There we enjoyed the first sight of Maria's uncommonly fine collection of art. The walls were hung, frame to frame, with dozens of superb examples of 20th century Cuban artists. As we began to savor this fine private collection, Maria handed to each of us a demitasse of robust Cuban coffee, with a generous dollop of sugar, as is customary and ubiquitous on the island. Some of her prints and canvases were so fine, she explained, "They would not be permitted to leave the country as they were considered to be national treasures." How this collection came to be is a remarkable story combined with a terrible tragedy.

One of Maria's four children was a promoter of many of Cuba's leading contemporary artists, assisting them in organizing exhibits at home and abroad. He was a friend of mine and as nice a fellow as one could imagine. Over the years he acquired many of the works in this splendid collection, and they were hung in the family home. A few years ago, the worst imaginable calamity struck. He was murdered in a botched robbery at the house. This was more than devastating to Maria. It collapsed her life, and only after several years did she begin to recover to a marginal version of normalcy. The murderers were finally caught, tried and imprisoned. But Maria had to relive the horror during the course of several court proceedings. "I saw the beasts that ended my boy's precious life," she whispered. "They are antisocial scum and, although they were sentenced to 28 years in prison, my son will never again live, talk or make plans for some day ahead."

Maria seemed to feel a need to vent about this terror, and each time it left her debilitated. Head down, she walked slowly to the kitchen to prepare more coffee for us. Our sadness left us speechless until we could shift the focus to her artworks, which are such an important part of her life. Each piece was described in detail: artist, techniques, provenance. She said she may need to sell some of her precious treasures in order to get by on her miserly pension of $7 each month. Understandably, she is bitter about that dilemma after a career of devoted service to her country. Our visit concluded on an upbeat note as we shared her joy arising from the artworks, her sweet dwelling, and her many friends. Leaving her a few Western news magazines, paperback thrillers and some medicine to share with friends and neighbors, we emerged back into the sunlit street and returned to our hotel both saddened and uplifted.

Santa Isabel's welcoming smiles greeted us as we deposited our morning's accumulation of treasures and mellowed in its cool shade after the blazing Cuban sun had taken its toll. A complimentary *mojito* with its mint leaves spilling over the top of the glass provided the perfect interlude before lunch. We walked the few blocks through and past Plaza de Armas, now bustling with vendors, tourists and small clusters of school children, with salsa music washing over the entire spectacle.

A left turn down a nondescript side street to Comendador, a small bar and restaurant that presented the finest array of *tappas* in Havana. After we were served a cool Crystal, Cuba's most popular beer, our table soon was laden with salads, fresh-baked bread and heaping plates of a variety of small servings of perhaps a dozen different *tappas*. It is beyond my culinary talent to name them. In fact, I could barely discern the ingredients beyond a few obvious ones, such as Chorizo sausage, potato quiche, and petite vegetable pastries. Well-fed and relaxed, we sat back in anticipation of the inevitable and tantalizing scoop of ice cream. Oops, I forgot. At this charming little *taberna* (tavern) the *tappas* are merely an appetizer and the main course follows.

Waiters descended with plates full of steamed vegetables, rice and a gigantic serving of grilled chicken. Quandary time. Do we politely send it back, after which it likely would be consumed by the staff or later by their families? Do we nibble at it, acting suave, as if we were expecting yet another course of food? Do we just run? Embarrassed and finding the simple food to be uncommonly tasty, we ate until we were just shy of bursting.

We paid the small bill and exited. We crossed San Francisco Plaza to meet our driver, noticing that Havana harbor's only cruise ship dock was occupied by a sleek white liner that sails the Caribbean with mainly European tourists. The great expanses and many possibilities of Havana had absorbed these 1,000 visitors without the slightest disruption of her normal routine. Our U-turn by Havana Club's splendid Museum of Rum took us back past harborfront warehouses, where sweat streamed from the muscular backs of workers who were unloading railroad cars laden with giant sacks of rice. Near the harbor entrance we dodged traffic and pedestrians to loop onto the access road to the tunnel under the harbor. It was a two-lane, two-minute drive through a fog of exhaust fumes. Before it was constructed by a French company in 1958, a circuitous traffic-jammed route that could last an hour was required to reach the eastern side of the harbor. Its opening enabled the construction of massive blocks of Soviet-style apartments, and later an extensive sports complex for the Pan American Games held in Havana in 1990.

A short drive with the rocky coast to our left and undeveloped land to our right brought us to the exit that would lead us to Hemingway's former home, Finca Bijia. Through the bustling neighborhood of San Francisco de Paula we went onto a side street leading to the gates of the farm. The serpentine driveway carried us up the hill, and soon the guesthouse and main house came into view. For reasons I could not explain, but for which I took full credit, a group of adorable schoolchildren in their red-and-white uniforms were singing Cuban melodies on the wide steps leading to the front door.

The Hemingway home, now a museum, underwent a much-needed restoration in 2006. It is a rather simple dwelling, neither huge nor ornate, reminiscent of his home in Key West. It sits on a hilltop, savoring the breezes, with a view to the sea and the city in the distance. Because the home is full of original furnishings and decorations, no one is allowed inside. No one, that is, except folks like us who charm the guards with a generous gratuity. All the rooms are on one level and can easily be seen well through the many open windows. We enjoyed the climb up the adjoining tower that Hemingway's wife had built for him as a sanctuary where he could do his writing. "He used it only once for that purpose" the guard volunteered to us. A stone path through verdant gardens led us to a huge swimming pool that must have been an unprecedented amenity when it was built in the 1930s. Adjacent to the pool we found a large shelter, formerly a tennis court, under which rested Hemingway's fishing vessel *Pilar.* It had been moored in the fishing village of Cojimar, some miles away, when he sailed on it. "Did you know that Hemingway had a machine gun mounted on the bridge and he went out in search of German submarines during World War II?" asked our guide. Hemingway, like most else about Cuba, was full of surprises.

As we left Hemingway's farm, we could not resist yet another kiosk overflowing with postcards and salsa CD's. In a dusty corner of the display case I found what was certainly my most bizarre memento of Cuba. In a yellowing plastic bag was a money clip, with an enameled little Cuban flag centered on a large silvery dollar ($) sign. What could possibly confirm better that Cuba is fraught with ironies? In a land where the dollar has gyrated among much sought, illegal, universal and now irrelevant, an official enterprise was manufacturing a souvenir celebrating it!

Still nodding my head in amazement, we departed to the fishing village of Cojimar. Presumably Hemingway chose this place to moor *Pilar* because it has a fine protected harbor and the town was only a short drive from his home. He thrived among the locals, especially the simple fishermen. I found only two landmarks there, but both are very special ones indeed. The monument to Hemingway, which has been described on other pages, stands by the sea and by a small 18th century Spanish fortress. It has guarded the harbor entrance for about 300 years, and even today it continues to house a few Cuban military personnel. Its occupancy is confirmed not by bristling weapons, but by the soldiers' laundry waving and drying in the ocean breeze. Just a few blocks away is La Terraza, a bustling neighborhood pub that served as yet another of the great author's favorite watering holes. There he dined and drank, but mostly drank, and spun fishermen's tales during many hours of very many days. The walls are hung with photos and paintings of the author and, if walls could speak, what wonderful stories we would hear.

As we sped back toward Habana Vieja, the entry to the fortresses, which guarded Havana harbor from the eastern side, beckoned us. El Morro, with its towering lighthouse at the very entrance to the harbor, was nicely restored to its original formidable presence, which threatened to rain cannon fire upon marauding pirates or invading fleets. From its ramparts a breathtaking view of Havana rolled out like a magnificent carpet into the far distance. A little father along the harbor entrance was La Cabaña, a massive complex of fortifications that housed 3,000 Spanish troops at one time and was a terrible prison well into the 20th century. The massive walls enclosed a green expanse where cavalry horses once grazed, and yet another stone wall served as the inner defense. Inside La Cabaña, restoration had progressed far and was continuing. Just inside the entry was the former office of Che Guevara, now a museum in his honor. The armory, chapel and other vast rooms were now museums, souvenir shops and restaurants. Only a little imagination called forth the sounds of soldiers marching in close order drill, the wails of prisoners and the echoing shots of execution squads. This window on the world of the Spanish occupation of Cuba was fascinating, and then the city summoned us to return.

As we approached the Plaza de Armas, children were riding slouching ponies in the nearby park, and the attractions of the vast handicrafts market drew us. I hardly knew where to begin to explore this massive display of art and souvenirs, so we chose the closest aisle, which extended for blocks and was dedicated to works of art. Each little stall offered a dozen or more colorful artworks, usually by the same artist. The styles and techniques seemed to run the entire gamut known to mankind. Watercolors, oils, prints, silkscreens, photographs and more. Colorful, monotones, abstracts, still lifes, portraits, landscapes, pop art, knockoffs of classics, some with political undertones and most without. It was a visual feast, and often the artists themselves were present for conversation and friendly haggling over price.

I purchased another oil painting by Mendiola, an artist whose works I had been collecting for years. The canvas of blues and browns showed an Impressionist view of a fishing village with skiffs tossing in the surf and royal palms bending to the wind. It disappeared, tightly rolled into a cardboard tube, and moments later it was returned with a broad smile, a firm handshake and the little export license that verified to the Cuban emigration officials at the airport that I was not smuggling a national treasure out of the country. Well-pleased with my latest acquisition, we continued past countless images of Che Guevara, La Bodeguita and Cathedral Square. All of these were certain to be considerably more lovely away from the chaos of the marketplace, hung on a wall in Europe or North America, to elicit sweet memories of Cuba for years to come.

The next aisle, with its bustling crowd, was home to scores more of vendors of every imaginable memento, and some that were beyond imaginable. Carvings from rare Cuban hardwoods, humidors, crocheted dresses, Che Guevara-style berets, ceramic plates, jewelry of beads and dyed cow bones, T-shirts, castanets and bongo drums. And that was just in the *first* several booths. Only the frequent hawkers of cigars interrupted the tsunami of possibilities. "Do you want a Cohiba? My mother works in the factory," said one. "Cigars, my friend? These are perfecto," said another. I told my friend that if he believed any of them, then I had a bridge from Brooklyn that I would like to sell him. Havana, and especially this marketplace, is awash in purveyors of fake cigars.

An hour later, our wallets only slightly depleted, but our minds numbed by the trek through all four aisles of trinkets and souvenirs, we wandered back to the comparative sanctuary of our hotel.

Two days in Havana provided me with a lifetime of memories, but I had only scratched the surface. Visits before and after added depth and breadth, and frustration. For the beauty and complexity of that city and its people may be observed but never fully appreciated, or even understood, by anyone whose origins are elsewhere.

CHAPTER 6

## FIDEL: SUPERSTAR

Havana enjoys a splendid modern international airport terminal with acres of fine marble and walls of soaring glass. It is the envy of many capitals in small countries the world over. In the huge passenger hall are endless rows of modern chairs, a dozen jetways and a towering ceiling adorned with the colorful flags of the nations of the world. *All* of the nations, including the United States of America. That struck me as odd.

Soon after this strange discovery, I met with an official of the Ministry of Foreign Affairs and revealed my bafflement. "How do you explain the flag of your 'arch-enemy' the United States hanging prominently in your airport arrivals lounge?" He responded succinctly, "There is only one person in Cuba who can explain that, and only one person who could have given the order for it to be done." Fidel Castro is renowned as a micromanager whose reach extends into every niche in his country.

Fidel Castro Ruz could reasonably be described as an unlikely revolutionary. Born to a wealthy family with more than

26,000 acres of sugar cane, trees for lumber and orange groves in rural Oriente Province, he was dispatched to the finest parochial schools and lacked little during his early years. (Ironically, among his first acts after the success of the Revolution was to order the government to expropriate his own family's farm, in conjunction with national land reform. In this case, the kid *literally* took away the farm. I was told that Fidel's mother barred the door with a Winchester rifle and was grumpy, *very* grumpy, and muttered about "my shameless son."

Castro's youth in remote Oriente, some 400 miles east of Havana, appears to have been unremarkable, characterized by a passion for baseball, self-consciousness about having been born out of wedlock, and an amusing letter he penned to President Franklin Delano Roosevelt in 1940, asking for ten dollars. (He got a perfunctory response, but no 10 bucks).

At the age of 11, Fidel (along with his older brother, Ramon, and his younger brother, Raul) was enrolled in the prestigious Jesuit boarding school Colegio de Dolores, in Santiago. Challenged by his peers, perhaps for the first time, traits took shape that would propel Fidel Castro to a lifetime as an overachiever. His keen mind and photographic memory enabled him to excel academically simply by last-minute cramming for exams; his reckless bravado to achieve personal recognition was illustrated when he leapt out of a third-story window to impress his classmates; his disdain for conventional norms was evident from his irregular adherence to Dolores' dress code, and his compulsion to be a leader was apparent both on competitive sports fields and in activities such as camping and hiking.

An example of Castro's extraordinary memory, which has enabled him to be a micromanager of practically everything on the island, comes to mind. A friend of mine who is an executive at La Casa de los Americas, a library and research center in Havana, told this anecdote: The facility, housed in a fabulous art deco building just off the Malecon, needed room for expansion and applied for permission to build an addition on the adjoining vacant lot. As is not uncommon in Havana, no response from the government was forthcoming. Years passed. "One day I was invited to a reception that was hosted by the president," my friend said. "I went through the receiving line and shook hands with him. He asked where I worked and I told him. He immediately responded, "Then you must be the fellow who, a few years ago, asked for a parcel of land next to your office.' I was amazed by the memory of the man." The last time I checked, he was still waiting.

After five years at Dolores, Castro was sent to another prep school, Belen in Havana. In the vibrant capital city he thrived and went on to enroll in the prestigious University of Havana. It proved to be fertile ground for dissent during an era of puppet dictators in a country rife with corruption and exploitation of a huge impoverished underclass. These troubling circumstances understandably radicalized Fidel, along with many of his schoolmates. Political activists on campus coalesced into often violent rival gangs that mirrored the country's turbulent political parties in the late 1940s. Historians and Fidel's former classmates agree that he packed a handgun. Frequent accusations that he actually shot a rival gang leader have not been proven. His growing reputation during those chaotic school years was that of a bully, opportunist, aspiring anarchist and still very much a rebel *in search of* a cause.

Being a political activist did not prevent him from gaining a law degree from the University of Havana in 1950, and certainly it motivated him. Among his early "heroic" acts, he appeared at the wake for a student who had been killed during a protest rally, and he volunteered to take legal action against the policeman who was responsible. A smart move despite the risks of incurring the wrath of a brutal regime that was notorious for bringing the hammer down on any nail that was sticking up. No doubt it occurred to Castro that such *pro bono* work would stand out on an aspiring revolutionary's resume.

Two years later, evidently having not yet forsaken all hope of political change shy of armed insurrection, Castro stood as a candidate for election to the National Legislature. His timing was bad. Just prior to the 1952 election, Fulgencio Batista, a candidate for the president's office, realized that he was doomed to defeat, so he staged a successful military coup. Proponents of democracy in Cuba were, predictably, devastated. Their morale sank further as the United States recognized the new government and, in so doing, legitimized the dastardly deed. Mired down in the Korean War and the increasingly ominous Cold War, the United States was content to know that its interests in Cuba were not likely to be disrupted. Democracy took a back seat to dependability as the United States supported right-wing, even despotic regimes throughout Latin America. In 1953, Castro upped the ante and led an attack on the Moncada military barracks, a dramatic repeat of a similar attack during an earlier movement for independence. It failed, and he was tossed in jail, sentenced to a 20-year term. Castro spoke in his own defense during his trial, a two-hour preview of much lengthier rhetorical flourishes that became his hallmark. He closed his remarks with the famous and prophetic words: "Condemn me, it does not matter. History will absolve me!"

Adding to his misery, while in prison in 1954, his wife, Mirta, sought a divorce and left Cuba for the United States with their son, Fidelito. A raging custody battle ensued, with Fidelito and Mirta zigzagging through Mexico, the United States and Cuba. Mirta ultimately remarried, and Fidelito now has a family and lives in Havana in relative obscurity. After two years in prison, along with brother Raul, Fidel was released in a general amnesty and returned to Havana. Soon the brothers chose self-imposed exile in Mexico rather than the possibility of again tangling with Batista's police and once more languishing in a dismal prison on the Isle of Pines. Down Mexico way Raul met, befriended and introduced to Fidel an Argentine physician named Ernesto Guevara. He shared the brothers' displeasure with the nouveau colonial scene in Cuba. During the next 17 months, they mobilized a band of revolutionary rogues, found a dilapidated yacht, renamed it Granma and limped to the eastern end of Cuba to launch their revolution.

Unfortunately, they steered off course, ran aground, had to toss their heavy weapons overboard, and landed far from collaborators who were waiting with supplies and transport. Three days later they were brutally attacked by Batista's troops. Said Fidel of the debacle, "There was a moment when I was commander in chief of myself and two others." In fact, the government proudly announced Castro had been killed. It was only months later that the adventuresome *New York Times* reporter Herbert Matthews, guided by the irrepressible revolutionary Celia Sanchez, found him alive and plotting serious mischief in his mountain hideaway. The survivors of the "invasion" and a handful of local revolutionary recruits had literally headed for the hills, the Sierra Maestra mountains. And even they surely would have been amazed had their crystal ball revealed that only two years later they would sweep across the country and march victorious into Havana itself.

During his time in the mountains, ironically, Castro was receiving secret funding from the CIA while the nascent Communist Party of Cuba had rejected his appeals for support. How very soon those roles were to be reversed! While he was leading the domestic revolutionary movement, Castro also was distilling his goals on a larger world stage. Reacting to the United States providing extensive support to Batista's armed forces, in 1958 he wrote, "I have sworn that the Americans will pay dearly for what they are doing. When this war has ended, a much bigger and greater war will start for me, the war I shall launch against them. I realize that this is my true destiny." Some bravado, perhaps, for a fellow leading a scruffy band of hungry rebels in the mountains, but it was clearly a preview of what was to become his lifelong struggle.

Castro emerged as a national hero, although tens of thousands of his countrymen who held him in lower regard fled the island in the months before and after the Revolution prevailed. His stature soared as he moved swiftly to rid the island of corruption, foreign economic domination and the vestiges of the colonial era. He initiated sweeping reforms, which today are his legacy. To overcome an unconscionable level of illiteracy, 200,000 "volunteers" were sent across the country to teach reading. Universal free education and health-care systems were launched. Roads, electricity and water supplies were improved, and rents were halved. Castro promised free and democratic elections (that were never to take place). And while many thousands of Cuba's best and brightest left the island in anticipation of the further reforms and radical changes that were soon to embrace the nation, others experienced an epiphany and became devoted to the Revolution.

A very close friend of mine, who will be called Gladys, shared her recollections of connecting with Castro as if it were yesterday. "My life changed in 1959, when I met Fidel at the Havana Hilton, where he was staying with his *barbudos*. I shall never forget his determination to end the era of tyrants, government corruption, the Italian-American Mafia taking over the economy, the illiteracy and poverty in the countryside, prostitution and the torture and killings," she said. She paused, breathed deeply, and continued, "I was transformed from my comfortable middle class life because I knew Fidel would devote his life to bringing the needed changes. I was flabbergasted, I had found my destiny. It was pure magic. A revolutionary was born."

Castro not only inspired millions, but he delivered on most of his promises. He came to be regarded as the father of modern Cuba, what George Washington was to the United States, Gandhi to India, Mao to China. Today he continues to be revered by all but perhaps a small number of intellectuals and those who favor progress toward political freedom and individual economic opportunity. A sensible, young, well-educated professional recently said to me, "I would lay down my life for Fidel." And while the rest of the world knows this man as Castro, I have *never* heard a Cuban refer to him by any name other than *Fidel*. He is family, he is a father figure, and he is embedded in the hearts of the Cuban people. Little wonder. He is the *only* head of state known to the two-thirds of the Cuban people who were born after he seized power, and along the way he has outlasted *ten* American presidents! So it should come as no surprise that when he rants about the dastardly United States, as that is the only posture that most Cubans ever have known, there is a natural tendency for it to be widely accepted. Conversely, almost half of the population of the United States was not yet born when Fidel Castro came to power. So when he is demonized in the American media it seems to most to be the norm, the only way they have ever known their country to deal with Cuba.

In part it is Castro's passion and charisma that has placed him so firmly in the hearts and minds of his countrymen. Whether he began his political ascendancy as an adherent of communism matters little, except perhaps to historians. It became his quest, and it has transformed his country and, to a degree, the entire world. He has not been shy about sharing his beliefs, whether in the United Nations, appearances in foreign capitals, in the domestic media or in his interminable public speeches in Cuba. To say that he has been a strong orator would be a huge understatement! Would you say simply that Goliath was a tall fellow?

What Castro may have lacked in mastery of lyrical speechmaking, he more than compensated for in duration. His public utterances routinely lasted for four to six hours, and his record was a 14-hour marathon! Woe be unto anyone who had the audacity to abbreviate or interrupt such a presentation. On one occasion, a visiting group of American VIPs was granted an audience with the masterful orator. The group, accustomed to meeting with world leaders, had made the grievous mistake of scheduling a dinner within merely a few hours of the start of Castro's chat. As you can imagine, the monologue flowed with no end in sight. So the leader of the visitors stood and explained to Castro that they would be late to their evening engagement. Big mistake. Indeed, Castro wrapped up his remarks. And the group has been in major disfavor on the island ever since. Would you interrupt a lion enjoying fresh meat? If not, neither would you attempt to shorten the comments of Fidel Castro.

In recent years, *El Comandante* has made crystal clear his concern with preserving his legacy. Many young professionals who are true believers in the driving principles of the Revolution have been inserted into top positions in the bureaucracy. Known for their ideological fervor more than for their talents as administrators, some in Havana have dubbed them "the Taliban." One conspicuous example was 40-year-old Otto Rivero, who was tasked by Fidel to reinforce socialist doctrine and boost the revolutionary mindset. To do so he was empowered with hundreds of millions of dollars for his free-lancing. Much of it was ill-spent and ineffectively used. After coming to power, Raul Castro trimmed his sails and returned that authority and responsibility to the traditional ministries.

Fidel Castro's image and platitudes began to appear on billboards around Havana and beyond after he passed the baton to his brother in 2006. And he seldom missed an opportunity to rant about the threats and abuses of the capitalist world – if only in the form of bulletins released to the media from his hospital bed. One Cuban skeptic confided to me in 2007, "He is squandering scarce resources that could better be used to improve conditions for the people."

As an aside, it is worth noting that Castro has succeeded in completely isolating his private life and family from his public persona. It is as if he fears that showing his human side would somehow erode his image as a pure revolutionary. It is known, of course, that he was married in 1948 to Mirta Diaz

Balart, who bore him a son named Fidelito. Soon after they were divorced, supposedly the love of his life became Celia Sanchez, a fellow revolutionary who shared the hardships in the Sierra Maestra mountains with him. She died in 1980 of lung cancer – perhaps a factor in Fidel's later decision to quit smoking his once cherished cigars.

Since the early 1960s, however, Castro has been with Dalia Soto del Valle, with whom he has five sons. For reasons that defy explanation (by me, anyway), all of their names begin with the letter "A." They are virtually invisible in Cuba, with none having any role in the government, nor ever being publicized in the media. As the government controls the media and there are no paparazzi in Havana, that's easy. Although from time to time I've heard rumors of one, who evidently is the "black sheep" of the family, being "assisted" by his security detail, out of a microbrewery on Market Square in the wee hours of the morning.

In May of 2006 there was a great splash of publicity when *Forbes* magazine reported that Castro had amassed a personal fortune of many hundreds of millions of dollars – placing him squarely in the company of many of the world's most notorious despots. What was evident only if one read the fine print, however, was that the methodology used in arriving at this unseemly conclusion assigned to Castro the value of state enterprises. Somehow they failed to assign to George W. Bush the value of the U.S. Postal Service, or to Tony Blair the value of Britain's national telephone service. In any case, Castro reportedly was enraged and spent hours on Cuban television denying the allegations. While he may have more than a few critics on the island, I know of no one who has ever accused Castro of helping himself to government funds, nor of *any* sort of corruption. Yes, I assume that he dines better than most of his countrymen, and he has a nicer home and car. And Cubans find that to be quite OK. Most of us wink at modest indulgences by our heads of state. But embezzling? Not likely. Few ripples followed the splash that the *Forbes* article had made.

During his 80th year, Fidel began to show signs that his age was becoming a limiting factor. He fainted (along with dozens of others) during one of his hallmark speeches after several hours of emoting under a scorching sun. A few years earlier, in October 2004, he tripped and smashed his knee, but he recovered nicely from the necessary surgery. Consistent with his awesome aura, the nation's only newspaper, *Granma*, reported that Castro was not only awake during surgery but also that he personally directed it. It was belatedly revealed, however, that in July of 2006 he had experienced intestinal bleeding that necessitated major surgery, which resulted in his passing the mantle of power to his brother Raul.

On the streets of Little Havana in Miami, joyful raucous celebrations erupted and traffic gridlocked with horn-honking cars full of expatriates waving Cuban flags. The people of Cuba were repelled by such morbid behavior. Said one Cuban official: "In Miami the reaction to Fidel's illness was sickening and disgusting." Not only in Cuba but also in America did the excesses of the Cuban-American community repulse most people. Congressman Charles Rangel, a New York City Democrat who has sometimes been critical of the Castro regime, commented, "I was so revolted by the behavior of my fellow Americans in Miami that I wrote a letter to President Castro expressing my sympathy and offering an apology for my countrymen's heartless celebration." The embarrassing display in Miami resulted in a further drop in support for the hard-line political positions that have characterized the exile community for 50 years.

During the following months various Cuban government officials and Castro's good pal Hugo Chavez of Venezuela all let fly with upbeat prognoses, which were followed by amendments of less rosy outlooks. When his nationwide 81st birthday celebration was held in early

December 2007, already having been postponed from August, Fidel was a no-show.

No, the citizens of Cuba did *not* rise up in revolution; the citizens of Miami did *not* board boats and race to Havana, and the U.S. government did *not* try to foment mischief on either side of the Florida straits. After the shocking reminder of Castro's mortality, all that was remarkable was that his long-awaited removal from power resulted in a quiet continuance of the status quo. Predictably, there are many who would use the words of Oliver Cromwell in 1653, "You have been sat here too long for any good you have been doing." Perhaps this bodes well for those who favor an easing of U.S. restrictions and new opportunities for the Cuban people.

Rumors that Fidel had cancer and perhaps complications were amplified by the government's shroud of secrecy surrounding the illness and its treatment. Once again it was confirmed that a government's ability to withhold information from the media does not automatically mean that is the wisest course to follow. Speculation ran rampant, and rumors flew regarding surgeons who had supposedly been flown in secretly from Spain and even from the United States. Some information was eventually revealed, and a consensus emerged that Fidel actually was stricken with diverticulitis, a painful inflammation in the intestinal track. It was subsequently complicated by several bouts of peritonitis, which is infection or inflammation in the abdominal cavity. Castro had multiple surgeries at the hands of both Cuban and Spanish specialists and was closer to death than to life on more than one occasion. A man of less fortitude would not have survived beyond the initial illness and surgeries, and Castro's prognosis was exceedingly grim during the fall of 2006.

Against all odds, Fidel continued to play a significant role despite being sidelined. Yes, he missed the summit of the Non-Aligned Movement in Havana in late 2006. Yes, he was absent at the Mayday demonstrations in 2007, Revolution Day on July 26 and his August birthday. His illness is not the sort that enables one to leap out of bed at will and he, no doubt, has cut back on his bungee jumping. Meanwhile, however, he met with the likes of the president of Venezuela and the president of China, and he periodically issued statements on major policy issues. For example, in April of 2007, he lashed out at the U.S. policy of encouraging ethanol as an alternative fuel, insisting that this would raise the price of corn and contribute to world hunger. This issue warrants a brief examination, as Fidel has placed himself squarely in the midst of an emerging international issue of great consequence.

In response to global climate change and political concerns about the availability and cost of oil, many nations are moving forward to expand production of biofuels. To the extent they are derived from corn and other edible crops, that will continue to drive up the prices of alternative edible crops. Such an upward spiral places a heavy burden on those least able to afford it, particularly in the developing countries of the world. Few would argue that Fidel is on the wrong side of this debate. *The Economist* magazine's food price index soared in 2009 to its highest level since it was created in 1845. Just from 2005 through 2008, these prices more than doubled. The supreme irony, or in this case perhaps tragedy, is that recent studies indicate that producing one unit of biofuel ethanol actually consumes more energy than it conserves.

The subsequent economic slump in 2008 and the related decline in oil prices predictably drove down demand for alternative fuels, resulting in a drop in world food prices to less burdensome levels.

During the fall of 2007, and into 2008, Castro continued to issue weekly editorial comments, including a continuing drumbeat about Bush's affinity for corn-based ethanol as an oil substitute, remarking, "The danger of a massive world famine is aggravated by Mr. Bush's recent initiative to transform foods into fuel." And he continued to meet with visiting heads of state, including Hugo Chavez of Venezuela (whom he warned against U.S.-backed assassination attempts), the president of Brazil, Luiz Inacio Lula da Silva, and the president of Angola, Jose Eduardo Dos Santos. Early in 2008, as the primary election contests got rolling for the U.S. presidential elections, Castro issued a statement denying candidate Senator John McCain's assertion that Cuban soldiers had tortured American prisoners in North Vietnam during the Vietnam War. (I personally had little difficulty deciding whether to believe the man who was imprisoned and tortured for five years in North Vietnam, or the commander in chief who sent soldiers to oppose the U.S. forces.)

In any case, by late 2007 Castro was indeed slowing down, almost to the pace of a mere mortal. For several months *El Jefé* had been alluding to his willingness to see the reins of power shift to others. Late in 2007, he said on Cuban television, "My eternal duty is not to cling to positions, or even less to obstruct the path of younger people." Yet he agreed to stand for re-election in January. He apologized to his constituents, saying, "I am not physically able to speak directly to the citizens of the municipality where I was nominated for our elections." The significant fact was that he was, indeed, standing for re-election – which raised real doubts about his enthusiasm for formally stepping aside. While pundits may long debate the nuances, there could be little question that, as noted in an editorial in *The Economist* in February 2008, "Real change in Cuba will start only after Fidel's death." So no meaningful change in the political framework of Cuba was expected just because the leadership was playing the game of musical chairs. Legacy rules in Cuba, and the formality of an election of Fidel Castro in Cuba would prove to be of microscopic consequence.

Fidel continued his campaign for relevance in early June 2008, when a videotaped interview showed him as healthier and chattier than in recent months. In mid-September he issued a surprising essay claiming that Cuba provided intelligence information to the United States that prevented an assassination attempt on President Ronald Reagan in October of 1984. *And* Castro appeared in an obviously very current taped television interview in which he continued to look a bit gaunt but talkative and lively as well.

So who is this guy, *really*, behind the beard and the trappings of power?

For openers, let me say that I don't personally know Castro, but my impressions have been gathered from talking with literally scores of Cubans who do. I do know that he has met with many groups of visitors, usually rather spontaneously. I suppose I came close one time, when I got a mysterious call from a woman in his office late one hopeful afternoon. "It is possible the president could meet with you later tonight. If so, I will call you very late, and you should have your group available at the hotel lobby at 11 p.m. We will pick you up and bring you to his office. He will speak with you, and return you to your hotel in the morning."

"In the morning?!?" I thought. Yes, it seems not only that the man likes to conduct monologues, perhaps four to six hours, and then wrap up evidently when he runs out of words, but also *he is nocturnal*. Anyway, the trigger phone call never came. Whether he meets with groups of Americans at all seems to depend on a variety of circumstances: Is he free that day or hanging out with some much more important folks? Does he want to send a political signal, especially to the powers that be in the United States? Less likely he would be munching popcorn in front of a rented video. Although, as you will read later, that is possible.

Despite being front and center on the world stage for a half a century, Fidel Castro remains an enigma. From what I've been told, there is a soft side to Fidel – and a stone hard side as well. Let's start with those character traits that are generally agreed to characterize *El Comandante*. From an early age he was described by family members and friends as single-minded, unconventional and driven to lead. His schoolmates at Dolores recall his enthusiasm for risk taking as well as his marginal interest in academics. At the University of Havana he seems to have amplified those traits and was known for his ruthlessness in seeking leadership, his conviction that he could achieve greatness, and a keen mind that enabled him to meet the academic requirements with a minimum of time and effort.

The "hard guy" feature of his character was enlarged and amply proven later as he endured many hardships, both on and off the battlefield. That can toughen up a guy. In the immediate aftermath of the Revolution he allegedly ordered the execution of thousands of people who were deemed to be hopelessly counter-revolutionary or who had done some terrible things to the Cuban people. I am unaware of Castro himself ever being the triggerman. In the years that followed he was not shy about throwing people in prison with only the most flimsy fig leaf of judicial process. And in perhaps his most notorious tough guy act, he ordered the execution of one of his top generals who also had been a lifelong friend, General Arnaldo Ochoa.

Throughout his life Fidel has shown a compulsion to lead and to win. In the category of "urban legend" comes the story of Fidel always demonstrating his need to prevail. While on an evening fishing trip with several friends one fellow was on a roll and catching more fish than Fidel. The hours passed, but at 11 p.m. Castro was still trailing. A mutual friend on the boat whispered to the fellow in the lead that he should stop baiting his hook because Fidel would not quit and lose. By 3 a.m. Fidel pulled even on the fish count, and at 5 a.m. Fidel caught one more and decided the boat should return to the dock.

Castro is a remarkably adept political leader and, as such, he radiated the image that suited his purposes. Ruthless, charming, charismatic. What's on the menu today? During former President Jimmy Carter's visit to Cuba in 2002, for example, the gracious host greeted the visiting ex-president attired conspicuously in civilian clothes – Mr. Soft Guy, if you will. And they scrambled around a baseball field tossing balls like a couple of kids. But when the visit concluded and Castro bid farewell to Carter at the airport ceremony, he was dressed in his starched military uniform. Just a little reminder that Mr. Hard Guy is always close at hand.

Being driven would not be unique to Fidel when compared with revolutionary leaders who have emerged around the world. You just can't overthrow a brutal military dictatorship while sitting on the sidelines. Some say that Castro also has been motivated by some "inner demons," such as his being born out of wedlock, his self-consciousness about possibly having Jewish ancestors – repeatedly denied, but his ancestors are from a Jewish area of Spain – and his own prosperous beginnings.

And how about the softer side? While Castro has relished the role of the hemispheric "bad boy," or the David stoning Goliath and the destructor of the Monroe Doctrine, his public persona may not totally conform to the private Fidel. In 2006, after he had relinquished the presidency and been hospitalized for five months, I had a most interesting view of the softer side of the man. A mutual friend confided to me that he was having a tough time figuring out what he could possibly give to Fidel for his birthday. After considerable hand wringing, my amigo recalled that, since childhood, Fidel had been quite the American movie buff. And could I possibly bring back a DVD of the film *Picnic* starring Kim Novak? "Of course, no problem." And a month later I returned with the video, considerably amused by my role as much as the selection of the gift for the rascal head of state.

Upon my return to Havana a month later, I asked if my contraband video had found its was to the top. "Absolutely," I was told, "and he couldn't have been more delighted. In fact, the man has another special request for you." Oh boy, I thought, it starts with 1950s era videos and soon I'm on the slippery slope to being asked for state secrets! Well, that's not even close to what happened. "The man asks if it would be too much trouble for you to bring back a DVD of James Dean in *Rebel*

*Without A Cause.* And several months later the wish list was *Moby Dick* and *Casablanca.* And the following trip the wish list included *Creature from the Black Lagoon* and *The Day The Earth Stood Still* (1951 version) – all classics, all enjoyed immensely according to reports!

I could barely contain myself. Not only had I become a modern day "Video Gunrunner" for a declining dictator but also for one who may forever be remembered as a rebel *with* a great cause wanting to watch a film about a rebel *without* one!

# CHAPTER 7

# ENDURING PERVASIVE GOVERNMENT

The government of Cuba has the odd characteristic of being simultaneously omnipresent and virtually non-existent. It impacts the daily lives of its citizens at every turn: food, housing, transportation, employment, wages, education, health care, media and most daily activities. Indeed, I have the impression that everything in the life of a Cuban is either prohibited or obligatory. Yet the typical Cuban seems less interested in politics than in his family and improving its standard of living in a land where economic opportunities are scarce.

Cuba's Constitution provides for grass-roots "democratic" elections to a National Assembly. A tidy line and block chart would show it as a key player in national policy, but in Cuba real power resides with the top leaders and the Communist Party. And many of those are the same folks.

To be elected to the National Assembly it is not necessary to be a Communist Party member, and some elected delegates are not. But neither are they in any other party, as the Communist Party is the only permitted political party in Cuba.

Not surprisingly, being a card-carrying communist in Cuba is a faster track to advancement, perks and a better life. Conversely, being critical of the Communist Party is at one's own peril.

And why does Cuba cling to communism? After all, of nearly 200 countries in the world, only Cuba, North Korea and Laos have kept the faith (although China and Vietnam still pay lip service to it). Despite some noteworthy social achievements, communism is best known today for its muddled economies and lack of individual freedoms. Why preserve it? Perhaps the explanation is no more complicated than inertia and the decaying dreams of old men.

The legal voting age in Cuba is a comparatively low 16, and voter turnout is consistently reported to be a remarkably high 96 to 98 percent. Members of the National Assembly are often elevated to higher positions in the government, not unlike a parliamentary form of government. Indeed, even Fidel Castro, to maintain his position as president of Cuba, formally had to continue to be elected from his obscure rural constituency in Oriente Province, where he was born.

The National Assembly, established in 1976, includes 614 (unpaid) elected members, who are all forbidden to campaign for office, and each of whom represents an average constituency of 18,000 people.

The National Assembly meets only for about a week twice each year, when its members address issues that are handled on a continuing basis by permanent committees of the Assembly. No, it is not a spectator sport of raucous debate and slick political maneuvering. They reportedly handle the people's business in an orderly way, and then all but a few return home to continue their employment (and wages) as farmers, factory workers, and many other occupations. During the 95 percent of the time when these elected representatives are *not* in session, apparently the Council of State (more or less the executive committee of the Assembly) and 34 ministries keep the ball rolling.

Interestingly, election to the National Assembly is not always "bottom-up" but sometimes appears to be "top-down." Some people just seem to enjoy a lot of name recognition and get a boost. For example, Juan Miguel Gonzalez, the father of Elian Gonzalez, was elected from his hometown of Cardenas in 2002. Perhaps being a restaurant worker provided excellent qualifications for becoming a member of the nation's legislature. A more plausible explanation, however, may be found in the close relationship he had developed with Ricardo Alarcon, the president of the National Assembly, his international celebrity status arising from the recovery of his son from the United States, and the public admiration of President Castro.

Among the Assembly's primary responsibilities is to select the real seat of power in Cuba, the 31-member Council of State. In turn, the Council of State elects its president and vice president, who also hold the top two executive positions in the country. Thus, Fidel Castro became president of Cuba as a result of being selected as the president of the Council of State. And his successor, Raul Castro, became president because he was previously the vice president of the Council of State. Along the way, I suppose being Fidel's brother may have given him a step ahead of the others.

Another key responsibility of the National Assembly is to select all of the judges in Cuba, except the top two posts in Cuba's Supreme Court, which are chosen by the president. Thus, the judiciary in Cuba is by no means an independent branch of government. Its principal purpose is to maintain "socialist legality," meaning the political status quo. It is not charged with protecting individual rights nor with interpreting the Constitution. The great majority of judicial activity in Cuba concerns criminal or civil cases. Those matters of a political content often are dealt with in Revolutionary Summary Tribunals where due process is observed mainly in the breach. Capital crimes, which can takes decades to resolve in the United States, somehow can be wrapped up in a couple weeks in Cuba. If, as the saying goes, "justice delayed is justice denied," then do you suppose that the reverse may be better? Does justice accelerated to warp speed provide a wiser outcome? Not likely.

In parallel with the government, but apart from it, is the powerful Communist Party of Cuba. The casual visitor to Cuba will not find the party to be of high visibility, and its membership comprises fewer than 10 percent of the island's population. But it's not exactly like your local garden club. It is elitist and, as guardian of the ideology that drives the country, it has a huge impact on government policies. The Constitution of Cuba describes the Communist Party as "the highest guiding force of society and the State." It reigns supreme, and the head of the Politburo, its first secretary, has always been Fidel Castro and then his brother Raul.

A friend who served her entire career as a government official became disillusioned with the apparatus and decided to resign from the CP of Cuba. This created a unique dilemma. Party officials met with her and urged her to reconsider and to rejoin the party. She said, "They came and begged me to return, partly to avoid an embarrassing and unprecedented situation, *but mainly so they could expel me instead!*" You see, no Cuban had ever before resigned, and officials were befuddled about how to deal with this anomaly! She declined, and she was forced into early retirement and quickly "disconnected" from friends and professional colleagues of many decades. People waggle their finger at the Communist Party at real peril to themselves.

During a trip to Cuba in 1998, I attended a Communist Party-hosted reception in Matanzas Province. I was surprised to find the event in a lovely modern dwelling, evidently dedicated to the comfort of the provincial Communist Party. And I was even *more* surprised, in fact, down right *amazed*, by the great variety of fine foods that covered a large dining table. By covered, I mean I could barely discern if the table was wood, had a tablecloth or was a magic carpet. Tempting platters of fresh fish and shrimp, huge bowls of fine salads, plates overflowing with rare tender beef, casseroles of steaming chicken and pork, and vastly more. It was a meal unlike any ordinary Cuban ever would see, even on a feast day. I am not naïve. I have dined in the White House and in the Kremlin, and the fare at this Communist Party-hosted luncheon was equally abundant and superb.

I was reminded on another occasion of the favorable treatment afforded to the "upper class" in the supposedly classless society of Cuba, meaning mainly top government and Communist Party officials. Having overcome a variety of challenges, I had arranged to charter a boat for a day of scuba diving on one of Cuba's wondrous reefs. Upon arrival at the dock on the appointed day and at the appointed hour, I was told, to my shock and great disappointment, "The boat you had booked is no longer available." Before I could launch into a justifiable tirade, I noticed Ricardo Alarcon, president of the National Assembly and confidant of Fidel Castro, and his family and friends, boarding "my" boat! I note simply that Cuba is not as egalitarian as the spinmeisters would have us believe. It is not uncommon for those in power to take especially good care of themselves. A more cynical view was expressed to me by a dissident friend who remarked, "All we have done is replace one elite class with another!"

One thinks of doctrinaire governments such as Cuba's as being constantly "in your face." I do not have that impression. It is not there every time you turn your head, as you think of North Korea or the old formerly communist Albania with propaganda at every turn. But do not doubt it. It is ever present in more subtle ways, often more pervasive than conspicuous.

Yes, Cuba is organized from the bottom-up on each block. Committees for the Defense of the Revolution (CDRs) are organized in every neighborhood, with an estimated 130,000 of them pervading practically every dusty village, town and urban area on the island. They have grown to oversee about 80 percent of the Cuban population since their inauguration immediately after the Revolution prevailed in 1959. Their ostensible purpose is to monitor health and education matters at the most local level. Yet they serve a chilling political purpose as well, providing a mechanism for neighbors to keep watch on each other and inform local officials of "counter-revolutionary" behavior. Each Cuban seems to have a story of a friend who has been the victim of a jealous or vengeful neighbor who snitched on them to the local CDR about real or imagined misdeeds. Even accumulating a few items for a household, if they arouse someone else's jealousy, can get you in trouble.

An amiga of mine who has a splendid art collection recounted with anxiety, "I must be careful to not make my neighbors angry at me. If they get mad they could call the police who could come and decide that my artworks are too valuable and then confiscate them." Urban legends abound in Havana about people who had been informed on by neighbors and then had virtually everything but the kitchen sink stripped from their dwellings by the police.

Late in 2007, a museum commemorating the heroic achievements of the CDRs was opened on Calle Obispo, one of Havana's busiest pedestrian streets – for both natives and tourists – on which vehicles are excluded. I have yet to see anyone enter it. It would be quite acceptable to most Cubans if the CDRs, and all their mischief making, were consigned to this dusty museum and removed from the everyday life of the Cuban people.

It is fair to say that there exists in Cuba today a palpable undercurrent of paranoia. Although seldom enforced, there are harsh penalties for dealing in the black market, which is a reality and practically a necessity for almost everyone on the island. So much of daily life appears to be dependent on skirting the law that taking those risks has become the norm rather than the exception. Do you have a (prohibited) satellite receiver? Do you have a (prohibited) video recording device? Do you have a (prohibited) copying machine? What brings the risk of non-compliance into a manageable realm is the reality of corruptible government officials. They are mostly to be found at the lowest levels where, for the equivalent of a few dollars, almost any indiscretion can be overlooked.

Burdening the daily lives of most Cubans is the continuous effort to scrounge for that little bit more of almost everything that would transform their lives from chronic shortages to marginal sufficiency. And how is that accomplished? Almost universally, employees of state enterprises, as well as their managers, pilfer, skim, overcharge and shortchange. Not because Cuba has become a national band of thieves, but because the needs are so widespread and dire. Moving up the "food chain," in this country where anything beyond basic necessities is unaffordable, I have found air conditioners, satellite dishes and computers to be available on the black market. A couple of typical examples may illuminate the way in which Cubans rise to meet their needs. An amiga was in need of a good pair of walking shoes, preferring something with a bit of style. Her search ended when she went into a store and found a friend who had, shall I say, "set aside" a nice pair. It was offered to my friend at half price, which was still beyond her reach. She negotiated it down to one quarter of the retail price and knew she had gotten the best possible deal when the sales lady told her, "You know I have to share some of what you pay." So my friend got her shoes, the salesperson got a hefty "five-finger bonus," and her boss skimmed a nice chunk of change. The bureaucrats probably just wrote it off as damaged merchandise or the proverbial "shrink" of inventory.

Another friend explained to me that a neighbor of hers was a hotel manager who had graciously provided to her family a gala wedding reception at no charge. When I asked if she thought the hotel fellow had paid from his own pocket, she laughed and said, "Of course not!" More inventory shrink, I suppose.

Periodic crackdowns have failed to suppress the instincts of people to provide adequately for themselves and their families. Surprise inspections of gasoline stations in 2005 revealed widespread theft by employees but probably only deterred it briefly.

Meanwhile, the upper levels of the government have been far from pillars of integrity. "We have a big, huge problem with corruption," one official told me. Scandals are periodically publicized, even about ministerial level officials who have been caught with their hands in the cookie jars. Big time. We're not talking about hoisting a lobster from the office freezer, but skimming vast sums or accepting kickbacks that would take the breath away of most folks. Fidel Castro has a low tolerance for violations of the public trust and has not hesitated to turn the guilty officials into national villains to illustrate the severe penalties for those who cross the line. In 2006, a Politburo member thought to be "untouchable" was sentenced to 12 years in prison after being found guilty of corruption. Speculation was that it involved big bribes, but Fidel never publicized details in such cases.

However, one can make a case that petty corruption like bribes are relatively harmless and are, in fact, one way to allocate scarce resources in a country that lacks a fair or rational system of distribution. Folks who really want to enjoy a lobster, if they have a few extra bucks, can get one. Inspiring a doctor this way can get urgently needed medical attention rather than waiting for months. A small donation to a policeman can allow one to keep a driver's license and avoid hours each day on a deficient mass transit system. Maybe then the policeman can afford that elusive lobster! This can be the grease that keeps a defective economic system limping along instead of grinding to a halt.

As I have moved about Cuba and met with hundreds of her people, especially in Havana, I have learned that there exists a deep and justifiable fear of the government's intrusive behavior in domains considered to be private in most societies. Among the most common examples of this is for Cubans, especially in conversations with Americans, to not use the name of Fidel Castro. Instead, most often they simply stroke their chin, alluding to the man by his renowned scraggly beard, or they make an obtuse reference to "Uncle Jose." They are more comfortable avoiding any overt reference to *El Jefé* in the context of a criticism of the government. Can you imagine being an American and being afraid to use the president's name? That could only be described as Orwellian.

But fear runs even deeper. There are more than a few intelligent observers in Cuba who believe there could one day be a resurgence of doctrine and revolutionary zeal and, should that happen, there could well be harsh retribution for those who have consorted with Americans. I have had numerous encounters with government officials who clearly were not inclined to develop more than a passing relationship. Worse yet, there have been a few who flat out refused to be with me, for fear of possible future reprisals against them simply because they associated with me. Even in the realm of what I consider to be personal friendship, invariably I am discouraged. More than a few times, for example, Cubans who became my amigos while they were posted to the Cuban Interests Section in Washington were intimidated. When they rotated back to Havana, I never was able to maintain contact by phone or e-mail. They simply vanished like wisps in the wind.

On numerous occasions while I was meeting informally with friends, government intelligence gatherers were not even subtle as they hung around trying to catch bits of our conversation. I believe this is called overt surveillance and is intended to intimidate the victim and deter whatever misdeeds they may be contemplating – like enjoying a beer and sharing a few laughs. In one case, my bold Cuban friend with whom I was chatting on the expansive veranda of the Nacional Hotel approached the government agent, put her hands on her hips and said, "Why are you bothering us? Don't you have anything better to do with your time?" With his role as a deterrent irreparably shredded, he quickly and quietly faded from view. Such bravado, however, is the rare exception and not the rule in a land where the Ministry of the Interior does not hesitate to dole out sanctions without explanation or a right to appeal, such as the loss of your job, your dwelling or your freedom from arrest.

Once I had an indulgent dinner with an academician and, although we failed to notice any curious observers, he was verbally "spanked" at the university the following morning. Ostensibly his sin was failing to distinguish between his personal observations and those that could be construed as representing the university. Clearly, however, he was being warned that hanging out with Americans could be hazardous to his professional health. My friend the professor was inconsolable. Being frail, elderly and gay compounded his alarm that this encounter with the government could imperil his job, apartment and modest perks, such as the car and driver that his academic achievements had gained for him.

A sadly humorous example of "Big Brother paranoia" relates to my quite innocently inquiring of a Cuban tour guide (a government employee) where President Castro lived. The home address of the president of the United States is not a very well kept secret, after all. It's a great big white house and millions of passersby ogle at it from behind a fence every year at 1600 Pennsylvania Avenue. Thousands get to tour inside every week. So I supposed it would be interesting to see *El Jefé's* digs. After pondering for a moment, he responded, "No one knows where the president lives. I think he moves around a lot because there have been hundreds of attempts to assassinate him." Let me clarify that this took place on a tour bus, and it is rumored that not only do guides have to file reports about foreign visitors, but also the bus drivers must report on the behavior of the guides. As the years passed and I became good friends with this fellow, one day when we were quite alone he confided in me about

Castro's residence – providing the details that are common knowledge among Cubans, that he lives in Siboney, near 220th Street in western Havana, in a lovely compound with a lake and guest houses as well as his own. Of course, it is unmarked and the access road is blocked by policemen. One telltale sign exists that does not take a James Bond to interpret. Starting close to the access road and continuing much of the way to the president's office at Revolution Square, one sees police kiosks along beautiful Fifth Avenue so cross traffic could be stopped when Castro's modest motorcade traveled by each day.

While Cubans have justifiable concern about their behavior being monitored by agents of the Ministry of the Interior, foreign visitors also are not immune from such invasions of their privacy. As a frequent American visitor to Cuba, I have no doubt that a fat dossier on me exists. I have been told that in many of the ministries with which I have had contact, there are people responsible for submitting reports on my activities. Since my ambling around Cuba always has been harmless, and I have never engaged in any sort of spying, I have never been shy about being very upfront about that fact. Nevertheless, as I am always assigned to the same fine rooms in the hotels in which I stay, I am reasonably sure that those rooms are equipped with devices that could be eavesdropping. One incident comes to mind that tends to confirm my suspicions.

During a visit a few years ago, an American friend who worked at the U.S. Interests Section visited me in my hotel room for a drink and a chat. The next day I received a visit from an acquaintance in the Cuban Foreign Ministry who cautioned me, "You are an American and have every right to meet with your officials at their offices, but we believe it is inappropriate for you to be having such meetings at your hotel." This was both disconcerting and offensive to me, and I was reminded of the paranoia that pervades Cuban-American relations.

Despite these examples, I am certain that the Cuban government has neither the inclination nor the manpower to monitor the activities of more than a very few foreign visitors. While some tourists have come back with tales of being followed day and night by government agents, this is probably more a reflection of their over-active imaginations than of purposeful intelligence gathering.

A more egregious example of government intrusion into what most Americans regard as the private realm concerned *Chicago Tribune* Havana correspondent Gary Marx. He is an aggressive reporter but, like other foreign journalists in Cuba, he knew the limits of expression and reporting well enough to avoid running afoul of a government that is known not to be keen on freedom of the press. Appropriately, he felt a responsibility to write about the dissident movement in Cuba, especially an energetic group of about 75 who operated overtly. While they attempted not to cross the line that would result in official penalties, they failed.

Meanwhile, Marx had become friends with one of the dissidents, about whom he wrote an uplifting article in early 2003. Shortly thereafter, and certainly not related to Marx's reporting, all the dissidents were rounded up and jailed, with practically worldwide condemnation of the government's action. All of the dissidents, that is, except about 10, including Marx's confidential source, who turned out to be a government informant who had moled his way into the dissident movement. This shocking revelation was devastating to Marx, who had been completely fooled and betrayed by the government spy. With admirable professionalism and a deep swallow of his journalistic pride, Marx then wrote a column about the duplicity and, more importantly, about his own victimization and misinformation in prior articles. As is recounted later, Marx continued to be a zealous journalist in Havana, although perhaps more skeptical of his Cuban sources. The Cuban government later revoked his official credentials as a foreign correspondent, and he was unceremoniously expelled from Cuba. Freedom of the press is by no means free.

# CUBA RISING

It cannot be denied that Cuba devotes a comparatively large amount of its scarce resources to monitoring (spying, to be blunt) the behavior and political compliance of its own people. For the most part, these activities are overseen by the widely feared Ministry of the Interior, which has increasingly blended with and come under the control of the Ministry of Defense (previously headed by Raul Castro). It has long been, and remains, a major feature on the domestic political landscape, with many people, momentum and seemingly a life of its own. After all, how many of us would like to tackle head on the FBI, or even the IRS, if they were on our case? But let us not lose sight of the fundamental underlying rationale for internal political surveillance. No one has put it more clearly or succinctly than Fidel Castro himself, who stated, "All criticism is opposition, and all opposition is counter-revolutionary." And if you are counter-revolutionary in Cuba you are *toast*.

The absence of a free press in Cuba is part of the larger effort by the government to limit open communication to, from and within the island. By 1961, all of the country's hundreds of independent newspapers and periodicals had been closed or fallen under government control. To this day there are no alternatives to the only government newspaper, *Granma*, which was first published in 1965. Its content is predictably, consistently and overwhelmingly pro-Revolution, pro-government and pro-Fidel. In fact, *El Jefé's* name seems to be on virtually every page, if not in every article. Only after his resignation in February 2008, were his written commentaries moved from the front page – all the way back to page two.

I recall a joke about the predictable content of *Granma,* told to me by a Cuban friend. "Napoleon is at a ceremony to honor and review the great Russian Army. He comments, 'With this great force I would have won at Waterloo.' Later he reviews the U.S. Army and says, 'With this I also would have won at Waterloo.' Later he has a chance to read *Granma* before reviewing the Cuban Army. He smiles and says, 'With this I would have still lost at Waterloo, but nobody would have known about it!'"

A freely admitted purpose of the media in Cuba is to promote official and ideological goals, and this extends to radio and television as well. There are no permitted alternatives, and to pirate foreign channels from the airwaves is to risk harsh penalties.

Visitors to Cuba will find that their hotels provide CNN and other news stations from various countries, without censorship. At first it occurred to me that the housekeepers and hotel bartenders could form a national network of purveyors of news. Had I discovered a leak in the national effort to contain the free flow of information? Such proved not to be the case. Invariably, when I return to my hotel room at the end of the day in Havana, I find that the maids have switched my channel away from CNN so they can watch music videos while refreshing the room. And the bartenders seem much more interested in sports or steamy films than in being up to date with U.S. newscasts.

For those with broader interests, government restrictions on communications can be stifling. In addition to restricting news to a predictable diet of government-operated television and radio stations, there are limitations on the possession and use of copying machines, video tapes, satellite phones, laptop computers and the like, and, perhaps most conspicuously in the 21st century, the government severely limits access to the Internet. Some of the most unpopular limits were eased by Raul in the spring of 2008.

Internet connectivity in Cuba, at 13 percent, is among the lowest in the world, lower even than in Haiti, which is the poorest country in the Western Hemisphere. This is no freak of nature, and it cannot be blamed on the American economic blockade. While Cuban officials mumble about the prohibitive cost, actually it is part and parcel of their effort to limit communication that potentially could undermine national policies and priorities. In a characteristically Cuban fashion, e-mail and Internet access is not flat-out prohibited. It is simply rationed by price. Those very few who can afford to pay $72 per month may have access. That sum, of course, far exceeds the average monthly wage of Cubans. If I, as an American, were to enjoy Internet access only if I could pay an equivalent several thousands of dollars for it each month, I surely would forego it. Underlying this style of "permission by price" in Cuba remains the basic policy: If it supports the Revolution it is permitted; if it could possibly threaten the Revolution it is effectively prohibited.

Ironically, as you may know, the origins of the Internet were premised on its ability to function in the event of a nuclear war. In other words, it was specifically designed to *go around and overcome* obstacles that could block the flow of communications. Will the Castros be able to overcome this powerful tool for people interacting? Is it even in their best interests to do so? How about the day soon coming when access will be wireless as well as inexpensive? Already there have been acknowledged complaints and protests from students, academicians, professionals and even high-level government officials in Cuba who do not have Internet access while some privileged others do. A high-level foreign affairs official recently asked me rhetorically, "Is it reasonable that I cannot have access to the Internet while many university professors and even students have it? That makes no sense."

Another domain in which the government provides a conspicuous presence is the local constabulary. A policeman patrolling on foot in the neighborhoods is both a common sight and a welcome one. No, it is not perceived as a grass-roots effort to dissuade folks from unwelcome political behavior. Rather, it is a necessary presence to deter petty crime, Cuban on Cuban. As one strolls the byways of Havana, lovely metal grillwork is found on virtually every door and window. While this is a legacy of Spanish decorative design, today in Cuba it serves a protective role as well. An unfortunate reality is that most of the people endure just a notch above the subsistence level, and petty theft and housebreaking are not uncommon. A good friend of mine enjoys a pleasant home in a modest neighborhood with a small patio facing the street. It is bountifully planted with greenery in the ground, in pots and in hanging baskets. Overhead was a splendid, old, very large and uncommon hanging fern – until one night it vanished without a trace.

This was the same woman whose son was a murder victim, as described earlier. Such violent crime in Cuba is rare, but less so than in years past. Confronting the reality of increasing levels of serious crime, especially in the major urban areas, the government recently has equipped some of the local police forces with sidearms. I daresay during my visits to Cuba in the late 1990s, I never saw a person in uniform with a weapon. Starting in about 2000, it became commonplace.

Speaking of crime, one cannot reasonably sidestep the issue of illegal drugs in Cuba. Yes, they do exist. One senior official confided to me, "Certainly, there has been an increase in drug-related problems." While there have been allegations of organized drug-dealing in Cuba and that the country is a significant transshipment point for drugs finding their way from Central America to the United States, no hard evidence of either accusation has been forthcoming. Some tourists have made the grievous mistake of bringing recreational drugs to Cuba and, when caught, they have been tried and imprisoned by the Cuban government. Drugs were sent into exile with the Mafia, and their return has been miniscule.

There remains a legendary, and rarely spoken of, tale of Castro's intervention in a high-profile case in 1989. In a widely publicized national scandal, numerous high officials of the Ministry of the Interior were convicted of trafficking in narcotics. It is said that Castro's childhood friend, General Arnaldo Ochoa, was involved in importing drugs for the military establishment, some of whom had become addicted during overseas adventures, such as in Angola in the 1970s.

After learning of this, *El Jefé* warned Ochoa that it must be stopped. And when it wasn't, he had his friend jailed and later shot, along with three others. The nation was shocked and, to this day, the incident is rarely discussed, even in private, and only with the greatest reluctance.

Understandably, because of their importance to the economy, crime against wealthy tourists, who are often tempting and simple targets, continues to be remarkably rare, although no one is immune from a jostling pickpocket. There is a widespread perception that the penalties for crimes against tourists, the lifeblood of the economy, are exceedingly harsh. What is striking to me, as a frequent visitor, is not that some petty crime may be on the rise – but that the Cuban people should be described as fundamentally *honest!*

I recall one occasion when I stopped at a café for a morning coffee and forgot to take with me a large bag of gifts and books that were destined for the people I would be meeting that day. I was more than disappointed by my carelessness, as these were special items that I had lugged thousands of miles for my friends. At the end of the day, easily six hours later, I revisited the café, I suppose to report my loss. To my surprise I was recognized by the waiter, and to my amazement he reappeared a moment later with my sack of goodies, completely intact. Time and again I have heard similar tales from fellow travelers who have misplaced jackets, cameras, and bags overflowing with souvenirs. The integrity of the Cuban people, if one may so generalize, appears to me to be of the highest order.

As the Cuban economy continued to struggle and tourism rebounded in the late 1990s, however, petty crimes against tourists began to emerge as an "Achilles' heel" in the government's high-priority efforts to attract hard currency. Stories of pickpockets and purse-snatchers became more common. And starting perhaps in 2006, short-changing tourists at the currency exchange *cambios* and overcharging for meals in tourist restaurants had evolved from rare to near epidemic proportions from 2008 onward. On several occasions when I was gypped, I scowled and scolded the perpetrators. They simply handed to me the balance due. No remorse, no eye contact. But as an amateur mind reader, I know the clerk was thinking, "Who cares if this one caught me, the next 10 won't have a clue!"

As I cruise around Havana, I often see billboards reminding folks of the grandiose achievements of the Revolution, salutes to Che Guevara and national hero Jose Marti, and provocative depictions of (George W.) "Bush plus Posada equal Hitler," referring to the 43rd U.S. president and to Luis Posada Carriles, who is wanted in Cuba for allegedly bombing tourist sites. Public sloganeering and reminders of the revolutionary underpinnings of the regime are not uncommon, including periodic mass rallies to celebrate a variety of revolutionary achievements. And only recently, I have found just a few posters and billboards honoring Fidel.

Speaking of those periodic million-man marches in Cuba, they are quite a spectacle and photo op that merit a little elaboration. I've been to several in Havana, where they seem much more akin to gigantic street parties than political rallies. First of all, in order to assure a great turnout, attendance is *required* from every enterprise and organization. Workers find comfort in the fact that it becomes a paid holiday with free transportation to and from the rally, an abundance of music and food, and a little paper Cuban flag for everyone to wave on cue. Is the atmosphere charged with political invective? Well, at a massive anti-American protest rally related to the little rafter Elian Gonzalez, I was invited to sing and dance my way along the route with a group of employees from my hotel. I declined!

Of course, the government does have a profound impact in terms of its many powers that tend to limit individual freedoms in exchange for expansion of the public good. By way of comparison, it is fair to say that most western governments guarantee individual freedoms, rights and even opportunity for privileges. Whereas in Cuba, I would describe it as somewhat upside down – the government has monopolized those individual rights and *doles them out* as privileges. For example, is a Cuban free to buy a new car? Nope – there is a law against it. Is a Cuban able to hop on a flight to Miami, Madrid or Mexico City? No – travel outside of the country is severely restricted. Can a Cuban buy a house? No – only the government can buy your house, or sell you one.

Indeed, there *are* new cars, travel abroad, and new houses for Cubans. But only at the discretion and allocation of the government. Personal rights seem to have become merely possibilities, rather like being in the Army, where the greater good requires the sacrifice of individual liberties. And just how do the people of Cuba feel about this sad state of affairs? Numb. "It has been a new type of struggle since the time of my grandfather," one young man said to me. "He was granted social rights which were gained through the Revolution. But at a cost of individual rights." In other words, the statistical health, education and welfare of the Cuban people have been on a meteoric rise. But their ability to go to Disney World or buy an air conditioner or freely express themselves is in the dumpster.

In many cases, government restrictions serve a political or economic purpose that may not be apparent at first glance. For example, regulations related to housing and employment make it very difficult for a Cuban to move from the countryside to an urban center such as Havana. Is this merely a whimsical policy? No, there are reasons related to "social engineering" that drive these policies. For example, Cuba already is highly urbanized with shortages of housing and other support systems in the cities. Meanwhile, more workers are needed in the countryside to fill essential but less desirable jobs, such as farming and processing agricultural products.

The tension between official policies and individual liberties is widespread, especially sensitive and below the radar of most visitors. An example: Government regulations long prohibited the presence of Cuban citizens in the country's many tourist facilities. Was this designed to prevent prostitutes from entering tourist hotels? To keep Cubans away from CNN and the Internet? To discourage Cubans and foreigners from spending time together? Perhaps all of the above. I asked a Cuban friend how he felt about this "apartheid" policy.

"It's more than disappointing, it's unfair and unnecessary," he told me. "How would you feel if you were a New Yorker and couldn't go to the Empire State Building or the Plaza Hotel?" Under new policies of the Raul Castro regime, in early 2008 Cubans were at last permitted some access to their country's finest facilities, such as hotels and resorts for tourists. That presumes, of course, that they can afford to do so. Said one young man in Havana, "What Cuban can pay a night in a hotel with a normal salary? If my girl and I having a *mojito* at the bar of the Nacional Hotel costs me two weeks wages, the fact that I was permitted to do something dumb doesn't mean I'd do it! A night in that hotel, which would cost about nine months of wages, would be way out of the question."

And how about political dissent and dissidents in Cuba? The government's harshest critics maintain that there are *thousands* of jailed political prisoners. The government admits to a handful, perhaps dozens. As is often the case, the truth probably rests somewhere (at the low end) in between. In 2007, Amnesty International maintained that Cuba held in jail a total of 72 prisoners of conscience. The organization's annual review of human rights concerns in Cuba continues to be a sobering litany of deprivations and abuses. It alludes to trampling on customary freedoms, including the imprisonment of political dissidents, limits on freedom of expression and association and assembly, arbitrary arrests, detention without due process, unfair sentences, harassment of critics, and use of the death penalty. With vague statutes, such as "social dangerousness," the government is able to penalize as well as deter and preempt behavior that it believes could threaten the status quo. While

Amnesty International's conclusions are rather mainstream (outside of Cuba), they cannot be verified because its staff members are routinely denied visas to enter Cuba. The U.S. Department of State issues an annual report on human rights abuses around the world, and in 2009 Cuba continued to be cited as an egregious violator.

Recall former President Jimmy Carter's visit to Havana in 2002, during which organizers of the so-called Varela Project presented him with a petition containing over 10,000 signatures urging greater freedoms in Cuba, including free speech, amnesty for political prisoners, private enterprise and more. Under Cuba's Constitution, such a plebiscite is permitted and must have the consideration of the National Assembly. In addition, Carter was permitted to make an uncensored live television broadcast to the Cuban people, and its unedited text was published the next day in *Granma*. Carter's tone was conciliatory, and he urged the U.S. government to initiate steps toward normal relations. His reception in Cuba was far beyond cordial. It reflected the importance to the regime of having a past U.S. president lend his prestige to progress between the two antagonists. Castro freed a high-profile dissident from jail during the visit, a step of no small symbolism. Treating Carter like a visiting head of state, Castro turned over the entire Santa Isabel Hotel to him and his delegation. This I can personally verify, as I was unceremoniously expunged from the Santa Isabel in the middle of one of my visits to accommodate the VIP delegation.

The reaction of the administration was predictable. It was annoyed. The Carter trip had proven to be highly visible and highly successful, to the unhappy surprise of the White House. Not only did it torpedo U.S. plans to tighten sanctions against Cuba, but it also induced Bush to do a turn about and endorse the Varela Project. High U.S. officials had tried to undermine the historic visit ahead of time by issuing statements alleging that Cuba was producing and exporting biotech weapons. No evidence was ever produced. After Carter's return he briefed

President Bush, who privately seethed at being upstaged on the Cuba issue. But no change in official U.S. policies resulted, and administration policies continued to march blithely out of step in the global parade.

After a nominal honeymoon period, Castro responded to the Varela Project with a contrary petition that demanded a constitutional amendment guaranteeing the eternal preservation of socialism in Cuba. He mustered over eight million autographs – many of which were, shall we say, "enticed" rather than reflecting an outpouring of national support.

The government has tolerated a modest level of dissident activity when such opinions have been under the auspices of the Catholic Church. Be aware of the delicate political dynamic between the global moral authority of the Vatican and a regime that is fundamentally uncomfortable with outside interference. But when inconsonant domestic voices reach an intolerable decibel level, a punitive response invariably is forthcoming. In 2003, 75 dissidents were rounded up, tried swiftly and jailed with long sentences. This both swept the streets of discordant voices and sent a strong message of deterrence to others who may have had unconventional thoughts in mind. The jailing of so many provoked a worldwide cry of outrage, which the government of Cuba casually dismissed as meddling in Cuba's domestic matters.

Perhaps sweeping the streets of dissidents was a miscalculation by Castro, who was accustomed to keeping the lid on at home and simply waving off grumbling from the United States. The international response derailed a variety of projects and progress with foreign governments. At home the roundup and severe penalties spawned yet another dissident presence. It never ceases to amaze me that governments around the world seem to be oblivious to one of the most profoundly important lessons of history: *If justifiable dissent is suppressed it will enlarge.* It is as predictable as a law of physics. Recall the Democratic political convention in Chicago in 1968? Protestors were literally banged on the head, yet their cause eventually prevailed. How about the U.S. civil rights movement? How many protestors were abused, even killed? They prevailed.

In Cuba, wives and relatives of the jailed ones have organized and become known as The Ladies in White. They attend services in St. Rita Church in Miramar each Sunday, then silently march the streets of Havana in white attire, symbolizing peace, to protest the harsh treatment of their family members. These courageous women were honored with the Sakharov Prize for Freedom of Thought from the European Parliament in 2005. Regrettably, the Cuban government prevented the leaders of the Ladies from traveling to France to attend the prize ceremony to which they had been invited. And that only amplified the publicity and moral suasion of their cause.

In an interesting departure from its past position, in late 2007 Cuba agreed to become a signatory to several U.N. covenants on human rights. While it is mainstream regarding many global issues, Cuba is widely regarded to *not* be in compliance with U.N. positions concerning political and civil rights. Observers such as Wayne Smith, earlier the senior U.S. diplomat in Havana, believe this higher profile may induce Cuba to reduce the number of its political prisoners. Perhaps a preview of such a policy change took place in Santiago, also in late 2007. Political protestors, an extremely rare sight in Cuba, sought refuge in the Santa Teresita Catholic Church. In the worst tradition of police abuse in Cuba, plainclothes officers followed the protesters into the church and proceeded to pummel them. The Catholic Church quickly and strongly protested to the government. And, in what was a significant departure from past practices, the government of Cuba issued an apology to the Roman Catholic Church and to its archbishop in Santiago. Keep in mind that "the government of Cuba" is not some amorphous blob, it is comprised of a very few people who are its top leaders. For sure, Fidel and/or Raul decided this conciliatory gesture was appropriate.

The fact that a low level of political dissidence characterizes Cuban politics cannot be interpreted as an endorsement except, perhaps, of the government's ability to marginalize dissent and dissenters. The official monopoly of the media combined with harsh rules against individual use of communications means, such as copying devices and videotapes and limits on public gatherings and access to the Internet, make it all but impossible to organize dissent. In those rare instances when it has occurred, the government's response has been rapid, predictable and harsh. Over the years, of course, the vast majority of dissenters have voted with their feet and their rafts and left the island permanently.

What is quite interesting is the Cuban definition of political dissidence and how it differs from most. In the West, for the most part, political dissent need be radical and/or violent to warrant the intervention or prosecution by the government. Oh yes, protestors get arrested with some regularity for trespassing or making a socially unacceptable ruckus. And usually they're back on the street as rapidly as the local constabulary can process some paperwork, with an arrest record for disturbing the peace that they generally regard not as a blight but as a badge of honor. In Cuba, however, political dissent is construed in a much broader and more threatening sense – matters that can undermine the national well being. In other words, if behavior is inconsistent with revolutionary principles, it is, by definition, regarded as a threat to national security. And the threshold for a punitive response is set comparatively low. All of this seems rather discretionary to those of us accustomed to more forgiving legal systems. But in Cuba, where the Revolution and its achievements verge on the sacred, it is no small thing to challenge even a thread of the national fabric.

One realm in which there is a conspicuous lack of freedom is the absence of a free press. The Communist Party newspaper *Granma* is the main print and online source of information about the country and the world. It is predictably biased in its coverage, providing the official spin in its articles, and publishing the government's choice of topics. Others never see the light of day. It is political correctness run amok, *Fidelista* cheerleading on steroids. It is always limited in scope, seldom more than 16 pages, which include a lot of photographs and advertisements of government enterprises. Formerly a daily paper, sometimes it is published less frequently as an economy measure.

What if I lust for a copy of the *London Times* or the *International Herald Tribune*? Just skip on over to the hotel newsstand? No, neither is to be found. Invariably when I visit Cuba, I bring along numerous copies of *The Economist*, *Time* and *Newsweek*. Said one my friends who sees them, "We pass them around for weeks; we read them until the ink has fallen off the pages."

In addition to this meager diet of news, the government broadcasts two official television stations and also pirates many channels of a non-political nature. While tourists can generally watch CNN in their hotel rooms, most are unaware that Cubans cannot receive that station and that there are criminal penalties for those who are caught trying to pirate the CNN newscasts with illegal satellite dishes. As a carefully orchestrated element of Cuba's foreign policy, television stations from some European countries, and more recently from China and Venezuela, are available on Cuban television. If you happen to like Chinese opera, for example, then you are going to *love* the frequency with which you can watch it in Havana!

A limited number of foreign media companies have been permitted to open correspondents' offices in Havana. In a meeting with Castro in 1996, Ted Turner and his celebrity wife, Jane Fonda, made such a hit that CNN was granted permission to open the first U.S. media office in Havana since the Revolution. It did so early the following year. In addition, the *Associated Press*, the *Chicago Tribune* and various third country media firms have had offices there for years. Until recently, that is.

# CUBA RISING

In the spring of 2007, a BBC correspondent and a Mexican journalist had their reporting credentials revoked. In addition, the *Trib's* correspondent in Havana, Gary Marx, was summarily invited to cease coverage, explaining only that his writing was too negative, and ordered him to depart the country on short notice. The office was padlocked. The Cuban government has long been hypersensitive about how it is portrayed in the foreign media, and it retains the right to revoke the accreditation of any journalist who shows "a lack of journalistic ethics and/or objectivity in their dispatches." Clearly, "ethics and objectivity" are in the mind of the beholder.

Marx appealed his expulsion because his wife and school-age children lived with him in Havana. In response, the Cuban government permitted him to visit periodically and allowed his family to stay until the school year ended in June. By coincidence I had a reservation on the same flight from Havana as Gary. As a bizarre conclusion to this episode, I noticed that when Marx and his family went to check in for their flight back to the States, they were hassled for hours by officials of the Interior Ministry. In fact, they nearly missed the flight. They evidently lacked some official piece of paper authorizing them to leave. Now one would think that after being unceremoniously expelled, official permission to depart would be superfluous. Then again, this was Cuba. Approval was finally granted and, like so many others that the government has chosen to "spank," they made the flight out with minutes to spare. Marx was down in the dumps, being shown the exit was not part of his plan for the future. Trying to offer comfort, I said to him, "For a journalist to be expelled from some places is a badge of honor."

In another example of high-handed official efforts to suppress the free flow of information and airport encounters of the worst kind, some friends of mine also got hammered when they tried to board their flights homeward. Each had brought with them a used laptop computer to leave behind for acquaintances. This is illegal, and the laptop is anything but ubiquitous in Cuba.

Although Cuban authorities had made note of their laptops when they arrived in Havana, none of the visitors suspected that departing without the devices would be a problem. Wrong, big time. Despite a fumbling bureaucracy that still relies heavily on carbon copies and rubber stamps, the Ministry of the Interior proved itself able to keep track of visiting laptops. And when my amigos tried to depart the country without them, they were summoned to a stark office for a grilling. Worse, they were threatened with fines and imprisonment.

"Where is your laptop?" each was asked. Being reasonably quick on their feet, one responded, "I forgot it in the taxi." Another claimed his had been stolen. And the third said, "I don't know, perhaps I left it at my hotel." These questionable responses were met with glares, interminable murmurings among the angry Ministry of the Interior officers, more threats and then silence. Ultimately, all three were allowed to scramble aboard their departing flight just moments before the plane's doors were closed. No penalties were levied, but it was made abundantly clear that their return to Cuba might not be welcomed.

The Cuban government's often ham-handed treatment of its citizens and its policies rooted in revolutionary nostalgia have resulted in shrinking empathy abroad. The common bond usually was a mutual antipathy for the United States more than an admiration of Cuba being "Velcroed" to communism. While dogmatism has resulted in more than a few conspicuous failures at home, in some areas government policies and practices have proven their worth and even propelled Cuba to rank among the top in the world.

Cuban health care, for example, is universal and free. It has achieved some remarkable successes, and not a few failings. This comprehensive effort begins at The International School of Medicine in Havana, with 23,000 students enrolled. It has an excellent reputation and draws students from all over the world, including the United States. None pays a dime, provided they agree to spend time practicing medicine in any under-served part of the world.

Cuba claims to have some 80,000 trained physicians (compared to 6,000 before the Revolution) and verifiably has more physicians per capita than any country in the world. So many, in fact, that the export of physician services has become a major source of export revenues for the country. Doctors and other medical specialists have been dispatched abroad by the tens of thousands. While away, they receive additional compensation, and their families left behind in Cuba continue to receive the physicians' usual salaries. This is a "triple win" proposition. The physicians benefit from higher income, the patients and beneficiary countries enjoy enhanced health services, and Fidel Castro has scored again with a rousing foreign policy success.

It is verifiable that the infant mortality rate in Cuba is among the lowest in the world and measurably lower than in the United States, 5.3 per 1,000 live births in 2008 in Cuba compared to 6.6 in the United States, according to the Population Reference Bureau. At the other end of the life cycle, life expectancy in Cuba is among the highest in the world, and comparable to the United States. It is apparent that key decisions were made early on to focus on preventive medicine, rather than postpone expenditures and deal with the significantly higher cost of remedial medicine years down the road. In the early months and years of life, a Cuban child receives no fewer than nine inoculations.

One health care issue that stands out has been Cuba's handling of AIDS. Infection on the island is at a comparatively low level, in part as a result of the very low level of drug use with hypodermic needles and comparatively low levels of prostitution (at least without prophylaxis!) and of unprotected sexual activity, straight or gay. A government policy of isolating known AIDS victims has been controversial, but perhaps effective. "Sanatoria" have been established where carriers are required to live, isolated from other people. When I visited one in Matanzas, it appeared to be a very comfortable community environment, somewhat mitigating the harsh reality that there are limitations on how often carriers can go out into the uninfected population. Overall, residents of these facilities seem to be more pleased with their treatment and accommodations than they are concerned about their limited mobility.

Its lapses notwithstanding, every Cuban citizen's entitlement to free medical treatment is regarded as a basic right. How sharply I remember the words of the late Julio Espinosa, a member of the National Assembly, as he recounted his experience while he was posted to the Cuban Interests Section in Washington. His young child had a mishap and had to be rushed to a hospital emergency room. "My child and I had to wait for hours until the hospital could verify that payment would be made for treatment. In Cuba people with illnesses are patients while in the United States they are *customers*," he angrily recalled.

Cuba's universal free health care system gets high marks, but it also has failed in some respects. Most conspicuous is the widespread unavailability of common medications, vitamins and remedies that are readily available over the counter in pharmacies all over the world. In Habana Vieja, on Obispo Street, there are two beautifully restored pharmacies dating back to the 19th century. Fine hardwood and glass display cases run floor to ceiling, beautiful antique porcelain apothecary jars line the shelves, and archaic lotions and potions are on display. Only after several visits to admire these sites did I realize that they actually were *working pharmacies*. Because of the lack of customers and the absence of medications for sale, I erroneously assumed they were no more functional than the many museums nearby.

During every one of my many visits to Cuba, my friends and I always bring a sack of household medications that are so common to us yet so scarce to Cubans. Ibuprofen, stomach antacids, eye drops, vitamins and many more. Invariably they are received with enormous gratitude, whether they are directed to churches, non-government organizations, or friends. But along the way it can be a heart-rending ordeal. At the airport, zealous inspectors of my baggage often give the first envious look. If they are particularly grouchy, they can find reasons to confiscate these items or, at least, create a long delay to let you know their disdain for your abundance in contrast to their needs. My next heartbreak comes at my hotel, where the housekeepers longingly eye my seemingly unlimited supply of desperately needed medicines. Then these gifts attract the attention of the bellmen, who carefully stack them in a baggage room, where they are gathered until we distribute them. Invariably, they plead for just a little bit for their families. Our gifts finally find their way to a reliable organization, where they will be passed along to those in most need. I am always reminded that we have had an impact on the quality of life for thousands of families, but they are comparatively few in a place where the needs are so great.

A friend to whom I often bring bottles of items such as aspirin, children's cold remedies, and antibiotic ointment, said to me, "You cannot imagine how important are your medical donations. Now I am known in the neighborhood to have a few medicines and people come to my house to ask for just a couple of aspirin." Why, in a country that attracts people from all over the world for specialized treatment and surgery, can its citizens not find an aspirin tablet? This is yet another of the great bafflements of Cuba, but one can surmise that a struggling economy has to include priorities, and evidently having enough petroleum or food has taken precedence over curing headaches.

The Cuban people justifiably complain about the deficiencies of the government-provided "social safety net." There simply isn't enough money to meet all the needs for which their government has committed to be the provider.

Consider the situation in the United States for a moment. The American government spends an estimated one trillion dollars per year just for pensions, health care and poverty reduction. That sum is approximately 25 times *the entire gross national product of Cuba!* Yet the United States has an estimated 35 million people still below the poverty line, almost 50 million people without health coverage, and *no one* believes that Social Security payments are sufficient to meet the basic needs of retired people. The world over, the reach of governments seems to exceed their grasp.

On a personal note, I was fortunate to be involved with the government of Cuba taking a step forward in the realm of global collaboration in medicine. A good friend is a founder of the National Marrow Donor Program. It has become a global network of donors of lifesaving bone marrow, actually considered to be a liquid organ that is essential in treating victims of certain types of cancer, including leukemia. What drives the importance of linking donors with stricken recipients is the medical fact that compatibility is most frequent among family members. So relatives are always the first place for physicians to look for donors. In the case of Cuba, many millions of people are from families that are divided by national boundaries. Thus, the problem is magnified to frightening proportions – especially in cases where the boundaries involve not only separations of thousands of miles, but also where there exist such formidable political, financial and legal barriers as between the United States and Cuba.

My friend traveled to Cuba and eventually arranged for a Cuban health organization to participate in the global marrow donor network. It was complicated by the fact that time is of the essence in transporting and administering the possible cure. And further complicated by the economic embargo and travel ban that meant that pilots as well as medical personnel were hampered in terms of ability to travel on a moment's notice and being required to pay expenses in Cuba. Obstacles were overcome, and the lives of victims in Cuba *and* in the United States (and in other countries) have been saved. The world is indeed a community of nations, and the demise of political barriers can only be welcomed, as these survivors certainly can attest.

Related to the high priority that Cuba assigns to medicine and health care is a substantial presence in the field of medical and biotechnology research. One result has been the development of the world's only vaccine for meningitis B. So if people are serious about prevention of this terrible disease, the path to prevention runs through Havana.

An unfortunate feature of medicine in Cuba derives from the egalitarian wage levels set by the government. While physicians may gain a few extra perks, their salary is likely to be as low and insufficient as that of most Cuban workers. In fact, undesirable positions like farmers and trash haulers may be paid *more* than a doctor, recognizing the lack of appeal of their daily routine. Two reality checks in my own experience give pause to the glowing reports about Cuban medicine.

First, a good friend of mine came to me to ask a huge favor. "I am in constant pain from terrible problems with my teeth," she said, "and I need corrective dental surgery." At the public clinic, to which she had free access, this would have involved a wait of many months. With cash on the barrelhead, however, the same dentist, in the same office, could do it within a few days. Actually, in the evening after normal treatment hours. The cash materialized so the surgery was quickly performed.

A second example may be even more telling. During one of my early visits to Cuba, I was introduced to a fellow who asked if I would like to have him drive me around town in his rattletrap car. As I recall, it cost $20 per day, which was substantially less, and vastly more convenient, than finding and using taxis in Havana. We did the deal, and he proved to be knowledgeable, friendly and exceeded my needs. After about one year, as we had become quite comfortable with each other, my amigo said to me, "Perhaps you do not know, but I am not a professional driver. Actually, I am a neurosurgeon. With you, I can earn in a day as much as I am paid for a month at the hospital." I didn't know whether to laugh or cry. This gave new meaning to the term "misallocation of resources" when a brain surgeon takes days off to work as a cabbie!

Although Cuba's highly educated work force cannot yet be fully utilized in a backward economy, few dispute that the educational system is excellent. It starts, of course, with literacy. Since the earliest days of the Revolution, when literacy was only about 60 percent nationwide, making certain that every Cuban can read and write has been one of the nation's highest goals. And it has been very well-achieved. Literacy in Cuba today is the highest in Latin America, higher than in the United States, and among the highest in the entire world.

School attendance is mandatory through age 15. The number of hours of class time per year is significantly higher than in most countries, and the teacher-to-student ratio is lower than in most countries – currently one teacher per 15 students in secondary schools. As children move through the grades, they are frequently tested for aptitude – starting as early as elementary school. Based on those tests they are set upon certain educational paths, and only strong academic performance will keep them on appealing career trajectories. Students who excel are able to continue to undergraduate, graduate and post-graduate specialties. At least one university exists in each of Cuba's provinces, with 40 altogether on the island, enabling most to continue their education without relocating or undue disruption to their families.

An unfortunate reality of Cuba's widely applauded universal free education is that the economy has failed to grow sufficiently to utilize these millions of well-educated people. In addition to my neurosurgeon driver, I have encountered a bartender previously trained as a helicopter pilot and a hotel bellman with a degree in civil engineering. Predictably, these citizens are counted as employed. For many years this enabled the government to make outlandish claims to having full employment. In recent years, official statistics have acknowledged some unemployment, but they fail to reflect the massive extent of underemployment, meaning folks whose skill sets are grossly under-utilized. For Cubans, however, having *any* job is vastly superior to having none. Simply because there is no such thing as unemployment benefits. If you quit a job in Cuba, or get fired, you are in a world of hurt. Not only are you without any income, but also you face formidable challenges to secure another job.

A complicating factor that is related to high education levels and the under-utilization of those people in the work force has been the low retirement age under Cuban law. Until late 2009, after 25 years of work or military service, a man could retire at age 60 and a woman at age 55. Sounds appealing. But that creates some serious problems today and in the future. For openers, a retiree's pension is apt to be about $7 per month, not exactly a rich reward for a lifetime of service. This has provoked a great deal of bitterness among those "true believers" who have loyally served their country for decades and then are put out to pasture with far less than even a subsistence level of income. "What sort of treatment is this for someone like myself who has devoted her entire life to the Revolution?" said a disgruntled retired friend of mine. Second, when you combine a comparatively young retirement age with a population that is, statistically, aging and shrinking at the same time, you are creating conditions for a perfect storm of problems a decade hence. Recognizing this looming problem, the government is encouraging larger families by means such as guaranteeing a full year of maternity leave to mothers of newborns. Although in a secular sense, as *The Economist* put it, "States should not be in the business of pushing people to have babies," many alternatives, such as inward migration, are not now viable options for Cuba.

Like so many other nations, Cuba is having to come to grips with the inevitable demographic fact that there will be fewer people working to support a growing population of retired workers. It is a clone of the troubling outlook in the United States. Today it's OK in some respects. Many educated young people are entering the work force, and they can have meaningful responsibilities only if the oldsters get pushed out of the way. When the economy develops, however, newcomers will be in high demand but so will those older experienced workers who would be removed from the labor pool by mandatory early retirement. Someone smarter than I will have to figure out how to deal with this dark cloud on the horizon. But serious thought must be given to providing a decent retirement pension to reward those who already have served, *and* a significant rise in wages to those who need an incentive to stay actively employed.

Adding to the complex issues of demographics and the economy is the impressive rise in the status of women in Cuba since the Revolution. Their presence in the work force has jumped from under 20 percent to nearly half today. The increase is even more pronounced in professional spheres, such as medicine. They are working more, at higher levels and are divorcing more frequently. In this respect, at least, Cuba already has an important characteristic of an advanced economy!

The facts and impressions of pervasive governance in Cuba suggest to me that it has been costly, even unaffordable, compared to most nations worldwide. A commentary on the achievement of revolutionary goals in Cuba is found in this popular joke: "What are the outstanding achievements of Fidel's Revolution in Cuba?" a Party official is asked. He responds, "Certainly, that would be health care, education and athletics!"

"And what would be the greatest failures of the Revolution?" a passerby is asked. "Certainly, that would be breakfast, lunch and dinner!"

Chapter 8

REAPING THE WHIRLWIND OF SOCIALISM

In a word, Ouch! The economy of Cuba is a Byzantine tale of some success and much failure, opportunities seized and missed, domestic and foreign political meddling, massive foreign debt, and the inevitable chaos when bureaucrats attempt to substitute their manipulation for the realities of the marketplace.

Prior to the Revolution, Cuba was, in the words of senior Cuban economist Rafael Roqueta, "A typical banana republic which was a wonderful vacation spot for Americans, but which had 50 percent unemployment and whose population was 40 percent illiterate." Its economy was nearly totally dependent on the United States, having 75 percent of its exports and 80 percent of its imports with the States. All of that was about to change radically.

In response to the foreign (read: American) domination of Cuba's economy when Castro came to power, radical reforms were high on the agenda of the new regime. Agrarian reform meant confiscation of the properties of large Cuban and foreign landholders and redistribution of that land to Cubans and for agricultural cooperatives. Across the economic spectrum, foreign as well as domestic companies were nationalized, spelling the end of a wildly profitable era for the likes of IT&T, American Fruit and Bacardi.

It also spelled, however, a period of massive challenges to the economy. Many top executives and professional and technical experts had fled Cuba just before and after the Revolution. At numerous enterprises, it was amateur hour with an inexperienced manager suddenly in charge of an entire factory. Production faltered as shortages of essential parts and supplies and personnel wreaked havoc. Not surprisingly, the economy was unable to turn on a dime from overwhelming dependence on foreigners to domestic autonomy. Cuba was self-sufficient in virtually nothing but grand intentions.

Along with Señor Castro came the mandate for a socialist economy. In a nutshell that meant all of the enterprises – from giant factories to the corner ice cream vendor – were to be owned by the government of Cuba. Or, to stretch a bit, they became owned jointly by the citizens of the country. About 11 million stockholders, if you will, in every enterprise in the country! Not all that different from the "Crown Companies" of Canada and England, you think? Hold that thought until I can describe what happens when you add a heap of political and ideological baggage onto that cart.

A socialist economy is an *administered* economy. Administered by bureaucrats in the ministries in Havana who do their best to reconcile national priorities with the immutable laws of supply and demand. In 2009, the conservative Washington think tank the Heritage Foundation released its Index of Economic Freedom. Hong Kong (recall it is part of mainland China) ranked first, the United States was sixth, Mexico was 49th and Cuba was 177th – out of 179 rated. That spells an enormous amount of government management substituting itself for the decision-making of customers and executives.

How has the dynamic between government mandates and free choice been faring in Cuba? While the government has been busy making five-year plans, setting prices and planning how many widgets would be made several years hence, the folks in the country often have been having different priorities and prices in mind. Creative and desperate people found some wiggle room among the sweeping official policies. While the "Ministry of Eggplants" was deciding how many to grow and to sell and at what cost, the people of Cuba devised an alternative mechanism, and it was administered not by bureaucrats but by the invisible hand of a black market. What would you like? How many? Trust me, it is available at some price in Cuba. Most likely the fellow with the green visor who drafted the national master plan is out buying some on the black market himself.

The failures of a wholly planned economy are evident everywhere, especially to a frequent visitor. On one visit I have found the breakfast buffet stacked high with packets of marmalade for my toast. The next time it will be strawberry jam, but no marmalade. Then comes apply jelly, with no sign of the previous flavors. Surely, not a calamity but an indicator of the planners' inability to be responsive to demand.

A case in point a couple years ago: I went to several cigar stores in search of the widely popular Montecristo #2. None was to be found. How could that be? It is one of the best and most sought after cigars not only in Cuba but also around the world. I asked an amigo, who was a top-level executive at the cigar export monopoly enterprise named *Habanos*. "What happened? How can my beloved Montecristo #2 be out of stock?" He responded, "You know it is an excellent cigar!" "Yes, for sure," I said. "You know it is a great value at its current price!" he said. "Yes, for sure," I agreed. "Well, then you can understand why we ran out!"

Actually, I didn't understand. Not to let him off the hook, I persisted. "In market-driven economies, if you have something really good at a really low price, demand would outstrip the supply, and then one of two things would happen: Either the price would be increased (more revenues) or the quantity for sale would be increased (more revenues). That way your customers would have what they want and you, the manufacturer, would have more money." Then came the "Aha" moment: "You forget this is Cuba, and we did not schedule enough production in the five-year plan that was prepared three years ago!" Now how could I argue with that?

Having challenged socialism as an inefficient economic system, let me note that many commercial ventures in Cuba not only are managed professionally, but also they thrive commercially. They have business plans, short- and long-term goals and accountability. There are numerous examples of enterprises that have under-performed and, as a result, management has been changed. In a phrase, the top guys got the boot.

A case in point is the huge business known to all as the Tropicana. Its large dining and entertainment facility in Havana is open every day of the year, offering a thousand seats. A similar club operates in the resort town of Varadero. Its performers include touring companies that have been successful in Europe. If you crunch the numbers, its total revenues could be approaching $50 million annually. Several years ago the success of this enterprise, especially the excellent results of the touring company, resulted in a decision by the top executive to send a touring company to South America. I was told the venture lost money. As a result, the top executive was relieved of his responsibilities and reassigned to manage a small salsa club out in the boondocks. Now that's hardball, more reminiscent of Wall Street than Obispo Street. It is my impression that, while a socialist economy remains sacrosanct as an ideological feature in Cuba, the realities of the marketplace, including rewards and penalties, are increasingly to be found.

Cuba's agricultural sector accounts for her two signature products: sugar and tobacco. Sugar cane production dates back hundreds of years and was a key to Cuba's prosperity during the colonial era. In modern times, however, sugar derived from cane plants has been largely consigned to the museum of agriculture as sugar beets have proven to yield far more per acre and they can do so in a variety of climates. During the Fidel Castro era, Cuba failed to achieve the ever-elusive 10 million ton crop despite massive efforts and diversion of resources. For many years, young people were routinely sent to the countryside to help with the harvest. Because the crop was subsidized at times by the United States. and later by the Soviet Union, it remained fundamental to the economy. By 2005 reality had set in and money was being lost on every pound sold. The sector was allowed to languish. The big push of nearly 50 years finally had ended. And wouldn't you know? The global market rebounded and the Cubans literally didn't have any sugar to sell! A close friend had an order booked from Asia for 80,000 tons *per month,* but Cuba could not provide so much as a teaspoonful for his client.

Most famous of all of Cuba's natural products, hands down, would be tobacco. Cigars, that is. While it may be only a sweet legend that Cuba's cigars were rolled on the thighs of virgins, their cigars' quality and reputation are unsurpassed in the world. Exports of *Habanos*, as they are known, contribute importantly to Cuba's export earnings, second only to nickel, according to Cuban statistics.

The process starts in the countryside, the most renowned region being in the western end of the island in the province Pinar del Rio. The soil is rich, the climate is fine, and the island's most famous growers have their *vegas* (farms) there. Cuba's most famous tobacco grower is certainly Alejandro Robaina, whose farm of only 42 acres is in the heart of the best tobacco country known as Vuelta Abajo. Not only does he grow the most sought after wrapper leaves in all of Cuba, but he also has received recognition, indeed has been made a national icon, by Fidel Castro. Robaina's craggy, sun-wrinkled face adorns advertisements for Cuban tobacco, and he has been rewarded with his own brand, named, of course, *Robaina.*

Robaina's distinctive face and calloused hands reflect scores of summers laboring in the sun, as they adorn one of the kindest gentlemen on the island. One sunny Sunday afternoon some years ago, I was driving through that scenic area with several amigos and we decided to seek out the famous *vega* Robaina. No easy task, but it was discovered – a modest stucco home in the center of a small farm distant from any highway. Having come so far, we approached the gate and were greeted by several workers and family members. "A thousand pardons, but would it be possible to offer our respects to Señor Robaina?" I asked. In only moments Alejandro, then approaching his 80th year, strode from the veranda, welcomed us and invited us to sit with him in the rocking chairs on the veranda overlooking green fields of thriving tobacco plants. So a remarkable afternoon unfolded. He shared his hand-rolled cigars, fine rum and coffee from his own plants as we bantered with his friends and relatives. It was leagues beyond memorable.

Knowing we would return to Cuba in several months, we presumptuously asked if we might visit again, on another Sunday that turned out to be *his birthday.* "Of course, you would be welcome, for Sundays are for relaxing with my friends on the porch," he said. I secretly asked his sister if there was anything that she could imagine he would like as a surprise birthday present from us when we returned. She thought, she nodded no, but she smiled sweetly. So I persisted, "Please let me know." And she reluctantly revealed that Alejandro, one of the most famous people in all of Cuba and someone recognized by millions around the world, had never enjoyed air conditioning in his humble home. Although we were aware that doing so would be illegal, we did not hesitate to adopt this mission as our quixotic quest.

To protect the not so innocent, let me simply say that on Robaina's birthday a few months later, we and a black market air conditioner magically appeared at *vega* Robaina. His reaction, along with his family, was far beyond mere disbelief. Tears, laughter, waving arms and dancing legs. The rum flowed freely. Almost a decade later, whenever I visit, just after a hearty *abrazo,* Alejandro and I point to the air conditioner emerging from his bedroom wall and burst into laughter, for we share a secret in a land with very few of them.

Just as Alejandro embodies the rich heritage of tobacco growing, his grandson, who is named Hiroshi, represents the future of the cigar industry. He is a handsome young man, passionate about baseball but even more about propelling the family business to worldwide prominence. His focus is on branding and marketing and growing the business. Already he has overseen the publication of an impressive coffee table book about his grandfather, created a line of distinctive Robaina humidors, and cultivated clients in Europe and Asia. His high energy and entrepreneurial skills illustrate the path that can shift the economy of Cuba into the 21st century.

Cuba's export of her world-renowned cigars continues to be a growing feature on her landscape of export revenues, providing almost half a billion dollars in 2008. Promotion of the country's most admired product has taken on a decidedly modern marketing flair. Havana hosts a festive cigar fair each year for its dealers and aficionados from around the world. Exhibits sprawl at its modern conference center, and exclusive visits are arranged to normally closed production facilities and to premier tobacco farms in Pinar del Rio. The days of good fellowship, fine dining and the hustling of more orders for cigars reach a climax at a gala dinner that Fidel Castro traditionally has attended. Each year an exquisite cedar humidor, signed by *El Jefé*, is auctioned. The high bids in recent years have been in the hundreds of thousands of dollars – all donated to charities in Cuba. Supplementing these types of promotions, Cuba's icon of fine tobacco, Robaina, often has been sent on grueling world tours to promote Cuban cigars. Such aggressive marketing efforts have paid dividends, as revenues from Cuba's tobacco exports continue to be high and rising. However, be careful what you wish for. It is far from certain that Cuba will be able to sufficiently increase production and maintain quality when demand for her cigars may *double* as exports to the U.S. market become legal.

Cigar factories are located around the island, with some of the largest and most prominent, such as Cohiba, Partagas and Romeo and Juliet, located in Havana. Despite, or perhaps because of, their seemingly antiquated production process, their reputation is unsurpassed in the world. For the best cigars the tobacco is not only aged, but the finished cigars also are aged like fine wine by connoisseurs. No visitor to Cuba should miss a tour of a cigar factory, which is truly like having a time machine take you back to one of her most unique and cherished traditions. Be aware that carrying a camera on such a tour is strictly prohibited. I overheard one tourist whisper to another, "Evidently, the Cubans are carefully guarding their 17th century technology!" In reality it is intended to guard her secret blends of various types of tobacco.

The process begins with nurturing tobacco leaves in the countryside, especially in the western province of Pinar del Rio, where soil, climate and growers dating back many generations seem to create a perfect mix. It is similar to the sum of environmental aspects known as *terroir* in the creation of the world's finest wines. Most growers start with seeds from the previous year's crop, to raise seedlings that are later transplanted into the fields. I was surprised to find many of the rolling acres of lush green tobacco plants covered with white cheesecloth. This protects the cherished leaves, especially the highly valued wrapper leaves, from the intensity of the direct rays of the sun. Continuing with my education in "Tobacco 101," I learned that the harvest involves stripping the leaves not top to bottom, but rather all of the bottom leaves in a field first, then the next ones up, with the top leaves harvested last.

This is not done in a rush, but at carefully calibrated three-day intervals. The crop of leaves is then gently placed on drying racks in distinctive wooden barns, where it rests for months before being shipped to cigar factories. Unfortunately, many of these barns, with their precious contents, get blown to bits by the occasional hurricane.

The tobacco of lower quality is made into cigarettes and lower value cigars, but the best of the best is further aged and processed for as much as five years. Production is in accordance with specific formulas for each type of cigar, and those formulas are as preciously guarded as the one for Coca-Cola. Particular leaves are included to account for flavor, aroma, flammability and the very important wrapper leaves, which must be flawless.

Factory workers are trained for months before graduating to even a simple, low-level production position. Then it can take a decade of experience until they are qualified to roll the most challenging and expensive cigars. These jobs are very desirable ones, as the pay is above average and additional incentives are provided for exceeding already ambitious daily production quotas. A skilled roller can be rewarded with cash bonuses or with cigars to take home (to smoke or sell). I sensed some creeping capitalism in the cigar factories of Cuba.

In the great open expanses of the rolling rooms I have found hundreds of men and women rolling cigars of many types. The well-worn wooden surfaces in each roller's cubicle reflect decades of meticulous handcrafting. Quality control is extensive, and rollers are accountable for perfection in every cigar they produce. To alleviate the boredom of the repetition of creating often over a hundred cigars a day, people read to the workers from elevated platforms in front of the rows of rollers. In the early days of the Revolution, political propaganda was the normal fare. Before that, traditional readings were more sophisticated, and some of the world's most highly regarded literature was routinely presented. As playwright Nilo Cruz said to me, "Illiterate workers could quote from *Don Quixote* and *Anna Karenina*." One of Cuba's premier cigar brands, Montecristo, arose from the affection of the rollers for the classic work of Alexandre Dumas, *The Count of Monte Cristo*. And what do you suppose was the origin of the brand *Romeo and Juliet*? Today, this special tradition of reading has expanded to include the daily newspaper and even steamy novels.

To the casual observer the production process seems unfathomable. The rolling rooms buzz with chatter and activity, supplies come in, cigars go out, and workers are in constant motion. To foreign businesspeople familiar with manufacturing processes, it is described as illogical, inefficient and chaotic. Rolled cigars go into a cedar box, then out of the box for quality inspection. Then back into their boxes, and again out of the box for wrapper leaf color matching. Then back into the box and back out of the box to have the colorful paper rings attached. Then back into the box. I mean to say those cigars have had some serious fondling before they finally get shipped out! No doubt a Western efficiency expert could come in and streamline, economize, and optimize the production process. And no doubt the finished product would be unimaginably worse as a result.

Only few foreign visitors are permitted to visit the elite Cohiba factory. It is located in a once fabulous, now crumbling, villa in one of Havana's most lovely residential areas. No sign reveals its presence. The expansive ballroom is now filled with the small work tables of the rollers. Formerly elegant bedrooms now house stacks of boxes, labels and other production supplies. During visits there, I discovered a surefire way to earn the friendship of the workers. I would take a Polaroid camera and snap roll after roll of film, with the instant color photos going into outstretched hands of the rollers. They would hoot and holler and giggle and pose for the snapshots, a rarity in Cuba. Without a doubt, sags in production at the Cohiba factory were directly attributable to my visits!

On one occasion I arrived with a small group of Americans. As a secret surprise we brought with us an enormous supply of equipment for the factory's baseball team. Work was suspended for a few minutes as we heaped our gifts onto a huge table in the marbled foyer of the villa. Baseballs by the dozen, a pile of players' gloves, protective masks and pads for the catcher, wood and aluminum bats, and more. The team captain yelled over the mayhem, "We have just become the best-equipped baseball team on the whole island!" Tears flowed from grown men, the women cheered, and we were astonished and delighted with the overwhelming reaction from our many new friends.

A footnote to the very important business of cigars to the national economy is the very important business that *counterfeiting* cigars means for the *personal* economy of many people. One can hardly take ten steps in the tourist areas of Havana without a Cuban walking by and whispering, "Cigars?" Why not buy a Cohiba for a buck instead of for 20 bucks at a store? They are invariably fakes. There are lots of ways that a cigar aficionado can identify the nasty ones. They can be too firm or too soft, they can smell wrong or the wrapper leaf colors may not match as in an authentic box. I had to chuckle on one occasion when I examined a box of "genuine" cigars from a street hawker. Inside was an assortment of lumpy, mushy smokes of various hues of green, brown and yellow, probably made of banana leaves instead of tobacco. The purveyor and I simply smiled at each other, and I walked away.

While most tourists are not too discerning, huge numbers of them want to take home Cuban cigars as a souvenir. Even I enjoy smuggling them more than smoking them! So the counterfeiters thrive. Meanwhile, the government is continuously attempting to suppress this underground industry, which not only deprives the government of sorely needed revenues but also tarnishes the brand reputation of Cuban cigars when low-quality ones are being passed around the world as authentic.

The government has taken countless measures to deter the crooks. Elaborate printed labels are used that are difficult to duplicate. So the bad guys just steal them. Special boxes and rings are used. They get stolen as well. Unique stamps and imprints are placed on the boxes. Those get duplicated. The most recent move was the government's placing of a holographic sticker on every box, and after a few years the counterfeiters seem thus far to be unable to duplicate those.

Another step the government has taken to avoid fake cigars leaving the country has been to require that anyone taking more than two boxes as they depart must show a numbered official receipt from a government cigar store. Once I got tangled up in the maze of regulations and had a terrifying and hilarious experience trying to stay in compliance with both the Cuban and the U.S. governments.

I was traveling with an American friend who had bought 10 boxes of genuine Cuban cigars, which generally cost between $200 and $600 for a box of 25, and was bringing them back home. Not permitted to do that, you say? Well, for a while Americans were allowed to bring back up to $100 of Cuban merchandise. So we would get to the United States and declare these were *fake* cigars that cost only five or 10 bucks a box. When leaving Cuba, it was essential to produce the receipts and declare them to be authentic. But when entering the United States, it was essential to have "lost" the receipts and declare them as counterfeits.

My amigo and I reached the emigration booths at Jose Marti Airport and were sent to a tiny office to confirm the authenticity of his cigars. My friend, confused by the contradictory requirements and intimidated by the inspectors, blurted out, "Don't worry, these are all counterfeits!" Ohmigod. As you can imagine, that attracted rather a lot of attention, which sent my friend, already in a state of high anxiety, almost over the edge. Inspectors were poring over his documents, examining all the cigar boxes, rifling through his luggage and emitting threatening noises. He was sure that he was about to be taken outside and summarily executed. By then I was doubled over with laughter, and the officials just wrote me off as a nutcase. We muddled through, everyone calmed down, and my friend probably still has heart palpitations when he is reminded of our great cigar misadventure.

In yet another ironic twist, among many that seem to be so characteristic of Cuba, a ban on smoking in public facilities was enacted in 2005. It is true that Fidel quit smoking his cherished Cohibas in 1985. But if his fingerprints are to be found on this new law, as most likely they are, it certainly took him a while to discover political correctness and health concerns that have been widely known for decades. Some of the time I have found the ban to be enforced in air-conditioned restaurants, but in a land made famous by its tobacco, the ban on smoking seems to be observed mainly in the breach. Said one waiter, indulging me in a no-smoking restaurant, "How can we not let you have a fine cigar here in Havana?"

Another signature agricultural product for which Cuba is famous is her sugar, which has been fundamental to its economy since the 16th century, and its downstream product, Cuban rum. Production surged in the 18th century when, almost simultaneously, the Haitian sugar industry collapsed and Spain allowed the import of slaves into Cuba and permitted the manufacture of rum. But it has been a bumpy ride. Its dependence on great expanses of cheap land and cheap labor has been pivotal in Cuba's history. In the 1960s and 1970s, when the romance of Castro's Revolution was sweeping the world, thousands of young people were drawn to the island to help harvest sugar cane in what became known as the famous Venceremos Brigades.

Until recently, Cuba was one of the leading sugar exporters in the world. From the 1960s through the 1980s, the Soviet Union – despite its own surplus of sugar production – imported millions of tons of Cuban sugar, to give the appearance of trading for her oil, which Cuba so desperately needed.

Even today, with sags more common than surges in world sugar prices, the lush green fields with their leaves waving in the tropical breezes are a common sight. Crisscrossing the expanses of cane plants is a vast national network of narrow-gauge railways that was designed and built to carry the bulky canes from fields to mills. On those rails rode more than a few old locomotives that had been imported from Hawaii in the 1950s. The sugar mills dotting the countryside could be transformed from industrial factories to museums at any moment. They are big, dark, hot, smoky, noisy and dangerous. They continue to operate with gigantic machines from the 19th and even the 18th centuries.

Upon reaching the mill, the sugar cane is moved into giant crushers that extract the juice, which then is filtered. Old iron boilers, fueled by discarded sugar cane fiber, provide blazing heat, which results in the evaporation of most of the water, leaving behind thick molasses-like syrup. Additional distillation and drying results in those familiar sweet crystals that we spoon into our morning coffee. In many respects this is not the end of the process, but just the beginning.

The huge amount of pulpy waste derived from the process is put to good use. In fact, nearly all of it is transformed into other products. Most of the fibrous waste is used as fuel for the sugar-processing line, and much of the remainder is recycled into wood-like material used to make furniture. Often those factories that consume the by-products are near to the sugar mills. Countless other derivatives have been put to use as ingredients in everything from medicine to perfume.

In 2005, in response to declining world sugar prices, the government finally threw in the proverbial towel. It closed two-thirds of the island's 156 sugar mills, replanted the tens of thousands of acres with other crops, and quietly let the annual harvest shrink to 1.1 million tons. This modest level would be sufficient to satisfy key export commitments and to supply domestic needs for sugar and the most profitable by-product known as rum. Along the way, however, hundreds of thousands of workers were idled. Some have retired, others have been redeployed to farm new crops that now thrive in the former cane fields, and most of the remainder were retrained for new jobs.

In a classic example of bad timing and the volatile nature of world sugar prices, the demand for sugar surged the following year. So the drumbeat for increased sugar production in Cuba was heard again. In order to meet rising demand, as well as provide for a rapidly growing ethanol production capacity in Cuba, the idle fields are being replanted and modernization of archaic refineries is planned.

While sugar itself continues to perform like a yo-yo in the Cuban economy, none of its derivative products rivals the most famous, and in ever-growing demand, Cuba's fabulous rum.

Made famous by the Bacardi family, which began producing it in Cuba in the 19th century, Cuban rum is unsurpassed, according to its legions of devotees. From the crushed sugar canes comes liquid sucrose, which undergoes natural fermentation at a distillery. The distillation and aging process result in the distinctive aromas and flavors of the rum. As the liquid ages in oak barrels and concentrates, it acquires deeper color and flavor as time goes by. The youngest emerges nearly transparent. It is called white rum and is ready to be enjoyed after less than a year. Amber-colored rums are aged three, five, or seven years in oak barrels. The most cherished is aged for as long as 15 years, and it has a strength and flavor more like brandy. During visits to the Bocoy Rum bottling plant in Havana, I have seen those massive old barrels stacked floor to high ceiling, much as they have been for centuries.

Cuban rum is delicious, available everywhere, and inexpensive. Illustrating the depth of rum in the minds and traditions of Cuba, a bottle is included in each Cuban's monthly ration allocation. An unfortunate consequence of its prevalence, just as with vodka in Russia, is the presence of alcoholism. Even some of the country's leading officials, athletes, and enterprise executives are verifiably victims of excess indulgence.

Purists insist that rum is to be enjoyed "neat," or straight. Said one such aficionado, "It doesn't get any better than sipping Cuban rum, not mixed or diluted even with ice." More familiar to Americans would be the *Cuba libre*. The hands-down favorite in Cuba, however, is the *mojito*. Arrive at your hotel and you are handed a refreshing welcoming *mojito*. At a party, restaurant or home, it is all but certain that an icy *mojito* will be handed to you. Perhaps the most impressive display of *mojitos* is found at Hemingway's famous watering hole La Bodeguita del Medio, near Cathedral Square. There skilled bartenders will mix dozens at a time, glasses lined up like a row of soldiers on the bar, before they are passed among throngs of enthusiastic and thirsty visitors.

So what is the magic of a *mojito*? Let's start with the recipe. Into a glass goes the following: half a spoonful of sugar, a tablespoon of lime juice, and a generous sprig of fresh mint leaves. Mix while crushing the mint leaves and add ice, sparkling water and a generous pour of white rum. You will find it to be much more than the sum of its parts. It is enhanced when consumed in Havana, with salsa music and laughter in the air.

When the Revolution loomed, the first family of rum, the Bacardis, left and took their vitally important trademarks with them. Production was reestablished in Puerto Rico, not surprisingly under the Bacardi label. Headquarters was moved from its fabulous Havana art deco building, with their logo black bat on its pinnacle, to Miami. While the new government in Cuba was stung by the loss of this Cuban hallmark, it responded by renaming the same product as Havana Club brand, upon that trademark becoming available.

For nearly 50 years the Bacardi family and the Cuban government have been wrangling over trademarks and legal use of the brand names. The dispute peaked again in 1998, when U.S. congressional action, with a strong push from the Bacardis and some reckless treatment of our obligations under international treaties on trademarks, denied trademark protection to Havana Club. Although that step was ruled illegal by the World Trade Organization in 2001, the dispute continues to simmer. Bacardi seems to be giving higher profile to its "Cuban-ness," and Fidel Castro has threatened to again bottle rum under the Bacardi label. Indeed, the Bacardi saga is a microcosm of the bilateral and worldwide avoidable fusses that continue to be inflamed by political hardliners in Cuba, Miami and Washington.

While the dispute over rum trademarks may appear to be a minor flap, the reality of politics intruding into the realm of trademark law has raised some troubling signals. In a tit-for-tat response, Cuba could cancel the hundreds of trademarks in Cuba of U.S. companies and begin to produce and distribute products under traditional U.S. brand names. "How would you like to see a Cuban soft drink with the name Coca-Cola slapped on the can?" asked one Cuban lawyer. This is indeed a slippery slope that could have disruptive consequences in law and commerce around the globe. It seems to me that governments would be well-advised to quit mixing global agreements on trademark law with bush league (no pun intended) political sniping.

The island of Cuba is not blessed with an abundance of natural resources. Aside from perhaps 35 percent of the world's nickel reserves, it is poorly endowed. In the all-important energy sector, Cuba is less than 50 percent self-sufficient, and petroleum discoveries off its north shore will take many years, even decades, to fully develop, if, in fact, they prove to hold substantial quantities. And if they do, they are likely to be high in sulfur content, necessitating additional expensive refining. A huge effort is under way to answer these vitally important questions. Meanwhile, Cuba is optimistically investing hundreds of millions of dollars in modernizing and enlarging its petroleum refining capacity. In early 2009, for example, a modern refinery came on line near the port city of Cienfuegos, a charming provincial capital on the south coast of the island.

In 2005, the U.S. Geological Survey estimated that Cuba's offshore unproven reserves could hold massive quantities of both natural gas and oil. At 6,000-foot depths, exploration has begun by companies from countries as far ranging as India, Norway, Canada and Spain. Some potential fields may be as deep as six miles beneath the surface. As world oil prices soared past $100 per barrel, U.S. policies of "let's shoot ourselves in the foot" prevented American companies from engaging in this hunt for liquid gold very close to its own shores and refineries. Just as American companies' lobbying efforts resulted in access to Cuban agricultural markets, it seems logical that American petroleum companies could secure a comparable exception to the embargo. After all, it can be argued, substantial Cuban revenues from oil could well be deployed to purchase U.S. products. Anytime Americans could stimulate their exports and have access to nearby oil would seem to be a double-barreled win for the U.S. economy. Even if this scenario were to not play out, Cuban oil could put its economy back on a healthy footing and reduce its reliance on regimes such as that of Venezuela's Hugo Chavez, who has made a career out of being hostile to the United States.

During Cuba's nearly 30-year honeymoon period with the Soviet Union, the Soviets promised to build a nuclear reactor at Cienfuegos to ameliorate Cuba's energy deficiencies. Construction was well along, but no nuclear fuel had yet been provided, when it was reported that the design was from the blueprints of the Soviet reactor at Chernobyl. U.S. experts looked at a map and charted the pattern of prevailing winds. They concluded that if the Cienfuegos reactor experienced a meltdown, as happened at Chernobyl, there would be massive amounts of radioactivity and widespread deaths as radioactive clouds moved up the East Coast of the United States. Enormous pressure was brought to bear on the Soviets by the United

States and its allies. As a result, construction was halted, and the nuclear power plant remains unfinished. Its white cooling towers in the distance across the blue harbor remain as a stark reminder of good intentions gone awry.

During a discussion of Cuba's energy dilemma, a government official elaborated to me, "We have no prospect of self-sufficiency in any sort of energy, except possibly solar." Thus the huge importance of the current oil deal with the simpatico regime in Venezuela. It is said to enable Cuba to purchase up to 13 million tons of oil annually at deeply discounted prices and very relaxed payment terms, valued at an estimated $2.5 billion per year. Of special value in this era of skyrocketing oil prices is said to be a provision that Cuba has an entitlement to that oil, but that it need not take physical possession of it. Said one cynic to me, "I'll bet a bundle that Cuba is taking some of its allocation at $30 per barrel and reselling it at $100 per barrel, making hundreds of millions without ever touching the oil."

And why is Venezuela so assiduously courting Cuba, when the Chavez government is facing rising political discontent and growing economic woes? Mainly because it can. Given President Chavez's desire to emulate Castro's socialist path and global legacy, oil revenues that have rocketed from $7 billion per year in 1999, when Chavez came to power, to $75 billion in 2008 enable him to do so. And what will happen when oil prices cycle downwards again as they started to do in 2008? Tune in then to see Chavez' balancing act between domestic tranquility and his egomaniacal tendencies abroad.

CHAPTER 9

THE LURE OF CUBA

In the long run, Cuba's greatest resource may be her fundamental natural one – the beauty of the island itself as a magnet for tourism. It is the largest island in the Caribbean, and its sandy white beaches outnumber all of the other beaches in the Caribbean combined. They run, unspoiled, for many hundreds of miles. In addition, Cuba is the proud designee of *nine* U.N. World Heritage Committee sites, each deemed part of the world's cultural and natural heritage with outstanding universal value – a remarkable number indeed that highlight many of her leading tourist attractions.

Those visitors whose focus is on Havana will find it to be a smorgasbord of delights. Its thousands of vintage American cars is a marvel, and landmarks such as the Tropicana cabaret (aptly described as musical mayhem in feathers and chandeliers) are not to be missed. The show at the Tropicana is reminiscent of its early heyday in the years after 1939, when U.S. mobster Meyer Lansky opened the world-famous casino, restaurant and showplace. With a live orchestra of over 40 players, 200 singers and dancers, costumes that dazzle, rum flowing freely, cigar smoke wafting upwards toward the star-filled sky, I couldn't imagine a more quintessentially Cuban evening of fun. As a pleased crowd departed after one performance, I overheard a smiling fellow comment, "I just saw more perfectly matched cinnamon colored buns than ever in any bakery!"

Following one particularly indulgent evening at the Tropicana, an exuberant friend, who was feeling no pain, thought it would be memorable to visit with some of the long-legged beauties backstage. Good idea, bad execution. We charged across the empty stage and headed for the gap in the curtain through which our friends-to-be had disappeared. Instead of finding a gaggle of beauties awaiting us, we literally bumped into a burly, frowning security guard. We were clearly not the first misguided visitors to go searching for an encounter of the best kind. The language barrier proved to be no obstacle whatsoever as he firmly assisted us in finding our way to the exit in the opposite direction.

One conspicuous absence in the existing array of tourism possibilities is, in a word, shopping. Yes, I have found an abundance of handicrafts like bongo drums, cheap cow bone jewelry and silkscreen images of Che. But there is an almost total absence of shops for upper-end mementos and expensive items for women. There are many plausible explanations: Catering to tourists is still a relatively new opportunity for Cuba, there are many higher priorities for imports that necessarily compete for scarce funds, and retailing itself is little known terrain. More importantly, however, seems to be the official view of Cuba as a marketplace. In a concept that is open to challenge, the prevailing official view is that retailing subtracts revenues from the economy without the retailer paying for that privilege. Yes, a store would pay rent, but that is seen as a disproportionately small price for the opportunity to profit from tapping into a thriving market opportunity. This approach, unfortunately, differs widely from the views of most economists.

Consider, for example, Walmart. Many small towns in which their stores were built were in a tizzy about the giant retailer. Indeed, some small, inefficient higher-priced stores did get knocked out of business. But overall in the United States revenues were hugely increased, millions of new jobs have been created, and enormous tax revenue growth in each community has proven the fears of its opponents to be unfounded. Retailing constitutes a cumulative, snowballing growth stimulus. In all likelihood, a similar transformation eventually will take place in Cuba, even with safeguards to prevent the "McDonaldization" of her beautiful neighborhoods.

An amigo who travels widely in Cuba said to me, in disbelief, "Do you know there already is a McDonald's restaurant in Cuba? I was astounded, until he explained that he had seen the golden arches soaring within the confines of the U.S. military base at Guantanamo Bay. That, of course, is regarded as U.S. territory and remains immune from Cuban regulations. Cuban officials, nevertheless, fear an onslaught of American fast-food retailers, as has happened across the globe. I am confident that the enormous sensitivity of the government to the country's heritage will prevent any such blight on her landscape.

Perhaps, above all, Havana is a living architectural museum. A politically correct tour guide may tell you that deep appreciation for these architectural treasures has resulted in their preservation. In reality, it's partly because the country has not had the money to tear them down and rebuild. Much like some cities in the United States, which, for reasons of cost, never tore up their archaic mass transit systems known as trolleys. A few decades later they had come back into fashion and economic sense. So they were rehabilitated and are serving well today.

The splendid result of historic preservation and rehabilitation in Havana is breathtaking and warrants some elaboration. The country's architectural heritage has emerged to be one of the supreme attractions of Cuba.

# CUBA RISING

In the center of Old Havana, one finds countless fine examples of colonial era buildings, including Cuban Baroque, Moorish and Neoclassical styles. Among the finest examples is the former palace of the Spanish Governor General at Plaza de Armas, surrounded by cobblestone streets of the same era.

Other major styles one can expect to encounter are art nouveau, with its more modern appearance, as well as eclectic, neogothic, beaux-arts, art deco (witness the fabulous Bacardi building) and modernism. I had assumed that with the Revolution and a pervasive Soviet presence on the island came a lot of functional, but really plain and ugly buildings. I was correct. In fact, the winner of the "Ugliest Building In Havana If Not The Entire Western Hemisphere" contest would be the edifice that the Soviets built as their embassy along lovely Fifth Avenue in Miramar as noted earlier. Soviet designs notwithstanding, many fine structures with distinctive architecture also have been added to the streetscapes during the past half-century.

Among Havana's most remarkable features is the Old City, Habana Vieja, which is densely populated with remarkable buildings as well as people. The tale of its preservation is fascinating.

Starting in the 1970s, when Cuba was struggling with its economic woes, a bright and energetic young man named Eusebio Leal made a seemingly preposterous proposal to Fidel Castro. As an architect, historian and engineer, he asked that terribly scarce government funds be provided for the restoration of the Old City. That part of Havana, which dates back as early as the 16th century, was crumbling from neglect as well as from the ravages of nature. Opposition to his concept flared. "When we are hungry, how can we afford to throw money at bricks and mortar?" was the rhetorical question. "How can we fail to?" was the response. Leal argued persuasively that seed money would lead to a great multiplier impact in terms of more jobs, growing skills, and above all drawing tourists and their hard currency to Havana. And he was exactly correct.

This entrepreneurial proposal involved restoring and developing hotels, restaurants and tourist attractions, some proceeds of which would be returned to the government coffers and the balance would be plowed back into further development.

Fast forward three decades and what a marvel is to be found. Dozens of disintegrating and overcrowded tenements have been beautifully restored, and their residents have returned. (The government guarantees their place, if they wish). A wide variety of community facilities, such as schools, clinics, parks, marketplaces and even a maternity hospital, have been built. Altogether, over 300 buildings have been restored with hundreds more in progress or planned for rehabilitation. Simple demolition has been avoided at all costs, even if the only remaining historic structure was a fragment of a façade. In one case, a splendid restored building had but a small area remaining above a new restaurant, and it was converted into a hotel with four, yes *only four*, hotel rooms. I wouldn't want to be the one to try to persuade Willard Marriott to do likewise. In another quintessentially Cuban innovation, one hotel was opened that caters to cigar smokers. It includes one of Havana's finest cigar stores, complete with an in-house cigar roller and a comfortable lounge for indulging in fine *Habano*s and Cuban rum and coffee.

The responsible organization, the Office of the Historian of Havana, now presides over more than 100 hotels and restaurants for tourists. They generate tens of millions of dollars each year, provide good new jobs, elevate the quality of housing for many, and continue to expand their impressive list of achievements and ambitious goals. While some of the estimated 65,000 Cubans who live within the 1.5 square miles of Habana Vieja remain unpersuaded of the direct benefit to them, the success of the restoration effort resulted in the area being designated a World Heritage site by the United Nations.

# CUBA RISING

During the first 30 years after the Revolution, tourism in Cuba was confined to a small domestic market, mainly sites where workers could be rewarded for outstanding efforts, and a few developments where select Soviets, Bulgarians and the like could enjoy some fun in the sun. This only slight attention to tourism arose from a scarcity of resources to be devoted to leisure and recreation, and the politically driven inclination to avoid attracting foreigners who might undermine Cuba's revolutionary fervor. Of necessity, these policies ended abruptly in 1990, when it was recognized that the struggling economy would benefit mightily from an infusion of foreign currency that filled the pockets and purses of foreign visitors. Thus began a concerted and successful effort to rapidly develop tourism with new hotels, beach resorts, airports that could accommodate international flights of jumbo jets, and the myriad of infrastructure and facilities to support this new industry on the island.

In a controversial step in 1993, the government, as a means to infuse the struggling economy with cash, reversed its longstanding policy of banning foreign currencies. Possession of dollars by Cubans was legalized. Offshore relatives began to send dollars to the island. This trickle turned into a flood of dollars carried in by an estimated 100,000 visiting relatives each year and through sums allowed to be transmitted by Western Union from the United States to Cuba. Estimates of those remittances run as high as $2 billion annually. Although this is but a tiny fraction of the roughly $300 billion per year remitted by migrants back to their home countries worldwide, it represents a massive and vital infusion of hard currency to cash-strapped Cuba. For many years, in fact, this was Cuba's largest single source of foreign revenues. It represented a significant offset to the loss of the Soviet subsidies, which totaled about $4 billion to $5 billion annually. What a deal! Cuba "exports" the pained expressions of needy family members, and it imports cash. The result is massive benefits to the home team, and *at zero cost!* For families whose annual income hovered around $200, even a very modest additional sum could provide for a huge improvement in their standard of living.

In order to soak up all that hard currency that suddenly was floating around, the government opened numerous stores where a fabulous array of food and household items were available – but only to be paid for in hard currency dollars. Food, appliances, clothing, children's toys, in fact, most anything could be had in exchange for the almighty dollar.

In one of the supreme ironies of the politically charged debates over U.S. policies toward Cuba, it is the Cuban-American expatriate community that is transmitting these vast sums to Cuba. At the same time, they demand the prohibition of travel to Cuba by other Americans because *their* dollars would be used to "prop up" the Castro regime that they so passionately oppose! It is not clear to me how the dollars of one group can be so objectionable while the dollars from another group are just fine. When Cuban-American politics gets into the game, not everything makes perfect sense.

As the dollar gained currency on the island, it became the universal currency of the tourism trade and the most valuable asset a Cuban could hold. With it, inadequate monthly food rations could be supplemented and numerous necessities again came within reach of many Cubans. Many, but not all.

*If* a family member had access to dollars, then life improved measurably. Being in the dollar stream was one stream every Cuban would like to paddle in. It meant that you or a family member might work for a foreign company or in the tourism sector. Often they could gain dollars through tips, permitted bonuses, or under-the-table incentives and rewards. More than a few visitors suspect that among the most prosperous people on this island are the bellmen at tourist hotels. As a result, huge and contentious inequalities have emerged throughout the economy, wherein bartenders and taxi drivers routinely earn 10 or 20 times as much as doctors, government officials and university professors. One official said to me, "Such disparities that penalize professional people cannot be continued." Exactly how to discontinue them will be a formidable challenge to the government. The transition from arbitrarily set penurious wage levels to market-driven ones will be disruptive, especially for those who inevitably will be left behind.

As the economy struggled, some people smiled and winked, saying they would endure with *fe*, the word for *faith* in Spanish. FE also happens to be the initials of *familia extranjera*, meaning family abroad. Thus the smile and wink. If you were a taxi driver who could flip off the meter midway through a trip and pocket the other half of the fare, life was good. The government collects fares that appear on the meter while drivers receive government-set wages and get to keep their tips. Otherwise, for the majority of folks, such as rural residents and Cubans not within the "dollar stream," the challenges of securing simply the bare essentials became overwhelming.

Meanwhile, the efforts to expand foreign investment in general and tourism investment in particular succeeded as the 1990s rolled along. Foreign hotel chains, such as Melia and Iberostar, built and secured contracts to manage dozens of attractive new properties across Cuba. In Havana and nearby Miramar, many beautiful modern hotels are now in place. Not traditionally Cuban architecture, perhaps, but fine facilities for tourists and businesspeople. In the historic town of Trinidad, a new hotel ranks among the best on this island. And a few miles away a new beachfront resort is open. Predictably, it is the go-to destination for visitors, replacing the Soviet era Ancon Hotel, where countless thousands of vacationing factory workers from places like Bucharest and Moscow once populated its now-decrepit buildings and endured its lumpy mattresses.

In addition to adding tens of thousands of new and refurbished hotel rooms to expand the opportunities to grow tourism and its revenues, starting in 1996 it has been permitted for visitors to stay in private homes as an alternative. *Casas particulares*, as they are known, are akin to a bed and breakfast and are considerably less expensive than customary hotels. They offer an uncommon glimpse into home life in Cuba. The government regulates them tightly to be sure the hosts pay their substantial taxes and, not always successfully, to be sure they are not being rented by the hour to the ladies known as *jiniteras*.

Billions of dollars in investments succeeded in attracting tourists, and along the way they created tens of thousands of desperately needed new jobs. According to Cuban data, the island hosted well over 2 million foreign visitors in 2009 and generated over $2 billion in revenues for the country. It is the leading growth sector in the Cuban economy. The largest single nationality group arrives from Canada during its frigid winter months and makes up over a quarter of Cuba's total tourists. The countries of Western Europe and Latin America accounted for most of the rest, each of the top six sending about 10 percent of the island's holiday travelers. The Cuban tour guides quickly came to characterize the visitors: The Germans are too fussy, the English are too tight with their money, the Italians are too exuberant, and the Americans give the biggest tips.

Although tourism from the United States is not legal, estimates are that tens of thousands of Americans find their way to Cuba annually, and there were far more when the restrictions were far fewer. There were 200,000 in the peak year of 2000. Who are they? You have a core group of folks doing good deeds in various arenas, such as religion, medicine and academia. I've also seen journalists, architects, librarians, photographers and even garden clubs, all of which enjoyed U.S. permission to travel. Celebrities have not been in short supply. Jack Nicholson, Jude Law and Muhammad Ali are among those I have seen in Havana. And there have been many others who are pleased to find a destination unencumbered by *paparazzi*.

A considerable number also travel illegally to enjoy the beaches, rum, cigars, sightseeing and more. And many who cannot resist the forbidden fruit of traveling to a prohibited destination. Forbidden how? Shortly after the travel ban to Cuba was put in place in the United States, angry prospective travelers challenged it in court. The good news was that America's highest court determined that its citizens could not be denied their right to travel freely. The bad news was that Americans *could* be denied permission to disburse U.S. currency along the way. Therein lies the answer to the frequent question, "Why is the embargo enforced through the U.S. Treasury Department?" Because it controls the money, and the money always seems to be at the heart of the matter.

When the inevitable day finally comes, when U.S. citizens are permitted to visit Cuba freely, another million or more tourists are expected in just the first year. Some optimistic Cuban officials have projected as many as 3 million. The Ministry of Tourism is ramping up as rapidly as Cuba's limited resources permit. Theme parks, marinas, golf courses, hunting expeditions, and much more are being planned. Special schools for training tourism workers have been established, encompassing everyone from kitchen workers to desk clerks to entertainers.

The repercussions for tourism in southern Florida and throughout the Caribbean could be anywhere from bad to catastrophic. American tourism to Cuba may become a "10"on the tourism Richter scale. In fact, there are more than a few observers who suspect that the Florida tourism industry may be quietly lobbying for the preservation of the travel ban to Cuba to avoid an incalculable blow to hotels, theme parks and a myriad of other tourism facilities and employers in the Sunshine State.

Will Cuba be ready for an onslaught of *Yanquis*? Not likely, in view of the huge need for additional hotel rooms and related supporting tourism infrastructure – everything from restaurants to laundries, buses to banks, minibars to doorknobs. Hundreds of millions of dollars of fresh spending in the tourism sector is planned, including new and refurbished hotels, highway improvements and modern planes for the domestic fleet. Despite ambitious plans, there remain real financial limitations on how rapidly the tourism sector can be enlarged. So how will the anticipated surge of visitors be handled? In the cautious words of a former foreign minister, "We may just have to put up some type of embargo ourselves!" In other words, a disruptive and unmanageable level of visitors could be rationed by limits on flights, visas, berths for cruise ships or other restrictions. How ironic that would be.

Cuba's Ministry of Tourism, in an effort to increase tourist income in a hurry, has focused on the mass-market opportunities, specifically inexpensive packaged tours on charter flights from Europe and Canada. In fact, Cuba has sought out and deftly attracted the so-called incentive tour market, which is widely regarded as the least profitable segment of the entire marketplace. Why? Presumably, low-cost package tours offered the fastest way to exploit the cash cow that is tourism. Less investment is required as is less marketing. So Cuba has become sort of the K-Mart of world tourism. I have asked officials of each of Cuba's leading tourism companies on numerous occasions if they are able to offer special opportunities at higher prices to visitors interested in a more upscale experience. Hot air balloon rides? Helicopter tours? Luxury train trips? Their eyes glazed over. After nearly two decades of promoting tourism to Cuba, the island still did not offer a single first-class golf resort or yacht marina. Forget about parasailing, and there are still no flights from Havana to most of her best tourist attractions like the cities of Trinidad or Pinar del Rio.

Another consequence of the mass-market approach to tourism development has been a paucity of fine dining opportunities throughout the island, nowhere more evident than in Havana. It is estimated by *Cigar Aficionado* magazine that there may be as few as 300 seats for good restaurant meals *in all of Cuba!* And all but a handful of those are to be found in *paladares*, which are small, family-run restaurants.

This stems, in part, from the packaged tour approach, which includes extensive pre-paid buffet meals at hotels. So the absence of excellent freestanding restaurants is noticeable and an unfortunate liability to those whose notion of cross-cultural travel includes nice dining experiences.

While dining in Cuba is not apt to be described as gourmet, frankly speaking, I have found it to be a barrel of fun and a distinctive part of the Cuban experience. Restaurant décor is almost always pleasing but certainly not elegant; wait staff is low key (sometimes it's *in absentia*), rather than hovering; dining is leisurely in the Spanish tradition, and, invariably, there are strolling troubadours or house salsa combos to add to the ambiance and offer you their CDs for sale. But I have never found it sensible to challenge the kitchen in Cuba.

Hold the veal cutlets, sweetbreads and chateaubriand until you get home. The traditional fare of pork or chicken and rice and beans seldom disappoints and sometimes amazes. Fish can be splendid, but beware. Much of Cuba's refrigerated distribution system is dedicated to perishable products for the export market. In fact, when I first began to visit Cuba, I was told that the country's *only* climate-controlled warehouse was devoted to storing tobacco. So I suggest you ask if their fish was swimming that morning and, if not, move on down the menu. And at the bottom you'll always find ice cream, which for me is one of the best-kept secrets in the country. No artificial flavors, no preservatives, and a butterfat content that goes right off the top of the charts. *Do not miss it!* The grand finale for every meal in Cuba is a traditional cup of *café Cubano*, a hearty espresso usually adorned with a massive spoonful of sugar and always served in a petite demitasse cup. It is ubiquitous on the island, to be found with every meal, snack, visit with friends, business meeting, and in street kiosks. In view of the late hours I keep in Havana, the words *café Cubano double* roll off my tongue automatically every morning.

The absence of golf courses on the island baffles me. In the old days, no doubt, golf was regarded as a degenerate bourgeois indulgence. But not today. After all, Cuba has plenty of available land, and plenty of need for the income golf resorts could generate. One of the iconic photographs of the revolutionary period was of Che Guevara and Castro enjoying a round of golf in 1962 in Havana. Written reports say that Che beat Fidel, who is not known to be a particularly good loser at *anything*. A *Granma* journalist who wrote about Fidel's loss on the links was supposedly fired the next day. Fidel turned one of Havana's two golf courses into a military school and the other into an art school. In 2009, the Ministry of Tourism was preparing to develop golf resorts to stimulate high-end tourism, with at least 10 developments in various stages of planning. One golf resort planned by a Canadian company is only now being launched after more than 10 years of effort. So golfoholics will have to settle for a marginal course near Havana and another funky one at Varadero until new ones open.

This spanking of Cuba's strategic planning for tourism done for the moment, I must recount one remarkable experience that may not be particularly instructive but which was an amusing eye opener for me. En route from Havana to Cienfuegos, we stopped at a wildlife attraction near Playa Girón. It was reasonably predictable: several souvenir kiosks, no restaurant, nasty restrooms, and some seemingly well-cared for native animals and reptiles on display. But for me the best attraction, and a complete surprise, was finding an older fellow who was hollering for attention, like a carnival barker, to his little setup under a tree. It seemed to be a bit more creative and entrepreneurial than I normally find in Cuba, so we went for a closer look. On a pedestal he had fashioned a whirling top, not unlike a roulette wheel. Around the perimeter was an assortment of bottles of rum. And in the center was a forlorn and somewhat raggedy looking hamster. The deal seemed to be this: Everyone places a bet of a buck next to the rum bottle they favor. The chatty master of ceremonies then spins the circular table top. As it slows, the dizzy hamster staggers away from the center and toward the edge. And, finally, the poor little critter wobbles into a tiny shelter next to one of the bottles. If it's the one you bet on, you get it as a prize. Everyone else loses, especially the hamster.

International airports have been built at Cuba's main destinations so tourists can flock to the beaches and often bypass Havana entirely. Joint ventures with foreign hotel chains have resulted in scores of modern tourist resorts being developed in the past 10 years. The leading player has been the Melia chain from Spain, with more than 30 hotel ventures on the island. Investing in Cuba during her hour of dire need, that being the early 1990s, has proven to be enormously advantageous to Melia. Fidel has a long memory. Rumor has it that Melia gets the last look at every hotel deal proposed for Cuba.

While most of Cuba's foreign visitors come for her sugar sand tropical beaches or sightseeing to mine some of her rich history and heritage, plans are afoot also to entice foreigners with more specialized interests. Medical tourism is already gaining traction as people find they can arrange for excellent and inexpensive medical treatments in Cuba's hospitals dedicated to their needs. In addition, the government has defined target areas for development such as ecotourism, hunting and fishing, scuba, and bicycle touring. Cultural festivals for art, dance, jazz, books and movies have been well-attended and likely will expand.

One specialized opportunity that I have not yet heard discussed is touring by motorcycle, as was favored by Che before he met the Castros. Some years ago friends urged me to organize a Harley expedition around Cuba. A complicated plan was devised. Bikes had to be shipped to Mexico and then secretly transported to Cuba. A chase vehicle with spare parts was a necessity. Identifying a route with food and accommodations at intervals was no small thing. In the end, because of its flagrant violation of U.S. laws, its "elitist" appearance to Cuban authorities, and its inevitable revelation on the front page of the *New York Times*, the plan was abandoned. I am confident, however, that a future group of Harley riders, under less burdensome circumstances, will find the highways and byways in Cuba to be an irresistible new adventure.

One of the island's most wondrous attractions for me has been scuba diving on her remarkable reefs. I recall such a trip to the Isle of Youth some years ago, when it became crystal clear how much effort still loomed to bring the facilities up to world class. The dive boat, using that term loosely, was a slightly reconfigured fishing vessel whose age abundantly exceeded mine. The divemaster's important briefings about the underwater adventure ahead were substandard. The diving equipment itself was antiquated, and I didn't have the courage to even look at the air compressor used to fill our tanks. The country's only hyperbaric chamber, in case of emergency, was a life-threatening distance away.

The above-water facilities were at a resort hotel named The Colony. In the 1950s it was the height of luxury and the premier destination for honeymooners. A Cuban friend who vacationed there described it as "the most beautiful and elegant hotel in Cuba." Likely then, but when I visited four decades later, it had deteriorated to the point that it was only marginally more appealing than the Bates Motel in the Hitchcock thriller *Psycho*. Like it was yesterday, I remember having to make a dismal choice between using the air conditioner to fend off the sweltering summer heat, or turning on the lights in the room. The available power was insufficient for both. And when I opted for the lights, even the dim fluorescent bulbs attracted land crabs the size of dinner plates that clambered in through the holes in the walls and floor. Anyway, the reefs were superb!

*Not* on the list of tourist attractions is sex. But an ugly reality of developing country economies is that a prostitute can earn in an hour a sum that otherwise might involve months of full-time work. It is not uncommon to find young women, often from the countryside, who ply their trade in Havana for a year and then can care for their families for as far into the future as they can imagine. Neither is it uncommon to see a foreign tourist with a beautiful young Cuban woman on his arm darting through a hotel lobby in the wee hours of the morning. Although hotel staff and security personnel could lose their jobs over this, they evidently take that risk in exchange for a generous gratuity.

For the tourism sector to thrive and remain popular after the initial wave of visitors, however, real advances in staff training, maintenance and even construction will be needed. Within months of the 2005 opening of Havana's lovely Saratoga Hotel, I encountered clogged drains, leaky water fixtures, low water pressure, unreliable hot water, electrical malfunctions and staff service which reasonably can be described as lackadaisical. And that's in a *new* hotel! During a recent visit to one of Havana's more venerable hotels, my shower was absent its head, leaving water surging out of a pipe as the memorable style of bathing. There was no way to plug the tub drain so the not functioning but abundantly advertised Jacuzzi was rendered useless. Light switches worked whimsically, at best. And the 1920s vintage elevators, well, let your imagination run wild. In one of her premier modern hotels, in response to a room service order for a pepperoni pizza, I received a pizza pie blanketed with heaps of *peppercorns* instead. None of these was a calamity. But *all* of these suggest that the maintenance and service levels that are essential to success in the tourism industry need to be vastly improved in Cuba.

While it may be a long time until anyone encounters a culinary tour of Cuba, one of the delights available mainly to tourists is an array of good restaurants and *paladares*. Traditional fare is dependably good, if not gourmet. However, paladares usually offer a unique dining experience. In the early 1990s, when Cuba's economy was in the tank and there was a desperate need to accumulate dollars, private restaurants became permitted. There were numerous restrictions, as previously mentioned.

*Paladares* became an overnight sensation. Thousands sprung up across the island, nowhere more than in Havana. Senior officials were taken aback by the popularity and success of this tiny sector of private enterprise. They reacted quickly. But the official response, based on socialist doctrine rather than economic opportunity, was to slash the number of permitted seats in half, to only 12 per *paladar*, and by reducing the number of such restaurants permitted. I suppose if the hamburger chain McDonald's had reacted to success in the marketplace this way, instead of over 30,000 locations worldwide there would still be just one lonely McDonald's burger joint in California.

One of the entertaining realities of *paladar* dining is that they routinely stretch the official regulations. Many have more than a dozen seats, employ non-family members and serve black market entrees. I recall enjoying a lunch of lobster at a sweet seaside *paladar* when there was a knock on the door. In a flash my meal had vanished from my table. You see, highly desirable fare, such as lobster, is prohibited to the *paladares*, for they have much greater value to the government in official restaurants or as high-value exports. Not only did my food disappear, but also the seats in excess of the permitted 12 were removed before the government inspector reached the upstairs dining area.

An emerging and somewhat surprising source of revenues for Cuba's struggling economy is linked to Cuba's strength in the health care arena. The country has found itself with not just abundance, but with an *excess* of highly trained medical personnel. In recent years, Cuba has been exporting these medical personnel and services, mainly to developing countries in Latin America, and generating substantial returns. The majority of the estimated 29,000 have been sent to Venezuela, as part of the deal that provides large quantities of oil to Cuba. The remainder have been dispatched to impoverished areas in about 70 other countries. The downside is, in the words of a retired Cuban diplomat, "Now that we are exporting one of our main assets, medical services, we have created a huge problem to maintain a reasonable level of domestic medical services." Such are the dilemmas faced by the bureaucrats in Havana, where the arbitrariness of an administered economy, combined with overriding political objectives, has boosted one sector of the national economy and resulted in a decline in another.

Of justifiable concern to the government is the possible defection of some of the health care workers once they have been sent abroad. "That is a fear which I share with you," said one senior government official to me. Although their wages while working offshore are vastly higher than in Cuba, the cash is frozen in a Cuban bank until they return home. Other incentives not to flee include the practically unheard of opportunity to buy a car in Cuba. Nevertheless, the temptations are great. None more than incentives offered by the U.S. government for Cuban physicians to defect. Since late 2006, American regulations have provided a tempting fast track to a U.S. visa if a doctor requests political asylum. About 500 have done so despite the threat of long prison terms should they ever return to Cuba. The U.S. policy has elicited an angry response from the Cuban government, with the regrettable side effect of depriving many elsewhere who are sorely in need of medical services.

Closely related to Cuba's focus on health care continues to be a major research and development effort in the fields of biotechnology and pharmaceuticals. Their facilities have developed numerous innovations, especially in immunology, and promising treatments for some cancers. Considerable success in applied research accounted for over $400 million in exports in 2007, primarily vaccines. Not surprisingly, hard-liners in the Bush administration tried to raise doubts about these achievements when, in an effort to undermine former President Carter's visit to Cuba in 2002, they were described as linked to research for biological weapons. No evidence was forthcoming, and the absurd allegations withered.

# CUBA RISING

In traditional sectors, Cuba's mining and minerals are virtually limited to nickel ore. That ore and its refined derivative, nickel sinter, rank at the top of Cuba's export earnings. And they account for some of her largest joint ventures, including major investments – in the hundreds of millions of dollars – from both Canada and China. Sherritt International, a Canadian company, has long partnered with Cuban enterprises in nickel mining and refining. It recently expanded into other promising investments in Cuba, such as hotels and offshore oil exploration.

I have digressed. Let me return to the realities of the 1970s and 1980s. Cuba's economy had transformed itself away from near-total dependence on the United States. It did not pass Go, it did not roll the dice and win the Monopoly game, and it did not achieve economic autonomy. What it did was become nearly totally dependent on the *Soviet* economy instead. From the frying pan into the fire, as it turned out, with nearly 90 percent of its international trade with the Soviet bloc countries. Because in 1990, with the collapse of the Soviet Union also came the collapse, nearly totally and instantaneously, of trade, aid and subsidies from the entire Soviet bloc to Cuba.

It was reminiscent of 1959, when near-total reliance on another foreign economic power, that time the United States, vanished almost overnight. Cuba had become, for all practical purposes, totally reliant on the Soviet bloc for imports and exports, even more so than her dependence had been on the United States when its trade went off the radar. Once again Cuba's economy went into a tailspin, more like a death spiral. Her economy collapsed, contracting by more than one-third in 1990 alone.

Cuba's imports, on which her economy was critically dependent, contracted from $8.8 billion in 1989 to $1.2 billion in 1993. Perhaps most disruptive was the absence of 13 million tons of oil that the Soviet Union had been providing to Cuba, its Cold War ally, which had practically no domestic supply at the time. The results were predictably grim: Transportation and many industries ground to a halt, and there were widespread power blackouts for years.

I recall an evening visit to a restaurant atop of one of Havana's tallest buildings in 2001, a full decade into electrical scarcity. Looking out the window all I could see was a black void, with an occasional pinpoint of light. If I had not known otherwise, I would have sworn that there could not possibly be a city of millions sprawling beneath me. Mindful of the huge disruptions to the lives of virtually everyone on the island, a retired government official who was in the thick of this mess at the time still managed to find a little humor about that national crisis. He joked to me sarcastically, "When streetlights go out in Havana, that is an inconvenience. But when a Cuban farmer cannot see the Brazilian soap operas on television because of a power blackout, that is no longer an inconvenience, but it is a major social problem!"

And that wasn't the worst of it. As the calamity rippled through the country, the Russian tractors ground to a halt and agricultural production collapsed. Unemployment soared to over 50 percent and dormant diseases reappeared. People lacked food and were hungry, considerably in the countryside and even worse in the cities. The government dedicated idle urban land for family vegetable plots (which are commonly seen even to this day). It was simply a national nightmare. And it took over 10 years (one Cuban expert told me *14 years*, until 2004) for Cuba's economy to rebound merely to the level it had achieved in 1989.

This unnatural disaster, known as the Special Period, ultimately had some positive consequences, even at the price of widespread and significant hardship. Almost simultaneously, many of Cuba's foreign military adventures were in retreat or collapse, Nicaragua, Angola and El Salvador among them. As a result, the government turned inward and switched its priorities to domestic issues. Of overriding importance was to achieve self-reliance to as great an extent and as soon as possible. In the health sector, for example, priorities shifted further from treatment to prevention. Ingenuity helped; hard work and sacrifice bridged many gaps.

In the context of responses to the dire economic straits of the Special Period, Cuba radically revamped her legal system to allow for and to encourage foreign direct investment. An infusion of foreign funds and technology was desperately needed to create new industries and jobs. This would enable Cuba to manufacture products that could be substituted for expensive imports, and to generate exports and increase revenues. Detailed provisions were prescribed that allowed for foreign investors to partner with Cuban enterprises. A few sectors were ruled out of bounds, including health, education and the military. A vast number of joint venture opportunities remained, and the government was not particularly discriminating, as the needs were so great in practically every sector of the domestic economy.

The response was encouraging. Results, after a few years, exceeded the government's expectations in some areas, such as tourism, where many deals were done that resulted in dozens of new hotels and supporting industries. In some sectors, the negotiated deals proved to be rather too beneficial to the investors, who were given considerable latitude and generous terms. As time passed, the Cubans became more discerning and better able to drive a hard bargain. For example, hotel companies could initially just about name their location and terms. Later, as the deals proved to be highly profitable, and the top locations had been claimed, the government was able to demand that new projects could include a prime opportunity – but also would have to include a secondary project with only marginal possibilities for profitability. In this same vein, the Ministry of Foreign Investment began to issue what, in effect, were "wish lists" that reflected national needs and priorities. Sure, you could drop by and propose a factory to make ping-pong balls. But if the government really wanted the manufacture of cell phones or plastic bottles, your ping-pong project was unlikely to get off the table.

The procedures for establishing these joint ventures were, and remain, somewhat cumbersome, at least in comparison to the norm. Elaborate proposals had to be submitted to the Ministry of Foreign Investment, and those predictably had to involve negotiations and coordination with both the proposed partner enterprise *and* the government ministry that oversaw it. Then a dollop of input from the Foreign Ministry and, finally, all the way up to the Council of Ministers, which was charged with reviewing every proposed joint venture and adding its approval. On a really fast track, such deals were autographed in a year. Most often they required two to three years. And I am aware of one that was still being wrangled over after *seven* years.

The new opportunity to tap into the Cuban market proved to be enticing to thousands of foreign firms. After almost 10 years, the number of approved joint ventures reached about 650. At that stage the government did a reality check, and it revealed that a large number of the ventures were dysfunctional and that many never materialized at all. A small number had simply provided a nice facade under which some foreign businessmen were able to spend most of their time hanging out in Havana. So the hammer came down. Cuba revoked the approvals for hundreds of the deals, and by 2007 the number actually open and operating had shrunk by almost two-thirds. There is continual discussion in Havana of a new set of investment laws, so this remains a major work in progress.

In the first decade of the 21st century, Cuba's economy remained troubled. Ironically, it achieved a significant lift starting with legislation passed in 2000, with President Bush's signature in 2001, enabling sales of U.S. food items to Cuba, ostensibly in response to Cuba being hard hit by Hurricane Michelle. In reality, this economic opening resulted from vigorous lobbying by American commodities companies, such as Archer Daniels Midland and Cargill. The modest beginning of

$35 million of grain sales to Cuba was climbing toward a billion dollars worth of food items by 2009. Astute buyers in Alimport, Cuba's agency responsible for these purchases, have expanded the range of items to include chicken, grains, fruit, vegetables, eggs, and even candy bars and dairy cows. For some items the scale has become enormous for both sides. For example, Cuba's imports of rice have grown to be nearly entirely from the United States, for whom Cuba ranks as the third largest market in the world for rice exports. This tidbit never fails to astound most Americans, who are unaware that Cuba and the United States are engaged in any trade at all.

The Cubans have proven to be shrewd buyers, knowing their priorities and competitive prices. U.S. law hobbles them to some degree, as payment must be made cash in advance and shipments cannot be on Cuban ships. Nonetheless, each year Cuba has hosted a commercial fair where hundred of American companies and purveyors are able to travel to Havana and engage in negotiations. Several years ago an acquaintance who was an executive with an American company that sold produce and meat had the opportunity to attend. He told me he was going to try to meet some Cubans and get a feel for future opportunities, and he asked me for some advice. I said, "These guys have a shopping list and are prepared to do deals, so take your order book." He did so and, to his amazement, he returned with firm orders for multiple shipping containers of his products.

The political calculation in the White House presumably went something like this: Although we'll incur some political flak from the hard-liners, this will defuse the growing pressure from Republican business interests (who happen also to be major donors to Republican Party campaign coffers). After all, the United States continues to sell foodstuffs to a variety of politically adversarial countries, such as Iran, Nicaragua, Venezuela and Syria. Why discriminate when it's not politically or financially convenient to do so?

From the Cuban side, although these arrangements entail uncommonly tough business terms, the savings arising from dealing with nearby sources of supply, instead of distant ones, are enormous.

Some sectors of the Cuban economy are showing signs of life and even vitality. But how are her 11 million people faring? Not so well, it appears. Although no one is malnourished, all but a few face a daily struggle to have adequate food and basic provisions.

Key to the "safety net for sufficiency" is the *libreta*, or ration book, held by every Cuban since 1962. It enables them to receive, from designated little *bodegas*, enough provisions at deeply discounted prices to sustain them for a month – *in theory*. Several kilos each of rice, beans, cooking oil, sugar; some chicken, beef, eggs and vegetables, and even some rum and toothpaste. And what is the reality? For openers, the items usually last, at most, for two weeks. And although items are on the ration list, they often fail to appear in the *bodegas*, especially those items that happen to have some protein. To bridge the gap there are semi-independent markets at which people can buy more or other items – but at significantly higher prices. Yes, even Cheerios can be found in hard currency stores in Havana – at about $7 per box. More appealing than breakfast cereal would be, for example, a kilo of pork for a family's dinner. And that would cost about 10 days' wages of a typical Cuban. I saw a robust frozen turkey for sale for $70 in 2009. With an average monthly wage of about $17, there is not a whole lot of wiggle room for such additional spending.

So how well does one dine on the economy? During July 2007, the *Associated Press* correspondent in Havana, Anita Snow, gave it a try for a month. She lost nine pounds. Perhaps we have stumbled upon a replacement for the omnipresent American diet fads. Let it be known as the Castro diet! No supplements to buy, just stick with the culinary delights afforded to the Cuban people.

Under the leadership of Raul Castro, the government has taken meaningful steps to provide for improved food supplies to Cubanos. For example, in mid-2007, farmers were finally paid some funds past due to them, and producers began to be paid 2 ½ times *more* than the prior sum for milk and meat destined for the ration program and for other institutional feeding centers. Heresy? No, merely a new grasp of the obvious economic reality that higher payments will elicit higher production. Cuban farmers began to receive more land as well as higher prices for their crops in 2009.

With Cuba's profound focus on family, second only to concerns about food are those for housing. Let's try some "d" words: deficient, defective, depleted, dismal, dilapidated and dire, as in shortage. The country has need for an estimated 1.6 million additional housing units. It is not uncommon to find three generations of a household in an apartment of only two or three rooms, with a few bathrooms shared among perhaps 40 families living in what was, in a bygone era, a villa for a single family. A friend who is hoping to get married soon summed up a common dilemma: "My only choices are to stay in the home of my family or to move into the home of my girlfriend. Either is a pretty miserable choice to start my own family!"

Most of the problem rests with government policies that 1) fail to allow construction of new private dwellings; 2) fail to build enough dwellings for its population, and 3) do not permit individuals to buy or sell their homes.

Cuban ingenuity, however, provides for a little flexibility in this realm that is largely frozen in time. You see, Cubans are allowed to *trade* their dwellings. This tiny opportunity has given rise to a huge semi-legal market of folks who try to structure multi-party swaps that can involve as many as a half-dozen or more families. The possibility exists for relaxation of the rules, which would enable more private housing. As a result, people are increasingly fixing up their dwellings, in anticipation of the availability of even better housing – whether for trade or purchase.

As the bureaucrats have struggled to develop a solid economy after a history of monstrous reversals, a multitude of incongruities have sprung up. The military establishment runs many of the country's most successful enterprises. Overenthusisam for foreign investment in joint ventures resulted in many failures. In the words of one Cuban economist, relaxed regulations "attracted all manner of carpetbaggers and scallawags." In other areas, all sorts of inequities and disequilibria are evident. For example, while many senior Cuban officials and students have laptops, countless others without them are frustrated. Sarcastically commenting on Cuba's infamous misallocation of resources, a friend confided in me, "Cuba has the healthiest and best-educated prostitutes in the world!"

Fundamental to a socialist economic system is that the government, through its enterprises, is the employer of all of its people. In a pure system, private companies and, therefore, private employment, simply do not exit. It truly boggles my mind to walk the streets of Havana and see an ice cream vendor (government employee), a salsa band (government employees) and stilt walkers (government employees). Bureaucrats all! And is this necessary or desirable?

There has been, for decades, a drumbeat of desire for an increase in the number of people allowed to engage in small-scale private enterprise. Although the laws were relaxed in the 1990s, they have been continuously constricted in recent years. Eliminated have been several job descriptions, including stonemasons, auto repairmen and even party clowns. As a frustrated aspiring entrepreneur asked me, "What kind of government is it that feels threatened by people earning a few pesos by entertaining children?" How much might it undermine the government for an individual to be self-employed by fixing bicycle flat tires? Repairing broken jewelry? Tutoring children? Not at all, of course. Yet the government permits children? Not at all, of course. Yet the government permits only about 2 per cent of the workforce, likely around 100,000 people, to be so engaged. That is a reduction from over 200,000 just 10 years ago. And for the privilege of being able to better feed and clothe their families, they labor under onerous government regulations. They must first gain permission to operate within one of the 118 categories that have been approved by the government. (Why not 117 or 119?). Often they must rent a small space for their micro-enterprise. Then they must pay hefty fixed taxes (not variable based on revenues) to the government for this "privilege." And, adding injury to insult, there have been numerous cases where an approved, successful self-employed business owner has been shut down without explanation, only to find his business replaced by an *identical* one under government ownership!

A young man who has become a good friend is engaged in one of the increasingly few permitted private businesses, and it may be unique on the island. Although trained as a lawyer, he has organized a network of traditional craftsmen who hand make humidors, the all-important means of preserving good cigars that are sensitive to changes in humidity and temperature. He is able to acquire high-quality cedar that is grown, then dried (to avoid warping), in Cuba. Other rare woods are accumulated to be used for the intricate marquetry inlays that decorate the outside of the boxes. Often the finishing work, including adding the hardware and humidistat gauges and countless layers of lacquer, is done in a tiny workshop in his home in Vedado. The result is masterfully crafted pieces that easily can be considered as artworks themselves.

My entrepreneurial pal sells these not only to tourists but also to the government for resale in their many cigar stores. And annually it has been one of his masterpieces that has been autographed by Fidel Castro, then auctioned during the annual cigar festival in Havana, to the benefit of local charities. Is he content to live comfortably in a small private home and earn an income that is surely higher than that of most breadwinners on the island? Absolutely not. He revealed to me that his goal "is to set up similar manufacturing on a larger scale in Mexico, and be able to serve markets all over the world." The seeds of capitalism may be beginning to take root in Cuba.

It remains indisputable that the economy of Cuba is in shambles. Yes, it is beginning to show impressive rates of growth, but from a very low starting point. As must be abundantly clear by now, official Cuban pronouncements place the blame for these unfortunate circumstances squarely on the U.S. *bloquero* of Cuba, now having lasted half a century. To some degree it is true.

But when I have asked top government economists why the other nearly 200 countries of the world have not swooped in to fill the breach, the explanations are few. "We are denied the lower prices, lower shipping costs and lower insurance expenses of dealing with the United States," I have been told. True, but not crippling. "We are unable to secure low-interest development loans from the World Bank and others," one has reminded me. True, but not crippling. "We can't have the revenues from millions of American tourists." True, but they couldn't accommodate most of them anyway.

In reality, there are many reasons for caution about jumping into the economy of Cuba. The country is insolvent and can never repay its foreign debt, which is estimated to be about $40 billion. Its currency is not taken seriously and is neither widely recognized nor convertible. In fact, it is unusable outside of Cuba. The country has a history of expropriating foreign property and not always paying for it. Joint ventures in Cuba, overall, have not been highly successful. The country has rather little to offer in terms of exports, and funds available for imports are extremely limited. And corruption permeates the economy as an imperfect means of allocating scarce resources.

Perhaps the most important reason why the capitalist birds have not flocked to Cuba, at risk of waxing polemical, lies in one of the irrefutable lessons of modern history: Karl Marx is dead, and so is the ability of non-market economies to function successfully in the beginning of the 21st century. The former Soviet Bloc countries, and their economic cooperation organization, Comecon, threw in the towel.

It's fair to say the economy of Cuba is a tangled web of manipulation, corruption, mismanagement and inefficiency. Sure, it has shown some flashes of brilliance, but fundamentally it is a mess. Can it be saved from itself? Of course, it can. Other countries have started from worse beginnings and prospered. China seems to be in the grips of capitalism, along with Vietnam and other former purely socialist economies of the Eastern Bloc.

The swift and efficient behavior of free markets simply performs vastly better than bureaucrats who attempt to substitute their designs for the immutable laws of economics. Indeed, the 2009 Nobel Prize for economics was awarded to two economists who contend that companies are superior to governments in rational economic decision-making. No modern economy, of course, should operate completely independently of its government. Businesses must serve purposes in society beyond their own profits. The key seems to be for governments to be able to strike a balance between a meaningful level of economic freedom and preserving vital national goals. Cuba needs to come to grips with this concept. She needs to muster the political will to bring about change and remove the man-made shackles from the market and its entrepreneurs. I predict that only then, and not before, her economy will soar and enable the country to prosper, in concert with the community of nations, to the lasting benefit of Cuba and her people.

CHAPTER 10

## CULTURE SHAPES THE NATIONAL PERSONA

Culture and religion in Cuba nourish the soul of her people. Both are rich in tradition yet contemporary in outlook. Both reflect the diversity of her history, the complexity of modern Cuba, and an underlying optimism that pervades the island. Nowhere is this more apparent than in the lively interest in and broad appreciation for her art.

The Havana art scene is vibrant, not unlike the energy and buzz I found in New York's East Village in the 1960s or in SoHo in the 1990s. In March 2009, the opening of an exhibit of 11 abstract artists at the spacious Acacia Gallery near the Capitolio was shoulder-to-shoulder with hip, nattily attired, and excited art aficionados. Unfortunately, this was an exceptional "happening," as the public gallery scene is rather sparse in Havana. Most artists exhibit in their studios, which usually are found in their homes or apartments. Prominent painters often are provided with their own studios and exhibit spaces, although these are usually off the beaten path, and I've found them only through friends. Once in a while I have been led to a treasure trove of Cuban artworks of the 1920s and more recent times. I found these to be priced at about half of the *wholesale* price in New York – and sometimes *double!* Therein lies an occasional opportunity, assuming I would be able to take such pieces out of the country. To avoid the stripping of Cuba's artistic heritage, a license is required in order to export a painting. The documentation is inexpensive and usually simple to secure. The good news is that, even under the repressive terms of the U.S. embargo, it is permitted to bring back from Cuba an unlimited amount of art.

Yet another source of excellent Cuban art is in the public areas of many hotels and tourist venues, such as restaurants. Not unlike in the United States, having fine art displayed in such high-traffic places both enhances the ambiance and enables artists to gain more visibility. Often it is a challenge to learn about the artists or prices, but such a quest has never deterred me if an artwork beckons.

During a visit to Havana in 2008, I was able to visit several galleries that were in the homes of artists and dealers. No signage, no advertising, just the word of mouth network that I call the "Havana telegraph." In one in Vedado, the exhibit space was on an upper floor of a crumbling old villa, occupying two of the three small rooms of the dealer's apartment. Tucked away in a dark and dusty corner I found an album of *American* prints dating to the 1930s. Many were wonderfully executed, but none was accompanied by a provenance, details about the artist, or any sort of marketing or explanatory information. And, unfortunately, Havana's hot and humid climate had taken a noticeable toll on these fine works on paper.

In a hilarious confirmation of the small space available for displaying art in already small apartments, it was not unlike Alice entering the rabbit hole in Wonderland. I actually had to crawl through a small hole in the wall of the first exhibition room, which led me into an old wooden wardrobe in the adjoining room. From that bizarre entryway, I clambered awkwardly into the second room through the small door of the wardrobe. Viewing artworks in most other countries is customarily a bit easier.

Another art gallery, overflowing with masterpieces of 20th century Cuban art, was accessed through an unmarked doorway on busy Obispo Street in Habana Vieja. Up a dim stairwell, through cramped living quarters, and into a vast room with soaring 20-foot ceilings. The walls were covered, frame to frame and floor to ceiling, with artworks that had already hung too long in an environment sorely lacking in appropriate climate control and with so little lighting that it was a challenge to study these paintings, which merited close and tender scrutiny. How a collection as remarkable as this one came to pass must be a fascinating tale to be learned. Suffice it to say that I could only have been there through the help of a friend of the dealer, who seemed to be more than a bit nervous that I was there at all.

In addition to the gallery and studio sources, much art is to be found in the many public, usually open-air handicrafts markets that are mainly for tourists. I have found hundreds of artists exhibited in a fun-filled, crowd-jostling, price-haggling atmosphere. While the artistic style may be described as mainly "tourist evocative," and the quality may be uneven, the diversity is remarkable and may range from Warhol knockoffs to abstracts, still lifes, colorful landscapes and the ever-present silk screens of Che. Usually a fun reconnoiter reveals some special and high-quality discoveries, and each day they seem to vary. Over the years, I have acquired dozens of finely crafted paintings and prints, mostly from a handful of artists whose works I have grown to admire. Invariably when I have collected the works of a particular artist, a personal relationship has developed, and I have been invited to spend time with them at their home, studio or favorite café.

There are rather few traditional public art galleries in Havana, but among the standouts is one located at a *taller*, or printmaking studio, just a few steps from Cathedral Square. The works are predictably contemporary and experimental, including some with political content. There I purchased, from the artist, a large print in the red, white and blue colors of the flag of Cuba. It depicted a shoreline scene with crashing waves and strands of barbed wire conspicuously crossing the image. "Are you not at risk by illustrating the inability of Cubans to travel freely?" I asked the artist. He responded imaginatively, "If necessary I will respond that the barbed wire is intended, of course, to keep the foreign threats from entering our country." While I was pleasantly surprised by his free artistic expression, I was saddened that he felt it necessary to have a political defense of his work at the ready.

As I have found among artists elsewhere in the world, the creative juices of Cuban artists are dynamic, seldom static. The artist whose landscapes I cherished a year ago has evolved into a painter of abstracts. Another whose whimsical style captured my interest seems now to be committed to realism.

The importance of art in Cuba is wonderfully embodied in Cuba's modern National Museum of Fine Arts. Actually, there are two fine buildings, one for the international collection and one devoted to Cuban art. Both were closed and meticulously restored during 1996-2001. Rumors that the Cuban government sold off some valuable artworks to fund the restoration remain unfounded and were indignantly denied by President Castro at the festive reopening of the museums. In the Fine Arts Palace, the galleries flow and carry you from the colonial era through *very* contemporary Cuban artworks. The atmosphere is serene, the galleries are uncrowded, and the artworks are masterfully displayed. A superb museum catalogue that describes the collections is available for sale.

Cuba's artistic heritage has been long, rich, deep and continuing. Surprisingly, it was only slightly skewed by political upheavals, such as those in the Soviet Union that gave birth to the dubious style known as socialist realism. In an apparent burst of revolutionary zeal in 1961, Castro cautioned writers and artists alike, "Everything within the

Revolution, nothing outside the Revolution." Again, during the 1970s, a five-year period of political consciousness-raising saw the government make it *clear* that there were *unclear* limits to artistic freedom. Dozens of artists and intellectuals were effectively blacklisted as "counter-revolutionaries" in response to their crossing an ill-defined line of acceptability. Overall, however, creativity has flourished and been nurtured by a special status which is afforded to accomplished artists in Cuba. Many painters, writers, filmmakers, dancers and their brethren in the arts are free to travel offshore and enjoy special privileges at home.

It cannot be denied that once in a while I have found a painting of a muscular gal beaming at her new tractor. But I recall that, even in the United States, there was an era during which handsome farmers and smiling factory workers were common subjects for murals, and they are still to be seen in many public buildings to this day. Mercifully, intermittent spasms of government intrusion never became the norm. In fact, Cuban art of the 20th century has become much sought after and widely collectible.

Some of the huge stable of superb 20th century Cuban artists whose works should be sought out in the museums are, in my opinion, the following: Eduardo Abela, Ramon Alejandro, Amelia Pelaez, Antonio Gattorno, Wifredo Lam, Servando Cabrera Moreno, Raul Martinez, Manuel Mendive, Rene Portocarrero and Alfredo Sosabravo. Yes, the works of these artists can be seen, in some cases, as reminiscent or derivative of earlier masters. Do any of us live in a vacuum? Of course, they have studied the artworks of others. The results, however, are technically impressive, full of vitality and distinctively Cuban.

Among the most impressive are works of Lam (1902-1982), an Afro-Cuban artist whose father was Chinese. Lam spent much of his life in Europe, including many years in Paris, where he became a student and close friend of Pablo Picasso. Some of his works are described as modern primitivism, while others reflect influences of surrealism. Many are evocative of Cuba, especially the island's Santerian religious beliefs.

In the spring of 2008, the Montreal Museum of Fine Arts presented an impressive exhibit: *Cuba! Art and History 1867 to Today*. As the name suggests, art and history are uniquely intertwined in Cuba in media. The exhibit included photographs, paintings, original works on paper and posters.

Among the art forms for which Cuba is world-renowned is her ballet. The National Ballet of Cuba, founded in 1948 by Alicia Alonso, included a school and was propelled to prominence after the Revolution. Castro asked Alonso in 1959 how much money she would need to establish a world-class ballet company. She responded, "One hundred thousand dollars." A short time later Castro gave her *two* hundred thousand dollars and, as they say, the rest is history. Dovetailing his enthusiasm for the ballet with an architectural renaissance that he fostered in the early 1960s, Castro approved the design and construction of a remarkable new ballet school and performance halls just west of downtown Havana. Its mushrooming domes and unusual construction techniques, however, proved to be overly ambitious. Its high maintenance needs and low ability to repel rain resulted in suspension of construction for decades, and its overgrown ruins were sad testimony to revolutionary reach exceeding its grasp. However, it has finally been completed, and it is a key center for the arts and architecture in Cuba.

The National Ballet of Cuba focuses on both classical dance and modern choreography, with performances in Cuba as well as abroad each year. In Havana performances are staged at the Gran Teatro, an elaborate architectural landmark across the street from Central Park. A performance of Balanchine's choreography of *Romeo and Juliet,* which I enjoyed early in 2008, was breathtaking. The physical control of the dancers, as well as their ability to express great emotion through dance, rivaled the best ballet performances I have ever seen, including those by companies such as Russia's Bolshoi and Kirov.

# CUBA RISING

Alicia Alonso has been the artistic force behind the ballet and the Cuban National Ballet School from the beginning. She had danced earlier with the American Ballet Theatre and New York City Ballet, where her roles as Giselle established her fame. Alonso also performed with the Bolshoi and Kirov and other great companies of Europe, returning to Cuba in 1948. She left Cuba to dance abroad during 1956-1959, reacting to suppression of the arts by the dictator Fulgencio Batista. She danced beautifully until almost 70 years old, despite failing eyesight. Infirmities notwithstanding, she continued in 2009 to be actively and deeply involved in every production. As she approached 90, Alonso remained a bigger than life feature on the Cuban artistic landscape. She is seen always elegantly dressed, with her hallmark scarf and dark glasses.

"Cubans were born to dance," said Alonso. Her National Ballet School, with continuing government support, searches the island for young talent and trains them in a distinctly Cuban form of ballet, known for its strength, vitality and joyous sensuality. Dancers soar and emote with superlative reviews. Training includes unique interpretation of both modern and classical ballet. About 40 students graduate each year, thrilled with the opportunity to earn a comparatively high salary, travel abroad, and enjoy glowing recognition both at home and overseas.

Reflecting Alonso's own international dancing experience, the National Ballet of Cuba enjoys a realm far beyond its national borders. Biennially since the 1960s, it has hosted the International Ballet Festival of Havana. In addition, rave reviews of the Cuban National Ballet have led to its touring worldwide to nearly 60 countries, including the United States, in recent years. An unfortunate result of this success has been the defection of many dancers while abroad. The temptation must be agonizing for professionals earning perhaps $50 a month, which is about triple the average salary in Cuba, to join a foreign dance company where a premier dancer can earn as much as $10,000 for a *single* performance. In addition, some have sought more contemporary works to perform and a greater diversity of choreography. Cuban stars have joined the American Ballet Theatre of New York, the San Francisco Ballet and the Boston Ballet, among others. Rolando Sarabia, a Cuban star often compared with Mikhail Baryshnikov, defected in 2005 to the embarrassment and chagrin of Cuban ballet aficionados.

A middle ground, however, has become possible. In recent years, some superior dancers have been permitted to dance abroad while remaining on good terms with the government of Cuba and returning, presumably with their huge earnings, from time to time. Current examples of this creative alternative to defection include world-famous dancers Carlos Acosta, of the London Royal Ballet, who performed in Havana in late 2009, and Manuel Carreno, who dances with the American Ballet Theatre.

Homage to her past cultural giants runs deep and, interestingly, includes American author Ernest Hemingway. Having spent most of 1939 until 1960 in Cuba, the Cubans perhaps rightfully consider him to be (nearly, if not entirely) one of their own. The room he occupied in the Ambos Mundos Hotel in the 1930s has been cordoned off as a mini-shrine. And his home, "Lookout Farm" in the village of San Francisco de Paula in the eastern outskirts of Havana, has become a national museum. After decades of neglect, it was nicely restored in 2006 with the assistance of American experts. It remains almost exactly as Hemingway last saw it, down to the bats and lizards in jars as he preserved them, to the bathroom walls on which he scribbled his weight for many months. One can almost hear the laughter and footsteps of his celebrity visitors, such as Ava Gardner, Errol Flynn and Spencer Tracy. Understandably it continues to be a destination for Cubans and foreign tourists alike.

The residence itself, a single story with an abundance of windows to capture the views and breezes, is bursting with Hemingway's hunting trophies and fascinating memorabilia.

His collections include a wonderful ceramic plate that was a gift from Pablo Picasso and countless other souvenirs of his travels, which proved to be too tempting to tourists. As a result, the interior of the home is no longer open to visitors. Unless, that is, the number of tourists is small and the gratuity is large. On such days I have been able to enjoy a leisurely stroll through the entire dwelling.

Ernest apparently chose this place, rather far from his cherished watering holes in Havana, because of its hilltop panorama of the capital and the sea and its proximity to the fishing village of Cojimar, where he moored his fishing boat *Pilar*.

Cuba justifiably boasts of it fine writers and poets, none with greater name recognition than Jose Marti. Although he wrote mainly from exile, he is regarded as the leading intellectual force behind Cuba's 20th century political upheavals and ultimate independence. His prominence as a Cuban author is unsurpassed, and his recognition as an inspirational force in Cuba appears to be second only to Che Guevara. Others, among many of whose works are critically acclaimed, include poet Nicolas Guillen and writers Guillermo Cabrera Infante, Miguel Barnet, Jose Lezama Lima, Alejo Carpentier and Reinaldo Arenas. Stretching the list to include an English author who spent time in Havana, one must mention Graham Greene, whose spy thriller *Our Man in Havana,* published in 1958, delivers wondrous images of Havana before the Revolution.

Celebrating the importance of literature in Cuba is the renowned annual International Book Fair, which draws publishers as well as authors from all over the world. It is staged in the historic expanses of La Cabaña Fortress, just across the harbor from downtown Havana. There I have marveled at the enthusiastic crowds, festive banquets and the inevitable clusters of literary types emitting energy and fellowship.

Of real prominence in Cuba, perhaps more so than in many cultures, is photography as a significant art form. Two legendary Cuban photographers stand out, Raul Corrales and Alberto Korda.

# CUBA RISING

I was blessed to know Corrales for nearly a decade, until he passed away in 2006. In many ways he was a calm and simple man, also one of great wisdom and extraordinary skill with a camera. We spent many hours together in his breezy house in the fishing village Cojimar – he, the great raconteur always in his favorite rocking chair and me, the rapt listener. Traditional metal grillwork filled the large void of a pane-less window in the little room where we sat, adjoining the small kitchen, where his wife, Norma, often was clattering about preparing a meal for their large family. From the metal spirals, only slightly interrupting the vista to the sea, hung a lifetime's collection of his artifacts. An old shoe, a battered license plate, a bit of colored glass – each item, no doubt, a reminder of a moment in a life fully lived.

Raul would graciously receive whatever token of my friendship I brought, sometimes photographic paper or chemicals for developing his photographs. I would always bring him copies of published books of his photographs that were out of print. Although he could no longer find copies, my friends on the streets of Havana always could rise to the need, and I dared not ask how. Raul would sit, pensively recalling his adventuresome life, place the stump of a cigar in his well-worn pipe, breathe deeply and relax. Then anecdotes would gradually emerge and come into focus, much like the images in his nearby darkroom.

Corrales was enamored with his little camera as a boy, as he wandered the streets and developed a keen eye for the perfect moment to capture a scene. "One day a white-bearded American fisherman asked if I'd like to spend a day on his boat," he recalled. He leaped at the opportunity, took many photos and thus began a friendship with a fellow named Hemingway. It wasn't until many years later that Hemingway became famous and Raul realized he had a treasure trove of photos of the American author who won both the Nobel Prize and Pulitzer Prize.

Some years later, in the 1950s, Raul clerked for a magazine in Havana, where one day he volunteered to fill in for a photographer. His work was so fine that he was immediately hired as a staff photographer. As revolutionary fervor began to stir on the island, Corrales was dispatched to the Sierra Maestra mountains to photograph Fidel, Che and their growing band of *barbudos*. From this period, under the most primitive circumstances imaginable, came many of his most celebrated photos.

The photography of Raul Corrales was anything *but* scenic snapshots. He could preserve a moment with great poignancy, drama and irony. Did I find images of soldiers in combat? No. But a weary soldier with a machine gun *and* his clarinet is striking. And rows of combatants in formation? No. But a scene from a balcony, showing an orderly array of sombreros and shouldered rifles on parade, artistically interpreted the scene.

During one of our many afternoons together I asked the great photographer what he would photograph at that moment, if he had a camera in his hand. He pondered, gazed in my direction and responded, "An image of your feet, of course!" His insight was penetrating.

After the Revolution prevailed, Corrales was summoned one day to the office of Fidel Castro. "I would like you to work for the Revolution," Castro told him. This was not an offer he could lightly refuse. "How much are you being paid now?" asked *El Jefé*. Corrales responded, "Five hundred pesos each month." Said Castro, "Ah, the Revolution cannot afford to pay you so much!" "Well, how much can the Revolution afford?" asked Corrales. "Half as much. Two hundred and fifty pesos." "OK" was the response that brought Corrales to the seat of power as Castro's official photographer. On the walls of his humble home hung none of the masterpieces that led to his fame. There was, however, a small framed photo of Corrales and his family. It was snapped by Fidel Castro, when, during a reception, Fidel had taken Raul's camera from him and thus created one of the photographer's favorite mementos.

During an interview for a feature article that appeared in the *New York Times* in 2003, Corrales was asked why he had joined the Revolution. "I didn't," he responded. "I *made* the Revolution." He was not being immodest, just keenly insightful. For his photographs, both during and after the Revolution, helped to focus the eyes of the world on the transformation of Cuba under the leadership of Fidel Castro.

Alberto Korda, perhaps Cuba's most famous photographer, passed away in Paris in 2001, just two days before I was to meet the legendary man in Havana. Although he served as Fidel Castro's personal photographer for a decade, Korda will forever be remembered as the photographer of the 1960 iconic image of Che Guevara that adorns books, postcards and T-shirts worldwide. I have been told that it, and the stylized silhouette version of it, is the most recognized image on the planet today – yes, ahead of Coca-Cola, Nike's swoosh, McDonald's arches and the others that transcend national boundaries. Although Korda never received a penny of royalties for his image of Che, a year before his death he successfully sued Smirnoff for its use in company advertising. Korda donated the entire settlement of $50,000 for health care in Cuba, commenting at the time, "If Che were still alive, he would have done the same."

And the music flows! The melodies of Cuba are a remarkable fusion of African, Spanish, jazz and other rhythms, which merge to create uniquely Cuban tunes and tones. Son, bolero, cha-cha-cha, rumba, mambo, and salsa sweetly bombard your ears – day and night. With its throbbing percussion and memorable brass melodies, Cuban music has enjoyed a worldwide resurgence in recent years. Its justifiable fame escalated with the music of the Buena Vista Social Club, which, contrary to what some people believe, is a band and not a place, and the sound track of the award-winning film of the same name released in 1998. This is hardly surprising in view of the country's long and rich musical heritage of musicians, such as composers and pianists Ignacio Cervantes and Ernesto Lecuona, violinist Brindis de Salas, and singer Benny More. In addition to these popular musical styles, Cuba continues to have a strong heritage of country music. Often it is in combination with traditional dances at celebrations by families, farmers or simply groups of friends.

Even before American jazz swept across Europe from the United States, it took root in Cuba as early as the 1920s. Then it became "Cuban-ized" by fusing recognizably with Cuban rhythms. I've enjoyed several intimate jazz clubs in Havana as well as its prominent International Jazz Festival. Started in 1978, it has included many of the great names of jazz, including Dizzy Gillespie and Chuco Valdes. A few years back I was in Cuba visiting the resort town of Varadero just after the festival. Arriving for dinner at Xanadu, the fabulous former DuPont mansion that has become a fine restaurant, I found American jazz great Herbie Hancock in the lobby, playing wondrous tunes on the piano. He was evidently with friends, waiting to be seated for dinner. But I told my amazed friends that I had engaged him to play for us before we dined!

Music seems to be one of the most pleasing and pervasive phenomena of Cuba today. It is always in the air and the souls of her people move to its rhythms. Mere words cannot begin to describe it. It has to be heard and savored, and if it does not move you deeply then you need to check that you have a pulse.

Among the most famous salsa bands on the island in recent years have been Los Van Van and Isaac Delgado. They frequently appear at the leading salsa clubs of Havana, and they invariably attract sellout crowds, which include a surprising number of Cubans despite the cover charge that would be a multiple of the typical monthly wage. Once I engaged Isaac Delgado and his band to perform at a party held at La Cabaña Fortress. While it was clearly a private group in a rather private area, word spread like wildfire that the band was in the area and going to perform. In short order hundreds of Cubans had gathered nearby, straining for a glimpse and to hear the fabulous music. Gradually, a few found their way into the party area, then a few more. Perhaps a little encouragement to the doorman helped. It occurred to me that enthusiasm was high, our space was large, and the excited fans should join us for free. So they did. Our group of a few dozen quickly grew to include a few hundred new friends with an unquenchable appetite for salsa tunes from the great Isaac.

Illustrating the fame and status of performing artists in Cuba is their tendency to begin their performances later than their scheduled time in proportion to their fame. Your garden variety salsa band can be expected to commence in the salsa clubs about as scheduled, usually around midnight. If you are still nursing your *mojito* at 1 a.m. you can be sure this is a group of some renown. I once paid my hefty cover charge to enjoy the rhythms of Los Van Van, scheduled to start at midnight. I was sure it would be worth losing some sleep to hear their *Timba* style, which merges salsa with hip-hop and R&B in what has admiringly been described as "salsa on steroids." After nursing my drink for three more hours with no signs of a live musician, I reluctantly abandoned my post, although I knew this was the most famous band on the island, magically fusing drums and guitars and blaring brass for nearly 40 years. My heartier friends reported that the band finally *did* appear at 4 a.m., just four hours later than scheduled.

While literally *thousands* of CDs of Cuban music are available on the island, not many are to be found abroad. Their best musicians do tour overseas, but only seldom have they been granted visas to visit the United States. To my great surprise, when I attended the Monterey Jazz Festival in 2007, as if by magic there appeared my amigo Isaac Delgado and his band! Other Cuba musicians have been barred from the United States in recent years, failing to gain entry visas, especially when their performance venues have been in the politically charged city of Miami.

In my own enthusiasm to take along some of this memorable part of the Cuban experience, salsa CDs are always to be found in my homebound baggage. On one occasion, not knowing who were the top performing groups at the moment, I went to a music store in Havana and asked the clerk for the best CD she had available. In a remarkable example of political correctness and bilingual misunderstanding, when I got home and unpacked the disc, it turned out to be the unedited recorded speeches of Ernesto Che Guevara!

Because most of us tend to not go to the movies when we are traveling, visitors to Cuba generally are blissfully unaware that Cubans are fanatical devotees of movies. Theatres are inexpensive and common, although most predate the Revolution and are in some disrepair. Cubans have long had access to films, mainly from the United States, both on television and in theaters. To this day, every Saturday night Cubans flock to their TVs to enjoy a double feature of contemporary American films. Courtesy of "pirates," some can be seen in Havana before they are released in the States. In the early years, predictably, the government produced and promoted movies with some inspirational or instructive political content. In recent years, however, cutting-edge Cuban films are more the rule than the exception.

Talented directors have created a small but impressive collection of award-winning Cuban films. Foremost among them is *Strawberry and Chocolate, (1994)* directed by Cuba's leading filmmaker, Tomas Gutierrez Alea. It is an artful plea for tolerance of Cuba's homosexuals, perhaps a bit dark and provocative for those whose tastes run more along the lines of *101 Dalmatians*. Cuban film critic Enrique Colina criticized the government in 2007 for failing to allow at least 30 films, including *Strawberry and Chocolate,* to be shown on Cuban television. Colina seemed to be skating perilously near the edge when he chastised officials for what he called "censorship that has unwritten taboos and codes of silence."

# CUBA RISING

Cuba has hosted the Havana Film Festival since 1979, with recognition comparable to the Academy Awards in the United States. Its worldwide appeal attracts celebrities and film buffs, including, on many occasions, Cuba's leading movie fan, Fidel Castro.

In sum, Cuba enjoys a rich diversity and depth in its culture and arts. Since the Revolution, the Ministry of Culture, its very existence being indicative of the commitment of the government, has been supportive of a vast array of schools, museums, art forms, venues and publications. The anticipated growth in tourism may well infuse Cuba's arts with still-needed financial support and propel Cuban culture to even greater heights.

Religion in Cuba has been shaped by the country's wild ride through history, and it subtly pervades society today. Along with the early Spanish *conquistadores* and settlers came the Roman Catholic Church and its missionaries. Their zeal has left an indelible imprint of Catholicism throughout the island. It is embedded in the people, and it is prominently visible even today in the hundreds of cathedrals, monasteries and churches throughout the land. Adoption of constitutional language referring to Cuba as an atheist state resulted in the cutback of religious practices, expulsion of many priests, and the closing of most places of worship by the new atheist government. While religion was never banned, the church was marginalized, and attending services was officially regarded as "antisocial" behavior. The church's schools, which ironically had played such an important role in Fidel's formative years at Jesuit and Catholic institutions, were closed. Communist Party membership was denied to practicing Catholics. The formerly active and influential church hierarchy remained in Havana, reduced to a remnant of a bygone era. But all of these challenges still failed to erase religion from the minds and hearts of the Cuban people.

Traditionally, the Catholic Church and communist governments have been antagonists throughout the 20th century, and Cuba was no exception. Concerned that priests, who generally opposed the new government, might disrupt a Castro family church wedding in 1959, Raul Castro ranted, "If anything happens to Fidel there, we'll kill all the priests in Cuba." Passage of time smoothed some of the very rough edges between the church, which is the largest independent institution in Cuba, and the government. Starting in the mid-1980s, the government began to relax its hostility toward religion. In 1992, language in the Constitution committing the nation to atheism was dropped, religious practices became permitted, and churches began to reopen as places of worship. This "rehabilitation" of the Roman Catholic Church in Cuba reached its climax in January 1998 with a four-day visit of Pope John Paul II. The pope addressed millions of Cubans, denounced the U.S. embargo and appealed for more religious, economic and political freedom in Cuba. In anticipation of that visit, the government reversed past policy and permitted Christmas to be celebrated for the first time in many years.

Castro's appreciation for the legitimization of his regime that was implicit in the papal visit was sharply illustrated to observers of Cuba when he appeared publicly in a business suit with the pope. Until then there is no record of Fidel being publicly attired in any other way than in military uniform in his own country. During the next decade, church and state appeared to be in not quite a truce mode but more like a standoff. The government has tolerated a low level of dissident activity associated with the church. As reported by the *Chicago Tribune's* Gary Marx, for example, Catholic layman Dagoberto Valdes had been active in Pinar del Rio. For over 10 years he conducted workshops focused, somewhat elliptically, on democracy and freedom. Although this resulted in his demotion at his workplace, he studiously avoided criticizing the government and, likely because of that, he was never imprisoned. Valdes is determined to seek change without leaving Cuba, which is the approach for those who have not abandoned hope.

In February of 2008, hints emerged from the Vatican that Pope Benedict XVI might visit Cuba. Cardinal Bertone, the Vatican secretary of state, suggested as much while he was visiting Cuba to mark the 10th anniversary of the visit of Pope John Paul II. Cuban Cardinal Jaime Ortega was ecstatic and issued his own invitation to the pope, echoing one made by Fidel Castro in 2005. When such a visit does take place, I am sure that Cuba will have made significant concessions, likely including permission for the church again to operate schools within Cuba, relaxing limits on the number of Cuban and foreign priests, unfettered Internet access, and greater freedom to print and distribute materials.

In the early 16th century, Catholicism began to show a uniquely Cuban face. The import of hundreds of thousands of slaves from Africa for trade and plantation work stimulated the inevitable proselytizers. The native religions of the Africans were largely animistic, and the Catholic Church was zealous and harsh in its efforts to groom converts. Meanwhile, with the arrival of black workers from nearby in the Caribbean came additional new and less conventional religious practices, such as voodoo. As has come to characterize Cubans in so many respects, a synthesis emerged. It is known as Santeria. This religion, very common on the island today, embraces beliefs and practices from all of the "competing brands."

Santeria, to the uninitiated such as myself, appears to be rather secretive and mysterious. This stems in part from the reality that there are no Santerian temples or formal places of worship, and virtually all rituals are performed out of public view, usually in private homes. There does exist in Havana the Yoruba Cultural Association, where Santeria can be explained, and a fascinating public street named Callejon de Hamel has been developed over the years by Santerian artist Salvador Gonzalez. It includes his 650-foot mural as well as smaller artworks, altars, artifacts and music and dance related to these religious practices. I have occasionally seen in public an aspiring Santerian priest, known as a *santero*. They are easy to recognize, as they must be attired only in white for an entire year.

I was once with an American visitor who was determined to witness a sacred private Santerian ceremony. With a considerable "donation," we were able to witness such a rare and remarkable event. Late one night we wound our way through the bowels of Old Havana and were led down a dark stairwell to a crumbling and barren basement, which was stripped of everything but a small group of Santerians and the loud rhythmic pounding of conga drums. Had we any sense whatsoever, we would have darted back to the familiar comforts of a tourist area, but we didn't. Dancers of all ages were swirling and twirling to the beat of the drums. One woman crumpled to the floor, with eyes rolled back, unconscious. Had she connected with one of her sacred spirits? What had she experienced in this trancelike state? Friends lifted her gently to the side of the room.

After only moments, I noticed an elderly woman who had been spinning in a circle suddenly went as rigid as stone. Her head spun in our direction, and she caught sight of my amigo. More than caught sight. Her eyes locked on him as she quickly moved across the room toward us, as if drawn by a powerful force. Without a word, she began dancing in a tight circle around him and chanting words that we could not understand but which sounded serious, even ominous. He looked at me as I backed away, and all he could say was, "Whaaat?"

As this ritual continued I looked about and noticed yet another dancing woman of perhaps 40 years who had collapsed to the floor in a dead faint. With the natives dropping like flies, and the drumbeats growing louder, my attention returned to my friend. His demeanor had transformed from shock to what seemed to me to be a spiritual connection with his mysterious admirer. After what seemed like an eternity, but likely was mere minutes, an English-speaking Afro-Cuban came up to us to explain these bizarre scenes and put our fears to rest. "The woman has great powers" he said, "and she is famous in our Santeria community. She has deep understanding and can know things about people which they themselves do not know."

While the ceremonial dancing continued among about a dozen Santerians, our new acquaintance began to translate the old woman's now torrent of words. Her special abilities, whether courtesy of a Santerian god or otherwise, had enabled her to somehow discern that my American friend was troubled, and sometimes debilitated, by a disorder that prevented him from sleeping normally. A physical ailment? A state of mind? That did not seem to matter. Her self-appointed mission, should my friend choose to set his doubts aside and cooperate, was to liberate him from this chronic disability.

The conversation, although inhibited by the need for translation, continued for another hour. My buddy and the Santerian elder had truly "connected." They agreed to meet again the next day and, in fact, they met several more times during our visit. At the conclusion of those sessions, my friend said to me, "There is no rational way for me to explain this, but I honestly feel that she has lifted my problem from me!"

In the weeks and months following our departure from Havana, my friend told me that, for the first time in memory, he was sleeping well and no longer was hobbled by the night. No, this outcome was not subject to empirical studies or clinical analyses. He feels better. He is convinced that the Santerian intervention is the reason. Sufficiently so that he had me take to her, on a subsequent visit, a tape recorder so that she could commit to posterity some of her remarkable thoughts, perhaps providing some insights into just one facet of the very distinctive, and perhaps elusive, religious practices known as Santeria.

Also present in Cuba, particularly in Havana and a few other urban areas, is a small but vibrant community of Jews. While the main synagogue in Havana, Beth Shalom, cannot afford a rabbi, a formidable woman named Adela Dworin presides over its activities, which include religious services, education and community health care. Although their presence has shrunk to only about 1,500 people, from over 15,000 in 1958, the Jewish community is active beyond its small numbers. Exceptions, as with so many religious groups, include a small number who seem to show up only when food is served, and Adela jokingly refers to them as "gastronomic Jews."

Adela is a remarkable woman. I have little doubt that other circumstances might have us watching her on late-night television instead of David Letterman. Her high energy and irrepressible sense of humor can only be described as extraordinary. One of her countless stories comes to mind, as she described her challenge to secure a van to transport people to the synagogue.

"I was fortunate to be visited by a family from New Jersey named Kaplan," began Adela. "They asked how they could help, and I explained our need for a vehicle in a city with no reason to brag about its mass transit system. They quickly agreed to provide one, and the *only* condition was that it have the name Kaplan Van lettered onto it." "No problem! We bought it and we stenciled the name Kaplan Van on it." "And then, well, you can imagine the Cuban Jewish busybodies and passersby! Everyone wanted to know what the words Kaplan Van meant! So rather than go through the whole story a dozen times a day, I decided just to tell them that 'Kaplan Van' was the Hebrew word for Mitsubishi!"

In 1998, Castro himself attended Hanukkah services at the synagogue, in response to an invitation from Dworin. He sat through services, gave a lengthy talk, and expressed his pleasure when he departed. "He kissed me on both cheeks, so I didn't wash my face for two weeks," she chuckled. Long before this symbolic visit, *El Jefé* was quoted as saying that he had Jewish ancestors. Both the name Castro and the origins of his family in Galicia in Spain suggest this may be true, official denials notwithstanding.

In a country where subtle signals can send powerful messages, I found it especially interesting that the government has recently restored and opened for tourists a fine new hotel named Raquel. It has distinctly Jewish themes, décor and souvenirs for sale. Perhaps this was done to confirm Fidel Castro's harmony with the Jews visiting and living in Cuba, for little in the country happens without his knowledge and approval.

There is one sad footnote to the history of Judaism and Cuba, in which the Jews were pawns and corrupt Cuban officials were players. In 1939, the German luxury liner St. Louis arrived in Havana harbor with over 900 Jews fleeing Nazi persecution. The ship evidently had Hitler's permission to sail with a nefarious plot that it would be denied safe harbor and have to return to Germany, this giving perverse endorsement to Nazi horrors already befalling Jews in Germany. After not being allowed disembarkation in Havana, the ship and her frightened passengers wandered the seas in search of a permissible port. Failing to find one, even in the United States, it sailed for Germany. At the last moment, however, the ship St. Louis was permitted to drop off passengers in Antwerp, Belgium. Tragically, most of the passengers died during the next few years at the hands of the Nazis when they overran Europe.

Although the historic antagonism between communism and Catholicism continues to simmer today in Cuba, with the 21st century has come a religious reawakening on the island. Celebration of religious holidays is again permitted and thriving. Worship services are well-attended, and the church hierarchy in Havana is able to operate with diminished restrictions. And, according to the *Chicago Tribune's* former

Havana correspondent, Gary Marx, the government seems to be tolerating some dissent and publications from the Catholic Church that challenge many aspects of Cuba's political and economic systems.

Another cultural phenomenon in Cuba that verges on the religious, in terms of its devotees, is sports. I am not alluding to simple recreation for players and spectators. It is a consuming and unsurpassed national obsession. From thwacking raggedy old baseballs in weedy neighborhood lots to the glitz of Olympic competitions, sports and its fans are always in sight in Cuba. Indicative of its nationwide importance, the government includes a Ministry of Sports. Similar to other communist governments, Cuba since the Revolution has promoted physical conditioning and competitive sports as national policy, although it abolished professional sports in 1962. The process begins with young children and continues to select, guide and groom promising athletes whose ultimate goal is to compete at the international level. In remarkable disproportion to the size of the population, Cuba continues to collect numerous victories and medals in such arenas as the Pan American Games, World Games and Olympic Games.

I found a monument to, or at least a monumental example of, Cuba's national focus on sports to be the impressive stadiums and arenas built for the Pan American Games that Cuba hosted in 1991. They sit slightly east of Havana, just past the fumes-filled tunnel under the harbor entrance. Unfortunately for Cuba, her economy had just crumbled the year before. But Castro was determined that the country would follow through with this huge financial and national commitment to the sports competitions. Cuba persevered with amazing results. The country accumulated an amazing 140 gold medals, more than any other country, and it was the first time a Latin American country had a better performance than the United States, which collected 130 gold medals.

# CUBA RISING

In the total medal count at the Beijing Olympics in 2008, Cuba ranked 12th. At the Athens Olympics in 2004, Cuba was 11th, It was ninth in Sydney in 2000, eighth in Atlanta in 1996 and fifth in the 1992 Barcelona Olympic Games. The Cuban medal winners always receive massive national acclaim, and they often were invited to congratulatory festivities with President Castro, whose own enthusiasm both as a sportsman and a sports fan is legendary. There is an iconic photograph of him in a baseball uniform, and an urban legend says that he tried out as a pitcher for the old Washington Senators. In the wry words of author Christopher Baker, "How different history might have been had his curveball curved a little better."

Baseball positively is the national sport of Cuba. It was introduced there during the 1860s from the United States, and it has only grown in popularity ever since, unlike most Latin countries, where soccer rules. From youngsters through oldsters, it is a consuming passion. Fortunately, the ardent fans can follow baseball year-round, as the Cuban teams compete in the winter, and the U.S. teams play during Cuba's off-season. I recall a friend, a deputy minister at the time, responding to my query whether I could bring anything for him or his family on my next trip. Without hesitating a second, he responded, "A good magazine about baseball, for sure!" National passions ran high in 1999, when, reflecting a momentary thaw in bilateral relations, the Cuban national team and the Baltimore Orioles had a home-and-away series of games in Havana and Baltimore. At the game in Baltimore, I was among the enthusiastic crowd that roared with approval when an anti-Cuban protestor who had run onto the playing field was decked by the Cuban second baseman.

Each of Cuba's 14 provinces has a baseball team, and Havana has two, which compete in the nationwide league. Not surprisingly, one finds huge ballparks dotting the countryside, and the largest in Havana can hold 55,000 screaming fans. Enthusiasm offsets the lack of amenities to which American fans have grown accustomed. After all, the modern parks in the United States seem to be more like family entertainment centers, often with many activities that children and adults can take part in and where one can take a break from a fine meal to glance at the game being played on the field below. In Cuba, tradition rules.

The entire baseball experience in Cuba differs markedly from what most Americans are accustomed to. In a stark example of the U.S. national pastime meets contemporary Cuba, I was surprised to see that foul balls, which are treasured by the lucky fans who jostle and catch one to keep in the States, are always returned to the field of play in Cuba. Their value is simply too high to sacrifice them as souvenirs. Cuban baseball stadiums seem like a throwback to the 1950s in America. One finds long concrete benches to sit on, rarely an opportunity to buy a beer or a snack, and a conspicuous absence of souvenirs to wave, wear or put on your shelf at home. I daresay when on some faraway day one can find a bobblehead doll of Cuba's leading player, *another* revolution probably will have occurred. Not merely because I am obsessive about souvenirs, I found it fascinating to find at a very few tourist shops, starting in 2006, one could buy "official" Cuban baseball jerseys for about $75 a pop.

Havana's leading ballpark does have at least one unusual amenity. At a game I attended, I was amused to find the team actually had a mascot. No, not some gigantic fuzzy purple creature that does somersaults along the first base line. Something improvised, a bit more authentically Cuban. A young man had a little dog, evidently a mongrel version of a beagle, dressed up in a tiny baseball uniform. It had a gaudy pink wristwatch on one foreleg and a set of tinted goggles as well. Their stage was the roof of the home team dugout. Remarkably, when the Havana team got a hit, or when its pitcher struck out a visiting player, the dog would bark like he had just treed a fox. And it would remain silent and sullen whenever the opponents did the same.

I recall an amusing occasion when the absence of Cuban baseball souvenirs at the stadium came head to head with American sports fans. We had watched a game won, as I recall, by the Havana Industriales. For those of us who wanted to buy a team cap as a memento, our inclination grew into determination when we discovered they were not available. As we were leaving the stadium after the game, we noticed the team was headed for its bus just a few feet away across a low fence. The stadium was apparently lacking not only souvenir stands but also showers in the locker rooms, as the players were still in uniform. Being typically gregarious and insensitive Americans, we hollered over and asked if any of them would like to donate their caps to us. The response was many quizzical smiles. One player responded in Spanish, "We only get one hat so we can't give them away." To us, the operative word was "give."

So one *Yanqui* whipped out a $10 bill and waved it gently. Suddenly the team's march to the bus swerved toward the fence line. Caps were flying off heads and $10 bills were flying over the fence. When the friendly frenzy finally subsided, the team headed back to the bus, half of them hatless! Our collective guilt feelings about a hatless team playing under the scorching sun at their next game was offset by our pleasure with our truly authentic souvenirs of Cuban baseball.

The national baseball team of Cuba, consisting of the best players from all the amateur teams in the country, has performed consistently well in international competitions despite competing against professional players from many other countries. Cuba had played in 40 international competition finals since 1952 and won 33 of them. When the United States was victorious in the World Cup in 2007, it ended Cuba's run of nine straight World Cup titles – and rumor was that *El Jefé* made his displeasure known to the team. Since baseball became an official Olympics sport in 1992, Cuba has won the gold medal three times and the silver medal twice in the five competitions.

While baseball reigns supreme as the leading team spectator sport in Cuba, boxing has comparable stature among individual sports. Cuban boxers have ranked high in worldwide competition since early in the 20th century. The country's boxing teams have performed remarkably in the Olympics, winning 32 gold medals, 19 silver and 12 bronze in the 27 Summer Olympics from 1896 through 2008. Two individuals stand out and have been unrivaled on the world stage, heavyweights Teofilio Stevenson and Felix Savon. Stevenson ruled in the 1970s and 1980s, winning Olympic gold three times and World Championships also three times. He was scheduled to have a bout with American champion Muhammad Ali in Houston in the 1980s, but political interference derailed what could have been the match of the century. Savon, a more recent legend, captured Olympic gold three times and six World Championships!

Today both famous boxers serve as coaches and are active within a special cadre of past Cuban Olympians, while their renown may be second only to Fidel Castro on the island. Their fame notwithstanding, both are true gentlemen and are happily accessible to their adoring fans. They truly believe in sports as an integral part of a healthy and well-balanced society. That view extends to the international domain of sportsmanship as well.

On several occasions when I visited Cuba with small groups of Americans, we had the opportunity to meet with Stevenson and Savon and enough of their Olympic colleagues to have a rousing game of beach volleyball together. No one was even remotely tempted to try a few rounds of boxing! Once when a sudden pelting rain interrupted our game, all of us retired to the veranda with *mojitos*. Overcoming both the elements and language barriers, a Cuban Olympic bicycler whipped out a deck of cards and entertained the group with mind-boggling tricks until the skies cleared. I think we caught a glimpse of what actually happens in the byways of international sports competitions in between events.

The athletes seemed to be ageless, despite some being decades past their prime. Faces were free of wrinkles, muscles were bulging like mountain ranges in a satellite photo, and fists at the end of long arms seemed able to reach my jaw from a mile away. They demonstrated the agility of young athletes a third of their age with smiles that radiated across the playing field and seemingly across town.

On the beach, in a true display of good sportsmanship, as well as mercy, the Cubans offered to mix the teams so we could avoid the likelihood of a dozen Cuban Olympians smashing a bunch of paunchy middle-aged Americans into the sand. Afterwards we enjoyed lunch together, sometimes including the spouses and kids of the athletes. We laughed and backslapped and relived in our conversations some of the great sports events of our time. Always we were mindful and respectful of the reality that, despite their status as modern day heroes, their earnings were tiny and their homes humble. Yes, they enjoyed more adoration and perks than normal Cubans, but their pride and humility always will be remembered above all.

One could explore the range of practically all sports in which Cuban athletes have excelled: soccer, volleyball, basketball, cycling and many more with the possible exception of bobsledding, where the Jamaican team allegedly reigns supreme among Caribbean nations. My goal is not to assemble a catalogue, but to emphasize the importance of sports to Cuba and Cubans, their passion for sports that has driven them to excellence and, above all, the human face and global outlook of the nation's athletes.

The culture of Cuba is a synthesis of innumerable disparate parts that blend the old and the new, the pensive and the raucous, and the hopes and fears of the Cuban people. It is not prescriptive, but rather a smorgasbord of tangibles and intangibles that shape the lives of the people. Is it unique? Of course, for no other place has been simultaneously the beneficiary and victim of identical circumstances. Is it transferable? Of course not, as is abundantly illustrated by the sense of homelessness of millions of émigrés who have left the island. To me, the national culture of Cuba is unrivaled in its richness, depth and diversity.

CHAPTER 11

## PROTECTING THE ENVIRONMENT AMID SCARCITY

"This is the most beautiful land that human eyes have seen," Christopher Columbus recorded about Cuba in his logbook in 1492. It remains a lovely island, although mankind has not always been respectful of its natural bounty, and today it is torn between the merits of preservation and the necessities of overdue economic progress.

Environmentally conscious travelers to the Third World uniformly return with horror stories of mountain ranges denuded of their forests for the lumber; topsoil stripped away and silting rivers because miners searched mindlessly for minerals, and species rendered extinct as a cost of economic development. Invariably, compelling short-term needs seem to prevail over the long-term costs of environmental degradation. I am reminded of the choking smog that blankets Mexico City, the once pristine but now poisoned rivers of China and the dangerous shrinkage of our planet's "lungs," the vast rainforests of Brazil. Cuba is no exception, although conservation efforts have become a higher priority in recent years.

# CUBA RISING

Starting in the colonial era, most of Cuba's forests were harvested in order to feed insatiable appetites for her lumber. It went for export, building and railway construction, shipbuilding and firewood for homes, and especially to feed the seemingly limitless needs of the sugar mills. Ancient stands of mahogany, cedar and ebony were decimated to serve as furniture, doors, panels and ceilings of many great mansions of Europe. Predictable results of deforestation have been reduced habitat for wildlife and the erosion of fertile soil in runoff from rainfalls. Some species of plants, birds and animals have disappeared forever, while scores of others have been categorized as threatened or endangered. Ecosystems have been damaged, some irreparably.

By no means has the government of Cuba been passive. Fortunately, it is sharply aware of the importance of environmental conservation and restoration. The Cuban Constitution expresses an impressive commitment to environmental issues, and subsequent laws have strengthened and expanded it. The existence of the Ministry of Science, Technology and the Environment gives continuing prominence to the problems and finding solutions. At least half a dozen other state bureaucracies have been created to address these issues. Commercial ventures with foreign companies routinely contain provisions to advance environmental stewardship. For example, the Canadian firm Sherritt International is actively involved in extractive industries in Cuba and has become engaged in reforestation, wastewater management and air quality enhancement. Such remedial and proactive efforts are necessary but not always sufficient. Reforestation programs initiated by the government, for example, have shown some success but also include the loss of millions of plantings from neglect.

Water pollution remains a major problem, largely as a consequence of Cuba's efforts to enlarge its industrial production and agricultural yields. Inadequate wastewater treatment, oil spills, industrial discharges into rivers, and runoff from animal farms are some of the leading culprits, not atypical in developing countries. In addition, massive withdrawals from natural water sources have resulted in the encroachment of seawater, rendering some traditional water supplies saline and some arable land irreparably damaged. Recall that Cuba is a rather narrow island, and the sea is rarely far from sight or mind or mischief. Many Cuban rivers and harbors are horribly polluted, and no worse example of the consequences of neglect can be found than in sprawling Havana Bay. With an oil refinery on its banks belching smoke and fire, one is reminded of Ohio's Cuyahoga River, which actually caught fire more than once as a result of its monstrous contamination.

Although of critical importance to Cuba's expansion of tourism, many of her beaches, including some formerly wonderful ones east of Havana, have been the victims of massive removal of sand for construction purposes. When a government is chronically short of funding for conservation and also has urgent needs for self-sufficiency in agriculture and industry, it runs the risk of creating a "perfect storm" of long-term environmental damage.

Cuba is surrounded by deep ocean that is rich in sea life and important both for recreation and the nation's commercial fishing fleet. Moving inward one finds thousands of small islands, known as cays, and coral reefs. Great flocks of domestic as well as migrating birds are found there, along with numerous species of reptiles. Her thousands of miles of mangrove swamps and palm-lined beaches follow, whose preservation is fundamental to Cuba's all-important tourism industry. As one looks further inland a variety of topography is to be found, including the savannah, rainforests, pine forests and mountains with their own unique flora and fauna. Cuba's abundant plants and animals include a reported 12,000 species – well over half which can be found only in Cuba.

Among the first of Cuba's environmental projects was an agricultural research center created in 1899 in collaboration with

Harvard University and American sugar cane grower Edward Atkins. From these beginnings has evolved the Cienfuegos Botanical Garden, which today offers what may be the world's most complete collection of palm trees, of which 85 species are native to Cuba. Predictably, it is modest, underfunded and understaffed. As the director said to me, "There have been times when we had no electricity for the office, no fuel for the tractors, and even no pay for the staff." But the endurance of this living collection through periods of great upheaval and widespread deprivation is an affirmation of the importance that Cuba attaches to the environment.

Included in the larger efforts to preserve and conserve, Cuba was a pioneer in protecting her underwater assets. Blessed with fabulous coral reefs on both the north and south coasts, Cuba was among the first to provide moorings on the reefs so fragile corals would not be damaged by the dropping and dragging of anchors from dive boats. Although the investment in such projects called for deploying scarce funds, there can be no doubt that it has proven to be a wise long-term investment. I consider Cuba's coral reefs, partly as a result of these early protective measures, the most pristine in all the Caribbean. Fish are abundant and unafraid of divers, corals are healthy and profuse, and the water is gin-clear and not polluted. These conservation efforts will pay compounding dividends as tourism, and its revenue generation, catches up with the foresight of ecologists decades ago.

Predictable trade-offs between the environment and economic growth can be expected to continue and even increase. For example, exploitation of recently discovered oil reserves off Cuba's north shore presents both the opportunity for urgently needed fuel and revenues *and* a demonstrable threat to the thriving tourist industry, which has been developed only miles away on her beautiful northern coastal coral reefs and hundreds of miles of beaches. Combine the facts that the recent discoveries are proximate to beautiful modern tourist resorts, that miles of undersea pipeline will be needed to bring the oil ashore, that the prevailing winds are from the north, that powerful currents sweep through Cuba's northern waters, and there should be a profusion of hand wringing about the potential for an environmental and economic disaster.

Above the sea, Cuba's conservation efforts have been comparably impressive. Across the country are 15 nature preserves and national parks, comprising almost a *quarter* of the entire country. And this is in a country of approximately 42,800 square miles, about the size of the state of Virginia.

Although they may be sparsely staffed and equipped, these national parks have successfully protected precious natural assets from the ravages of pollution and development. Among the most impressive is the huge preserve near Playa Giron (Bay of Pigs) named Cienaga de Zapata. Although this massive swamp was largely drained by Cuban engineers decades ago, it has rebounded well and remains a vital part of the natural flyway for dozens of species of birds migrating between North America and Latin America. I have seen there great flocks of pink flamingos, Cuba's national bird (the colorful parrot Tocororo), the world's smallest bird (the endangered Cuban bee hummingbird), and the Cuban crocodile, whose brush with extinction has been reversed thanks to a successful government initiated breeding program.

During a visit to Playa Giron years ago, my friends and I stopped at the extremely humble park ranger station. We found just one devoted but lonely fellow, no literature and no maps. Remarkably, one in our group had brought along a wonderful book about the birds of Cuba, published by Cornell University. After an enjoyable and informative chat about the park, we gave the ranger the book as a gift. "Never in my life could I have dreamed of having such a beautiful volume," said the grateful guardian of the preserve, nearly in tears.

Another remarkable preserve named La Mocha is just an hour west of Havana. On a site once devoted to a coffee plantation, tens of thousands of trees have been planted in the fields and adjoining hillsides. Ecologists have established a thriving research center, environmentally friendly tourist accommodations and attractions, and even a resident community of artists and craftspeople. Most revenues derived from this type of environmental tourism are funneled into the growing conservation efforts.

As is reasonable to expect in any developing country, efforts to restore and conserve the environment are comparatively costly and must compete with needs for basic provisions, such as food, fuel and medicine. There was a painful reminder of these trade-offs during the Special Period of the 1990s, after the Soviets and their largesse departed the island. Already dwindling forests were ravaged for firewood, and sustenance took precedence over environmental concerns. Following the rebound of the national economy, some impressive steps have been taken. On the island one can now find wind farms for power generation, small methane production facilities on pig farms, aquaculture for raising shrimp and fish, and successful organic farming. Cuba is frequently cited by U.N. officials for its impressive achievements on environmental issues.

Cuba has become a world leader in progressive sustainable farming techniques, shifting away from chemical fertilizers and pesticides as a matter of national policy. The genesis for this was more chance than choice, as manufactured stimulants to enhance agricultural yields have proven to be unaffordable. Especially after the end of Soviet assistance, farming reverted to natural methods with a predictable fall in yields. It is reported that, after more than a decade of innovation, crop yields climbed back to their previous levels. The island is fortunately blessed with an abundance of rainfall to grow crops. As in many countries, the problem was not so much the quantity of rainfall, but rather the ability to conserve and redistribute it. A national network of reservoirs and pipelines has opened up hundreds of thousands of acres to productive agriculture. I have often seen these blue lakes in the countryside being enjoyed by families along the shore. One not far west of Havana also serves as the practice site for Cuba's Olympic rowers.

Another combination of circumstances has resulted in the improvement of the level of air quality. Unfortunately, this results more from a lack of industrial development than from proactive efforts by the Cubans. Yes, there are oil refineries, steel and sugar mills, nickel smelters and very many vehicles belching smoke and particulates. I visited a steel mill not far from Havana and found no pollution control devices whatsoever. The lovely valley adjacent to the mill was laden with smog to a degree that made Los Angeles on a bad day look pristine by comparison. But heavy industry is conspicuous mainly by its absence. With the island's comparative lack of natural resources to feed the enormous appetites of industrial processing and manufacturing industries, it is possible that Cuba may be spared the environmental nightmares such as occurred in Pittsburgh in the mid-20th century, where skies were dark with smoke at mid-day and the white shirts of office workers looked grimy after just a few hours. Many foresee the economy of Cuba expanding its provision of services and "intellectual" items, which already exceed half of the national economy, and leapfrogging past the dirty heavy industries, which characterize the early stages of most developed economies.

The passion for preservation runs deep in Cuba, and it extends to a variety of man-made historical assets as well. Nowhere is this more evident than with the effort to preserve and restore the historic treasures that comprise Habana Vieja. Time takes a terrible toll on buildings whose construction dates back to the colonial era and the ensuing five centuries. Scorching sun, salt and torrential rains inflict a wicked toll on buildings of limestone. In a race against time and its ravages, a remarkable story of preservation is continuing to be written in Havana today.

Ever aware of the richness of its history, shortly after the Revolution the government established the Office of the Historian of Havana. Appointed to head the office was Eusebio Leal, an architect, historian, engineer and, perhaps most importantly, an entrepreneur. Leal recognized not only the imperative of preserving the buildings of the crumbling old city but also the area's potential as a magnet for tourism and its related economic growth.

While the process of conserving Old Havana's buildings seems to be accelerating, the same cannot be said for her environment-related infrastructure. The pipes that carry water date deep into the 20th century, some earlier. Whenever I walk the streets I am sharply reminded – because of foul odors – of the crumbling sewer lines beneath the streets. Power lines dangle precariously from buildings and are draped across streets like spider webs. Debris, oil slicks and the absence of fish characterize the water in Havana's harbor. So little time, so little money, so many urgent needs must be consigned to the future.

In an extraordinary redefinition of priorities, Cuba has in recent years attached considerable importance to stewardship of its natural endowments. Beyond Havana, recognition has come from across the world. Reflecting both good intentions and solid achievements, the Rio Earth Summit, in 1993, awarded Cuba top marks for its sustainable development practices. In addition, Cuba holds a remarkable nine U.N. World Heritage sites. Among them is the charming 16th century south coastal town of Trinidad. It is low rise, a palette of pastels, and an architectural marvel now hosting busloads of tourists instead of shiploads of marauding pirates. Trinidad was selected for this important status in 1988, and Havana had been so designated in 1982. How well historic Trinidad can withstand the onslaught of increased tourism remains to be seen.

Cuba faces enormous environmental challenges and opportunities. The country is handicapped by very severe limits on how much money she can dedicate for protection of her natural assets. Yet she may be blessed, in one respect, by the possibility of being a "post-industrial" state. Not because of her prosperity, mind you, but because her economy appears to be migrating toward the less-polluting service sectors. To Cuba's credit, there is a high level of official and public awareness of environmental issues. This combination of factors suggests to me that Cuba will be able to overcome its history of environmental decline and become a champion of conservation and sustainable growth.

CHAPTER 12

## BEING CUBAN

Above all, Cuba is its people. Surely, you will find remarkable its lush landscape and tropical climate, its striking features as a living museum of architecture and vintage cars, and its rich history and sensual rhythms. But all of that would be nothing, *nada,* just an aftermath of an imaginary neutron bomb, were it not for the very special sum of all of its parts – from the magical to the mundane – embodied in about 11 million souls.

The beauty of the women and the handsome men impress me, not just the first time but *every* time I see them. They stand tall and proud, agile and resilient, carefully groomed and with skin tones that reflect the richness and diversity of Cuba's history. Their happiness and friendliness have buoyancy that cannot be disguised.

Perhaps this is not so much a revelation as a grasp of a key facet of the Cuban culture. It brims with humanity. I can think of many tropical islands whose people also endure tough economies and lack political freedoms. But Cubans distinctively embody pride and joy, seemingly with no bounds.

I could argue that some limits actually might not be such a bad idea. Infidelity seems to rank somewhere between the norm and a national pastime, and the rate of divorce in Cuba exceeds 50 percent. One very close friend at age 36 already has been divorced *six* times. Sounds to me like Las Vegas and Havana could make a good partnership, one with 24-hour a day wedding chapels and the other with convenient divorce drive-throughs.

On many warm Havana evenings I have found the sidewalks of the Malecon, the seaside boulevard that runs for miles along the waterfront, crowded with young people socializing and enjoying the cool breezes. Strumming guitars, sipping rum and smooching. While it is a tender sight, it speaks of the precious few venues where they can gather. It may be that the fewer the opportunities are for them to meet and cultivate relationships, the weaker is the likelihood of forming enduring bonds.

Speaking of human bonding, it is noteworthy that homosexual behavior in Cuba, perhaps reflecting its Catholic heritage, is not well accepted. However, public understanding has grown vastly since the 1960s, when Fidel. Castro had homosexuals rounded up and punished. Some were jailed, others were denied customary social benefits, and many chose exile. Even today, gays and lesbians are well-advised to not flaunt their lifestyles. A turning point may have been in 1992, when Castro expressed a change of view and encouraged tolerance toward gays. A year later the award-winning Cuban film *Strawberry and Chocolate*, which beautifully portrayed the dilemma of two gay men in Havana, was widely acclaimed worldwide. There are some spots in Havana where gays routinely gather, but they tend to follow the advice of a gay friend of mine who is on the faculty of the University of Havana: "Follow the policy of the U.S. military, 'Don't ask, don't tell,' and don't show off."

Not simply common but seemingly universal is the profound love of Cuba by its people. This goes far beyond patriotism, for it appears to include even the most politically disgruntled. A dear friend, a retired professional woman, is fortunate to be allowed to travel abroad frequently. Each time she goes through a paper chase for the necessary documents, both to leave Cuba and to enter another country. She has experienced more than her fair share of personal suffering in Cuba, and she is far from being a cheerleader for the regime. Yet, as surely as night follows day, she always experiences deeps pangs of homesickness while abroad. She flourishes upon returning to her homeland, her home, her friends, her Cuba. Travel seems to bring her peace of mind, but only Cuba can bring peace to her soul.

On every flight I have taken to Havana, the expatriates returning to their homeland show unbridled glee. These are people who have extracted themselves from their country for a variety of painful economic or political reasons, yet they cannot contain their joy upon coming back. Conversely, tears flow in torrents in the Havana airport departure area, as Cuban-Americans again prepare to be separated from home and family and from the country that binds them so tightly. Under the George W. Bush administration, they faced a minimum separation of three years. And seeing so many frail and elderly people, who would certainly never return, broke my heart. Fulfilling a campaign promise, President Obama relaxed those punitive restrictions shortly after he was sworn in, early in 2009.

What else binds the people with their unique country? Above all, it is family. This is a cultural tradition and to some degree a necessity. With housing chronically in short supply, I have often found three or more generations sharing a single dwelling or apartment. It is common to find once grand villas now housing dozens of families. In those fabulous buildings with elaborate architectural details, an additional floor of living space has frequently been cobbled together between the original high-ceiling levels of the villas. Frankly characterizing this national calamity, a government official admitted to me, "The main domestic problem in Cuba is a shortage of housing."

This dilemma is compounded by government regulations restricting both an individual's ability to sell their home (if they are fortunate enough to possess it as private property) and their freedom to move within the country. Roots run deep when they are not able to spread far.

A splendid aspect of the Cuban family is its fanatical devotion to its children. Sure, kids are something special the world over. But in Cuba they are even more so. Adorable small clusters of youngsters in their pristine school uniforms are guided in organized chaos along the sidewalks by their teachers; they frolic with inner tubes in the shallow waters offshore; they clamor for tiny paper cones of peanuts from street vendors, and they scuttle about like little crabs, laughing and screeching, as they scoop up precious handfuls of tiny ice pellets after experiencing a rare hailstorm.

The tales of adult sacrifices in order to please their children are so commonplace as to have become normal. I often ask my Cuban friends what can I bring them on my next visit. The invariable response is a dream to have even simple medications for their children: cold remedies, cough medicine, vitamins. Beyond that, perhaps a pretty dress for their daughter or a baseball for their son. In anticipation of a visit in 2008, I asked a friend whose wife was *very* pregnant what I could bring. Their needs were many, but the shy request was for a baby bottle sterilizer – a simple item that is readily available in any drugstore in the States. Or so I thought. While it is true they are available, what I discovered is that virtually all are now designed to be used in microwave ovens, which, until recently, have been illegal for individuals to own in Cuba. After days of searching I located an "archaic" style with an actual heating element and electrical cord. My friends in Havana were thrilled, and I spared them the details of my shopping ordeal. On another recent occasion, when I asked a friend what her loftiest financial goals were, she said, "Just a few extra dollars each month so that I can buy little gifts for my grandchildren."

A sweet example of the attention lavished on children is found in the *quinceañera*, a special celebration for young women on their 15th birthday. This Spanish tradition goes far back in time to the era when it celebrated girls having matured into women and becoming available for courtship and marriage. The festivities usually include a party with special food, music, dance and gifts, as well as a religious ceremony. One occasionally sees on Havana's cobblestone streets a horse-drawn carriage with a young woman in a colorful floor length gown, family and admirers nearby, fresh flowers in abundance, and *always* a photographer to record the special event. There can be no doubt that Cuban families save for *years* to provide this important extravagance for their daughters.

Data shows, however, that there are fewer daughters, or sons. Cuban couples have been having a smaller number of children. Common explanations I've heard include that a high proportion of women who are well-educated and employed (by choice or need) choose vocations rather than home-making; the profound shortage of housing results in most young couples having to live in the small homes of one of their parents; low wage levels that make child rearing a financial burden; the high rate of divorce; the surprising fact that a significant majority of those who leave the country are men, and the ease with which a woman can have an abortion in Cuba.

Confirming some of these explanations is data from the Swiss-based World Economic Forum that annually ranks countries according to their "gender equality." Factors such as education, economic opportunity, political empowerment and health and survival are evaluated. In their 2009 findings, Cuba ranked 29th in the world while the United States had slipped to 31st, edging ahead of Namibia. (Iceland ranked 1st, Russia was 51st, and Malaysia was 101st.) Although machismo may characterize Cuban men, her women are fully involved and respected.

# CUBA RISING

In response to the declining rate of population growth, the government has enhanced an incentive for making babies by increasing paid birth leave to one full year, up from the 12 weeks that went into effect in 1963. Either parent may exercise this right. Even if this might reverse the trend, Cuba's aging population will have consequences for generations to come. As in much of the Western World, fewer young people will be responsible for paying for government programs designed to meet the basic needs of growing numbers of elderly.

Despite a history of hardships and deprivations, some of which continue to this day, Cuba exudes magnetism on its people unlike I have witnessed elsewhere in the world. It is like air they must breath, it is balm for their souls, and it is unalterably home.

Some of the difficulties, of course, relate to the discord with the United States and its economic embargo of the island. Is there hostility to U.S. visitors? I never have experienced any. Is there bafflement that the world's greatest power would endlessly punish its small poor neighbor? Certainly. Yet there is fundamental affection for Americans that transcends harsh political realities. Of course, government officials are pleased to describe a litany of grievances with the U.S. government. But this does not extend to personal relationships that seem to thrive despite ample grounds for grumpiness.

A simple gesture confirming this tight bond between Cubans and Americans never fails to amaze me. Each time I travel to Havana I bring along a handful of little lapel pins that show the crossed flags of Cuba and the United States. I have never been able to take as many as 20 paces in public without having a total stranger approach me and ask for my pin. Including times when the political scene was inflamed, such as during the long battle over the future of little Elian Gonzalez, Cubans find this tiny symbol of Cuba-U.S. friendship to be irresistible.

Perhaps because of the hardships they have endured, or despite them, the Cuban people are proud almost to a fault. You can read it in their erect bearing, keen awareness of their success in overcoming the daily challenges linked to the U.S. embargo, and those caused by the abrupt exit of the Soviet Union and its billions of dollars in economic assistance. Time and again I have witnessed the pride that has driven the Cuban people to some of their greatest achievements.

Conversely, a couple of personal incidents illustrate when their stubborn, even if admirable, pride has worked to their disadvantage. In international airports around the world there are containers into which a departing traveler can drop a few coins, usually those "leftovers" after converting money back to the visitor's native currency. Who among us does not have a jar around the house with those orphaned coins from foreign lands? I suggested to an official that such an opportunity for little charitable donations by people in the departure lounges of Cuba's many international airports seemed like a worthy idea. "If each of your 2 million visitors dropped only a dime for charity, at the end of a year Cuba would have accumulated more than $200,000 for people with dire needs," I proposed.

I imagine this idea wound its way up the ladder of officialdom in Havana. And it was rejected. There is little doubt that the negative response reflected Cuban pride rather than the merits of the proposal. Cubans likely felt it would make them appear that they were beggars. But really, if anyone has to choose between another coin in a Mason jar in a closet and life-saving equipment for a hospital, could there be a more obvious choice? Cubans insist, however, they can meet their own needs on a level playing field, and soliciting donations is not in their repertoire.

On another occasion, I was involved with the Cuban Chamber of Commerce as it organized a day-long program of briefings and meetings for foreign businesspeople. At the conclusion I handed an envelope to the Cuban fellow in charge, explaining I simply wanted to help offset the costs of materials and a luncheon provided to us. Had I handed him a coiled viper he could not have dropped it any faster. No, he absolutely refused sharing the cost of the program, although a comparatively meager sum to the attendees could have had a meaningful impact on other important activities of the Chamber. More Cuban pride.

A little known but politically charged example of such Cuban pride rests with Castro himself. As you know, the United States has a military facility at Guantanamo Bay, at the eastern end of Cuba. It is leased, based on a treaty more than a century old, for the paltry sum of $4,000 per year. In accord with its treaty obligations, each year the U.S. government passes to the Cuban government a check for the annual rent. *And not once since the Revolution in 1959 has the Cuban government cashed those checks.* Perhaps they are all in a neat stack in a wall safe in Castro's office. Why? To accept the payments could be perceived as legitimizing the presence of a foreign military base on their soil, against the wishes of the current government. No, another $200,000 would not make a huge difference for the economy of Cuba. But the many hundreds of wheelchairs it could buy would be an appealing alternative to checks gathering dust.

On a personal level, one poignant example comes to mind. It is the remarkable story of Mariella, a Cuban woman whose pride and determination enabled her to overcome massive obstacles. Her quest is described in detail Chapter 14.

As you can imagine, the Cuban people are fully engaged day to day, way beyond enjoying the company of folks like you and me. Indeed, millions of Cubans may not even see a tourist for months or years at a time. Their lives are busy, their routine is demanding. Their work comes second only to family. Most are employed with a five-day workweek, but the daily bookends are the challenges of commuting. Mass transportation is scarce, crowded and time-consuming. For many it adds several hours to each end of the workday. In the city, that is. Out in the rural areas it is much worse.

During a trip through the countryside a few years ago, I picked up two women who were hitchhiking to the hospital where they worked as nurses. It was a long haul on a small country road. I asked how they normally get to work and what they'd have done if I hadn't come along. "Sometimes there is a bus, but mostly not," one of them said with a sigh. I asked, "What if you are hours late to work, or if the person for the next shift doesn't appear?" Another sigh emerged from behind her starched white uniform. "Often we are delayed for hours, and many times we have to work two, or even three, shifts."

In addition to such grueling daily routines, long lines are an ever-present feature of life amid scarcity. Everywhere I go I see lines of Cubans in front of open and closed doors, banks and ration *bodegas*, and post offices and, above all, waiting at bus stops. Often people will jump into a line simply because they assume that something desirable and scarce awaits at the front. To my surprise, those in line seldom have the frown of frustration and consternation that I would expect. They are usually smiling and chatting with new acquaintances. Nowhere is this better illustrated than in the hours-long lines people routinely experience at the Coppelia ice cream store. And, trust me, *that* line never fails to have a happy ending.

On the job, a centrally administered socialist economy leaves scarce space for innovation, extra effort, or reward. Salaries deviate little from a prescribed norm. While in the United States a CEO may earn hundreds of times more than a factory worker, in Cuba it would be surprising for the head of an enterprise to be paid even double the wage of the lowliest employee. In fact, some of the less appealing jobs, such as farming, actually are rewarded with *higher* monthly wages than those paid to urban workers. Incentives are rare. Frustration results.

It is reported, on the employment front, that virtually every able-bodied Cuban is working. While the official unemployment rate is marked at a low 5 percent, I am mindful of the words of the famous English economist Adam Smith, who said, "I have no great faith in political arithmetic." Close scrutiny is not required to see that one feature of this so-called full-employment economy is an abundance of underemployment.

Another daily challenge is to feed the family. Supermarkets, as we know them, simply do not exist in Cuba. There are some independent (read: "more expensive") markets, especially for produce. But the principal source of food continues to be small storefront ration stores, where every Cuban can receive an allotment of rationed food each month at minimal cost. How wonderfully Cuban that the authorized list includes not only items such as rice and beans and cooking oil but also cigars and rum. As noted earlier, many items are chronically out of stock, and none actually meets a full month's needs. Despite this literal struggle to find one's daily bread, it is surprising to learn that so many households have a pet, often a small dog or cat or bird that is almost always well fed and lovingly attended. A friend of mine of modest means dotes on her two small Pekinese doggies, who could not be better cared for if they were royalty.

So is all in perfect harmony in Cuba? Of course not. Despite official policies and denials, there remains a small undercurrent of racial discrimination against the darkest skinned Cubans – probably a vestige of Cuba's own sad history with slavery that ended in 1886, more than two decades after the U.S. Civil War ended. Issues of skin color are more evident on the eastern end of the island, where there are more darker-skinned people as a result of their historic inward migration from nearby Caribbean islands, such as Haiti and Jamaica.

Occasionally in a conversation about race issues, a Cuban will lightly tap their forearm with two fingers, their discreet way of alluding to dark-skinned people. Overall, I have the impression of remarkable racial harmony. In part this arises from Cuba's historic mixing of the races and the absence of racial discord and violence that characterized 20th century race relations in the United States. Racially mixed couples are commonplace, and in the professional realm, darker-skinned people can be found occupying a proportionate number of senior positions in government and enterprises. Racial discrimination, which is mindless at best, would verge on the ludicrous in Cuba because the skin color reflects a full spectrum of beiges and browns, and trying to draw a line at one hue would be so arbitrary as to be laughable.

On an early trip to Cuba, I visited the sprawling beach resort of Varadero. Among our small group was a black activist from the United States. Over lunch in a fabulous new resort hotel, he noticed that the wait staff was mostly dark-skinned. Well, he went off like a rocket. "Here we have blatant discrimination, this is unacceptable, I demand to see the hotel manager!" So we asked if the manager would talk to us as we tried to calm our colleague. Graciously, the manager soon appeared. Well-dressed, articulate, *and definitely black*. While our friend was sputtering and searching for words to allay his embarrassment, we were impressed that a black professional Cuban had been selected as the chief executive of this new multi-million dollar facility.

A Cuban official confided to me with unusual frankness. "Blacks are still in a subordinate position in many parts of Cuba. There are still remnants of racism. Discrimination is not a problem that can be solved in 50 years, as your own experience shows."

Havana and the entire nation of Cuba appear to be ethnically homogeneous. That differs from many major U.S. and Canadian cities, such as New York and Toronto, where you find conspicuous groups of Asians, western Europeans, contemporary Africans, Slavs, Middle Easterners and others. Immigration to Cuba in the 19th century included an estimated 150,000 Chinese laborers. Early in the 21st century that figure has shrunk to a population of fewer than 10,000 for reasons of death, departure and inter-marriage. A vestige of a once-thriving Chinatown can still be found in Havana, but there is nothing more than a shadow of this once robust community. And it's easy to imagine why I have found no evidence of inward migration of ethnic groups during the 20th century, when so many millions were expressing their hopes and fears by fleeing Cuba.

Also to be found, of course, are individuals who have cause to be unhappy, such as criminals and a gaggle of ne'er-do-wells. They are the exceptions, however, in a country whose national character includes a buoyant happiness, affection and respect for others.

Indeed the Cuban people are the country's greatest asset. Beyond their genetic good fortune they now rank high among nations in their health, education and welfare. They radiate pride in self and family and country. Their individual and collective sense of friendliness and joy is infectious and is one of the most remarkable facets of Cuba to be discovered and savored.

CHAPTER 13

# EMIGRATION: A NATIONAL TRAGEDY

In no respect has the post-revolutionary history of Cuba been sadder than the emigration of millions of Cubans from their cherished homeland. There are countless tales of hardship, tears, financial deprivation, divided families and death. Each is its own story.

It is estimated that as many as 3 million Cubans have left the island between 1959 and today, creating a diaspora around the world with none larger than the estimated million-plus now in Florida, and another 200,000 in Spain. From infants to grandparents, from some of the best and the brightest to Mafia thugs, from political opponents to some of the country's most famous artists and athletes. No stratum of the society was spared, and practically no family on the island fails to have a relative who chose, or was forced by terrible circumstances, to leave. Even Fidel Castro has not gone unscathed: His own sister Juanita fled to Miami in 1964. And later she revealed having worked with the CIA against her brothers since 1961.

Being aware of the profound bond between Cubans and their country, I have tried to understand what reasons could possibly motivate such a huge proportion of the country's population to flee. Many of us have borne witness to calamities such as the massive destruction of war, the ravages of widespread disease and the consequences of natural disasters that have prompted populations elsewhere to exodus en masse. But Cuba has been spared those harsh realities, and before the Revolution emigration was in very small numbers. So what is the explanation?

The causes of emigration of millions of people from Cuba during the past half-century reasonably can be divided into two broad categories: economic and political. Both have been amplified by fear, often of the unknown, and both have been amplified by the proximity of a familiar and friendly alternative just a short distance across the Florida Straits.

It began quietly enough in 1958, when those who feared the outcome of the Revolution began to pack, liquidate their assets and depart in an orderly way, mainly to the United States. During the months just prior to Castro's victory in early 1959, the reasons for many to flee became clearer. Officials of the old dictatorship and their active supporters flocked away like migrating birds. Momentum grew rapidly after the Batista government was toppled, Castro's forces prevailed, and it became certain that opponents of the Revolution and people of significant wealth would not be welcomed by the new regime. Many of those who remained behind were dealt with harshly, including executions.

During 1959 and 1960, as the new government actively imposed political and economic reforms, tens of thousands more fled. The unwelcome mat was extended in Cuba to private business people, foreign companies and the Mafia. Many of those who left naively believed that it would be only a temporary evacuation, anticipating Castro's removal by American pressure or intervention. Of course, they were totally wrong and most, to this day, have never returned to Cuba.

Unfortunately, one result was a massive brain drain of many of Cuba's leading professionals: physicians, lawyers, architects, engineers, business owners, senior managers, intellectuals, and dozens of other prosperous, educated and specialized upper-class people. For example, more than half the faculty the University of Havana emigrated in the months following the Revolution. The consequences of this flight of professionals easily can be imagined. Suppose *your* community was suddenly absent its senior public safety officials, most of its physicians, the great thinkers and finest minds, the folks who run the schools, the water system and most of the businesses in town.

A conspicuous, but not atypical, example is to be found with Nilo Cruz, Cuban playwright and author of the Pulitzer Prize winning play *Anna in the Tropics*. Although his father was imprisoned for trying to leave Cuba, eventually the family emigrated, and Nilo grew to be an author of world renown. Said Cruz to me, reflecting on his painful separation from Cuba as he described El Morro lighthouse outside of Havana Harbor, "It is the blink of a light like a woman winking, flirting, inviting you in." But the last time he saw it he was leaving. Sadly, to this day he is fearful of returning to his homeland because bureaucrats in Havana consider his writing "anti-government." I wonder how many of them have ever read his wondrous prose.

Among the earliest and most poignant of the waves of emigration were those dubbed the "Peter Pan" flights of children from Cuba to the United States. In general, they arose from monstrous uncertainty about the future of Cuba under Castro and, in particular, from rumors that children were going to be sent to Russia for indoctrination in communist ideology. In all, over 14,000 children were put onto flights by, and to, family and friends. At first it was covert, and it continued to be allowed from early 1959 until the autumn of 1961. The notorious Bay of

Pigs invasion prompted the new government to end this gesture of tolerance. Some children subsequently waited as long as 20 years to be reunited with their families. Others never were. Most have not returned to Cuba.

The next surge of emigration took place in 1965, by small boats from the north coast village of Camarioca. Thousands more fled, and they were followed by hundreds of thousands more on the so-called "Freedom" flights. The exodus surged and sagged for years, and then suddenly ballooned into what became known as the Mariel Boatlift. In 1980, with the Cuban economy struggling, the government actually encouraged the improvised exodus of an estimated 125,000 Cubans in boats, rafts and literally anything that would float. Castro took advantage of the opportunity to vacate the prisons and mental institutions of thousands more. Estimates are that as much as 10 per cent of the entire flotilla embarking on that perilous journey consisted of Cuban society's "undesirables."

The trip proved to be frightful to all, fatal to many. On the best of days ramshackle vessels disintegrated and sank, and inner tubes deflated. On the worst of days foul weather proved to be catastrophic. A short 90 miles, the voyage entailed seas tossed by storms and ripped by dangerous currents, blistering sun above and man-eating sharks below. Thousands perished at sea. In the prescient words of Ernest Hemingway, "Brother, don't let anybody tell you there isn't plenty of water between Key West and Havana!"

The chaos and loss of life was of concern to both the U.S. and Cuban governments. After yet another mass exodus from Cuba, an estimated 40,000 people in 1994, both sides reached an agreement soon after to provide a safety valve and allow for the orderly and safe emigration of Cubans to the States. The key elements were the United States agreeing to accept an unprecedented 20,000 Cuban immigrants annually and the Cuban government agreeing to allow a national lottery for those entry visas to the United States. In addition, the

United States adopted the controversial policy known as "wet foot/dry foot."

The wet foot/dry foot provisions constituted a momentous departure from past practice of the United States, and it afforded favorable treatment to emigrating Cubans that was unrivaled in the world. Actually, it was a huge expansion of the provisions of the Cuban Adjustment Act of 1966, which provided that any Cuban who managed to get to the United States and stayed a year would be granted permanent residency. Under the liberalized policy any Cuban who was *able to reach U.S. soil* (not territorial waters, not a bridge, not bobbing in the surf), was entitled to remain there. Of course, this was specifically intended to accommodate rafters who survived the perilous journey, most often to the nearest U.S. landfall, the Florida Keys.

During the national lottery in 2008, over 600,000 Cubans applied. Assuming most applicants represented a family, that could be extrapolated to mean there are perhaps two million Cubans who would like to emigrate to the United States. That is an overwhelming and frightening statistic. If you apply that proportion to the population of the United States, can you imagine 60 million U.S. citizens lined up to leave the country? That would approximate the *entire* population of California *and* Texas, or *everyone* in the least-populated 28 states.

Those emigrants who have a near miss – meaning those who are intercepted on or in the water – are repatriated to Cuba by the U.S. Coast Guard. Predictably, the Cuban government officials have not been too keen on the "wet foot/dry foot" policy. In fact, they regard it as an outrage. It reasonably can be seen as an incentive for Cubans to leap onto flimsy excuses for watercraft, often little more than a few barrels and some old boards, in an attempt to depart the island "illegally." To depart the country legally, it is necessary to apply for, pay for, and secure a Cuban exit visa and a U.S. entry visa. Other detractors point to the obviously discriminatory nature of the policy, wherein a Haitian floater, for example, who touches U.S. land may as well have hit a rubber wall. For they are immediately bounced back to Haiti without appeal, receiving just a bottle of water and a friendly wave goodbye.

Enterprising boaters have found yet another way to enable the exodus of Cubans to the United States. They depart in fast boats from southern Florida, and only a few hours later, in the dark of night, pick up pre-arranged passengers to whisk back to Florida. Very neat and very profitable. For this service, they charge anywhere from several hundred dollars to $10,000 per illegal émigré. The coast guards of both countries have conspicuously failed to interdict this traffic in human cargo, so it continues to thrive.

Applying for an exit visa from Cuba, or even having the government become aware of one's desire to leave, often has had consequences. Elderly people who may no longer be productive members of society are able to leave with relative ease. Younger people who have benefited from the largesse of the government, mainly in terms of their free education and health care, face greater obstacles. Routinely, they have been required to "repay" the government for those investments in their future. Usually those sums are far beyond their ability to pay, effectively blocking their emigration from Cuba. Worse, however, are the many tales of Cubans who have sought to leave and subsequently lost their jobs and found that their family members have been harassed or penalized. Even harsher fates have befallen families of Cubans back home who have defected while traveling abroad.

From those who decide to leave the island, I have learned of a variety of motives and misconceptions. Surely, U.S. immigration laws, particularly the Cuban Adjustment Act of 1966, as expanded during the Clinton presidency, enormously favor (and even entice) Cubans who can legally remain in the United States if they can get there. Many have relatives in the States and reasonably expect a soft landing in their chosen new land. Most often that is the Miami area or northern New Jersey, where there are large enclaves of Cuban émigrés and Cuban-American representatives in Congress.

The transition to life in another country is not always as easy as expected. The need for individual economic self-reliance, unlike recent generations have had to face in Cuba, has been particularly challenging. Significant numbers of émigrés simply cannot cope with the comparative absence of government subsidies, their misconceptions, the realities of living in a new land, and they return to Cuba. They do so despite their awareness that others who have left and returned sometimes have been subjected to penalties, even jail sentences.

The painful experience of Jorge, a close friend of many years, a young Cuban man of great energy, drive, ambition and intelligence, may be illustrative. My amigo was seduced by the economic possibilities abroad in contrast to their absence at home. He was a natural entrepreneur. He said to me, "I am suffocating with no opportunities, I cannot breath here." After years of trying, he and his friends and I rejoiced when he finally succeeded in securing an exit visa along with an entry visa to Mexico, where he had friends and relatives.

Jorge left the moment he was allowed. And what was the outcome? Did he become a captain of industry in a free market economy? Did he thrive once away from the restrictions of Cuba? Sadly, neither. Within six months he had returned to Cuba, embarrassed and frustrated, but joyful to be back. Such can be the magnetism of the Cuban homeland. And it does not apply only to émigrés. I have two good Cuban friends, and no doubt there have been numerous others, who were born and raised abroad and could have remained in their second country. Yet they freely chose to relocate to Cuba. While, admittedly, these cases have been rare, there has been, in fact, a tiny amount of such "reverse emigration."

Often I have asked Cubans why they wish to leave – as well as why they are content to *not* leave. I recall the response of a young fellow, perhaps 15 years old, when asked why he wanted to go to the United States. With enthusiasm he said to me, "Surely, you know that along the streets in America there are wonderful machines. All you have to do is push a few buttons and they give you money." I tried to disabuse him of this wacky notion, to inform him that you had to have money in a bank account before an ATM would share it with you. But he would not hear of it and remained delusional about the bounty just beyond the sea.

Over the years more than a million Cubans have settled in and around Miami, including a large area that has come to be known as Little Havana. Unlike most arrivals, the Cubans seem less inclined to assimilate than to duplicate their native surroundings. The streetscape is crammed with stores full of familiar foods, the signage is entirely *en espanol,* and not a word of English is to be heard on the streets. It will be fascinating to see how many Cuban-Americans decide to leave their comfortable but new perch and return to Cuba someday.

Another less conventional and less common form of emigration, but far more dramatic, has been political defections. Recent decades have been punctuated with stories of Cubans, both famous and ordinary, defecting while traveling abroad. Most conspicuous have been various athletes, such as *El Duque,* a pitcher by the name of Orlando Hernandez who was once Cuba's most famous baseball player. He defected on Christmas Day 1997 and was enticed to join the New York Yankees for a four-year contract worth a cool $6.6 million. In all, Hernandez pitched for nine seasons in the major leagues for four teams and won two games in the World Series for the Yankees.

More recently, in 2007, star Cuban boxer Guillermo Rigondeaux apparently sought to defect while he was in Rio de Janeiro to compete in the Pan American Games. He and a teammate were caught and returned to Cuba where, to the surprise of many, they were not arrested. Castro rose from his sick bed to lambaste them, saying, "They have reached a point of no return as members of a Cuban boxing team. An athlete who abandons his team is like a soldier who abandons his fellow troops in the middle of combat."

The consequences rippled beyond the two boxers, who had been judged politically unreliable. The *entire* boxing team was punished as the government pulled them from the world boxing championships scheduled for Chicago later that year. Such penalties being meted out to associates of "unreliables" are not uncommon, and they result in enormous peer pressure for Cubans who are allowed to travel abroad to return home. But the beat goes on. In the spring of 2008, one-third of the Cuban soccer team defected to the United States while playing Olympic qualifier soccer matches in Tampa, Florida. And in late 2009, a Cuban volleyball player defected to the United States while competing in Puerto Rico, and his inspired teammates reacted by defeating the U.S. team to win the gold medal and then triumphantly returned to Cuba.

The sadly long list of defectors, with so many people having to deal with that wrenching dilemma, includes people from almost every walk of life: artists, ballet dancers, athletes, academicians and even air force pilot Orestes Lorenzo, who flew to the Florida Keys in his Mig-27 in 1991. (*And* he later returned in a daring adventure in a small plane to whisk his family off the island). As a deterrent, the Cuban government often responds with serious consequences for the families of defectors, such as losing their homes or jobs in Cuba.

Elpidio is a dear friend of mine who was a Catholic priest in Havana. He chose to leave. His case was more singular than instructive but no less disturbing for him, his family, friends and parishioners. In part his frustrations arose because he grew up in the humblest imaginable circumstances, in a milieu that included keen awareness of the religious practices of Santeria to the Afro-Cuban community. In combination with the reality that he was a *gay* Cuban, church officials let it be known that his destiny was to serve in obscurity in a little remote village far from his attachments in Havana. With a broken heart, he chose to leave forever, and he defected while on a sanctioned visit to Miami.

Although the root cause of Cubans desiring to emigrate – the dismal economic conditions and low standard of living – has diminished during the 20 years since the departure of the Soviets and their massive subsidies, discontent continues to be widespread. In early 2002, it manifested itself again. During an inflammatory broadcast on Radio Marti, whose listeners in Cuba are mainly those with a higher level of curiosity and frustration, comments by the Mexican foreign minister created a huge flap. He said, "The doors of the embassy of Mexico in Havana are open to all Cuban citizens in the same way that Mexico is open," and his words were rebroadcast repeatedly.

Wishful thinkers in Havana interpreted that to mean that Mexico would accommodate people wishing to move there. That misconception swept over Havana like a tidal wave. A crowd gathered outside the embassy and soon crashed through the gates onto what is perceived, under diplomatic protocol, as Mexican territory, which would be immune from Cuban intervention. An earlier embassy invasion, that time involving the Embassy of Peru, had triggered the calamitous Mariel Boatliftt in 1980, and no thoughtful person wanted to contemplate a repeat of that chaotic catastrophe. Responding to a formal request from Mexican embassy officials, Cuban police entered the grounds and forcibly removed the hundreds of intruders. A larger crisis had been averted, but the undercurrent of unhappiness in Havana again was made starkly apparent to the world.

Defections often have been high profile and embarrassing to the government. As a deterrent, the regime has periodically taken extreme measures, as was the tragic example in 2003. Three teenagers mindlessly hijacked a harbor ferry in Havana and set out to the north. Just a few miles offshore the vessel ran out of fuel, and the Cuban authorities easily captured the boys

– and executed them a short time later. Mr. Castro certainly had an instinct for getting the message out.

Despite possible terrible consequences, a few have resorted to fleeing the island by hijacking aircraft from Cuba. In recent years, this has become a no-win proposition. Failure to escape has led to severe penalties, even execution. And success was likely to result in being sentenced to jail in the United States, as was the case in 2003, when a hijacker diverted a domestic flight to the States. As recently as 2007, a trio of fugitive Cuban soldiers tried to hijack a flight to Miami. They killed a hostage in their failed attempt, were captured at the airport, and there can be little doubt about their fate.

What is remarkable is not that Cubans are sufficiently disgruntled to vote with their feet to leave their families, homes and homeland, but that so many have succeeded despite their high visibility positions of trust and political dependability.

Not surprisingly, Fidel always has been at the center of the many emigration storms. Under some circumstances he encouraged his fellow Cubans to leave, other times people fled because of him, and most of the time he has made it a massive challenge for Cubans to depart. His role always has been decisive: basically to allow the oldsters and undesirables to depart, but keep the young and productive.

There is in Cuba a yarn that goes like this: Inevitably, the day came when Fidel Castro passed from life and moved into the great hereafter. To his great shock, he found himself in Heaven and had a chat with St. Peter. "Mr. President, it is a great honor, but mostly a great surprise, to see you here. Always The Big Guy and I assumed that you would be spending eternity not in Heaven, by way far down south of here," said St. Peter. "Amigo, I am pleased but even more surprised than you are," responded Castro. St. Peter scratched his head, thought a few moments, and said, "Although it's nearly closing time, almost 5 p.m., let me check with the VIP office and learn if there has been a mistake." So the reluctant host got on the phone and inquired, and sure enough there had been an embarrassing blunder. "Mr. President, I have checked and indeed our travel agent angels got the paperwork confused and you were dispatched upstairs instead of downstairs. But I am sure we can get you on your way to your correct destination right away," said St. Peter.

Sure enough, as the tale goes, Castro was zoomed straight to Hell with no further delay. There he was greeted personally by the Devil: "*Hola*, President Castro. We have waited for you for such a long time, and we are delighted that you are with us." "Thank you" responded Castro, "I am not entirely amazed to be here. But would you check on my baggage, which I believe may have been lost when my travel arrangements went off course." Señor Devil checked upstairs and indeed Castro's luggage was still in the waiting room in Heaven. "I will send our little devil baggage men up to Heaven right now, while you are settling into your new quarters," said the Devil. So up went the little demons, only to find that by now the gates to Heaven were closed and locked for the day, as it was well after 5 p.m. Undeterred, the little devils circled around the gates and windows to Heaven, searching for a way into the baggage claim area. By chance, St. Peter glanced out a window as the devils were flitting about in search of an entryway. "Oh my goodness!" he exclaimed. "Fidel Castro has only been in Hell for a few minutes and already there are émigrés!"

Millions have left, and millions more have expressed their desire to go by applying for the lottery for the required entry visa to the United States. This horrific exodus has unfolded over a span of about 50 years, not unlike watching a tragedy on the screen unfolding in slow motion.

The equally baffling and intriguing question, however, may be why do the vast majority of Cubans want to *stay*? Of course, they have a powerful connection to their homeland. For some it may be the richness of the nation's history, the powerful ties to family, the opportunity to live a lifestyle that suits them, professional satisfaction or a host of other reasons. For most it is a melange of these and more.

It is my impression that there is another compelling reason, perhaps the single most powerful one, which is less recognized. Emigration from Cuba has been a million variations on a theme of dissatisfaction. The flip side of that coin is the reality that the great majority of the folks in Cuba do *not* want to leave. And why is that? To understand, we must remove one of the filters that may slightly obscure a clearly focused view of the Cuban people.

Americans are blessed to live in a land of unimaginable bounty compared to most of our cohabitants on the planet. Upon reflection, many if not most of our daily dilemmas stem from this bounty and not from insufficiency. "Should I splurge on a new car or live with the perfectly adequate vehicle I own. Or can I afford both? My neighbor just bought some fabulous lawn furniture, and I *must* upgrade my own. Or should I keep saving for a swimming pool?" Onward. Each day millions of Americans have choices among great abundance. I would describe this as "horizontal" thinking. We are continually comparing our well being with others and the countless choices before us.

Cubans, on the other hand, tend to think "vertically." Surely, they are aware of the wealth and all it can buy just 90 miles away in Miami. Indeed, most have relatives who share the bounty of Walmart with their relatives "stranded" in Cuba. By thinking "vertically" instead, it seems to me that most Cubans focus not on what could be available to them somewhere else, but they think more historically. Typical was the response from a young Habanero named Enrique when I asked him why he chose to *not* leave Cuba, and why was he not frustrated and discontent.

His response was, "Do you realize that my grandparents were illiterate peasants in the sugar cane fields owned by greedy foreign companies? They worked every day, lived in a terrible shack with a dirt floor, had no education, no electricity, and they died young of preventable diseases. Then came my parents, who were young at the time of the Revolution. With new reforms they were able to become literate, have health care at no cost, enjoy a small apartment with electricity and a refrigerator and a radio. And maybe I am typical of my generation. My life expectancy is greater than that of an American, I was able to complete my education through a graduate degree at no cost, I have work and I am paid enough to get by with some extra efforts, and I have a small apartment in a fairly new building, *and both a refrigerator and a color television!* You ask how I can be content? And I ask you how I could not be amazed as well as content. Look at the progress since 1959. I am moving at warp speed, my family has leaped from a feudal existence to a modern society in only two generations! I can have a healthy and fulfilling life and my children will have even more than I."

Emigration has been a tragedy of epic proportions in modern Cuba. Few nations have been more disrupted, even by wars, famines and natural disasters. It is part of the remarkable tapestry that is Cuba, and knowing why so many have left, and why so many more have chosen not to leave, is essential to understanding Cuba itself.

CHAPTER 14

AMAZING MARIELLLA

Her name is Mariella, and she lives alone in a tropical wonderland she created on the rooftop of a decaying apartment building from which she was expelled more than 30 years ago. I have known Mary, as she is generally called, for a decade, merged gradually into her diverse circle of friends, and we have talked late into many Havana nights. But this night was different, for my goal was to learn from this very private woman the details of her struggles to overcome massive obstacles along her life's path in Cuba. How her oasis of tropical plants, singing birds, subdued lighting, fine artworks, hand-wrought furniture and splendid cuisine came to be is a tale worth the telling, for in a land where obstacles are common, overcoming them is rare.

My 1956 lime green Chevy had lumbered down a darkened side street, guided by a single headlight and the intuition of my driver. Streets failed to reveal their names, and dwellings failed to reveal their numbers. We ground to a halt in front of a nondescript gray apartment building noteworthy mainly for its peeling paint and shattered sidewalk. Far from evident was that, in only minutes, I would be comfortably settled in one of the most secret and magical domains in Havana's ample repertoire.

We had wound our way through Vedado, the central area in Havana that rests between the Old City and modern Miramar. While the Old City hugs the harbor and was founded in the 16th century, Vedado emerged centuries later as the city expanded westward beyond the walls of Habana Vieja. It includes the renowned University of Havana, the "grand dame" Nacional Hotel, office buildings, and a sprawling residential neighborhood.

I recalled my instructions, a hybrid of a spy thriller and Hansel and Gretel: "Follow the path alongside the building and enter the doorway you will find." After doing so I found myself in a dimly lit stairwell with once marvelous but now crumbling white marble steps leading up several floors and into the darkness beyond. Onward. A locked wrought iron gate near the top barred the way to my destination – the roof. Anticipating my arrival, a buzzer sounded, a lock released, and the barrier opened. I scrambled up the remaining steps to find an ornately carved wooden door. It swung wide, and there emerged the beaming smile and warm greeting of Mariella.

My gasp at the vision before me was expelled by the firm *abrazo* of Mary – chef extraordinaire, divorced mother, skilled artist, overseer of her rooftop domain, and woman of incredible determination and strength.

I was uplifted by Mary's smile, so broad that it seemed to rise from her soul to embrace me. Her smooth skin was the hue of a rich *café au lait*, and her colorful flowing dress could be worn by a woman much younger than her near 60 years. "Welcoming you again is like a deep breath of fresh air," she said sweetly as she chatted and guided me to an area surrounded by plants, soft lights and colorful little birds singing from their swaying bamboo cages. She set before me a demitasse of thick rich Cuban coffee and added a generous spoonful of sugar. I stirred and reminded her that this was to be an evening of asking many questions and unveiling many mysteries.

"Above all, know that I am a *cimarrona*," she began with conviction in her voice. In one of the darker chapters of Cuba's history, when this colony of Spain was a trader and user of African slaves, *cimarronas* was the name for slaves who escaped from their masters. They found refuge in the eastern mountains, where they survived under the most primitive conditions, for capture spelled severe punishment or death. As decades turned into centuries and slavery was abolished, the *cimarronas* returned to the villages and towns and have become part of mainstream Cuba today. Part, but still apart.

"Also know that I hate interviews. I can't explain why I said yes to this one. The Cuban media and TV keep asking to interview me, and they always get a big 'NO!' I don't know why I'm doing this. I cherish my privacy. I have never been interviewed before today, and this will be my first *and* last one!" I squirmed, I sweated, I persevered.

Mary is an intensely private person, yet she becomes exuberant among close friends; she is gentle, yet she has proven to be strong and resilient in rising to overcome difficult circumstances. She is profoundly reluctant to discuss what she describes as "the painful journey I have traveled through time." Reluctantly, Mary began softly speaking a stream of consciousness about her life, her dreams, her realities.

"I was still a youngster when Fidel Castro's Revolution prevailed on New Year's Day of 1959. My interests were not in politics but in the arts, and I experimented with watercolor painting." Although she came from a working class family, with universal free education Mary graduated in painting and sculpture from the prestigious San Alejandro Institute of Fine Arts in Havana. Next she secured a bachelor's degree from the Fine Arts University of Havana, followed by a Ph.D. in history and philosophy from Cuba's finest, the University of

Havana. She said modestly, "I have spent so many years of my life studying."

Soon after university, Mary fell in love and married a leathercraft artist. "We were both very young," she said wistfully. "Two wonderful children came of our marriage, Alejandro and Adria, both now living in Spain." But the marriage did not last. In fact, it ended soon and badly in the late 1970s. As was customary at the time, the children stayed with their father. Mary was literally put out onto the street. And this is where the amazing story of Mariella, a Cuban *cimarrona*, really begins.

Mary's rising trajectory was launched from all-too-familiar circumstances: penniless, unemployed, aspiring artist, divorced mother, and homeless. Compound the dilemma with a "macho" society, meddling government officials, no social or financial safety net, and more obstacles to overcome than there are salsa tunes in Cuba. But then add some rocket fuel: ambition, intelligence, determination, persistence, natural talent, a dream, incomprehension of the word "no"– and a dose of desperation.

"Housing has been a big problem in Cuba," Mary said. So when she was divorced and forced to leave her apartment, she found shelter with a friend. "Days of terrifying anxiety followed, and then the phone rang." It was a friend and neighbor from her former apartment building. "Come back to your old building," she said. "You can use the flat roof of the building. Surely, the neighbors will complain, but the roof is as much yours as it is anyone else's."

Mary was thunderstruck. "What nonsense. It's just open sky above and tar underfoot! It was ridiculous, but immediately I moved to the roof with only a tent and my few possessions." Foolishness took a back seat to decisiveness.

Under the brutal Caribbean sun and through torrential downpours she toiled, scraping the roof on her hands and knees, creating a toehold on the route to survival, to normalcy and perhaps even to happiness. "I lived in that tent for three years." The long arduous days passed, salved by the balm of painting artworks at night.

During the course of many months, one brick at a time, she built a small room and a tiny bathroom. "When this was done, it was like Heaven to me. I had a home," she said. Predictably, there were complaints, adverse reports to government officials and worse. "They tried to declare that my little room was illegal, and I was ordered to move out more than a dozen times. But I always refused. I told them the only way would be for them to carry me out. That, too, almost happened, but I was able to avoid it."

Slow forward, 30 years. Mary persisted in her quest. One small room became two, then three, then four, each with better materials and finishes and décor. Along the way came an additional bathroom, a well-equipped kitchen, numerous dining and chatting areas separated by countless planters overflowing with tropical plants and flowers. The foliage thrives in the tropical sun and has created a luxuriant green canopy overhead, with orchids cascading down the walls. Scattered among the flowers and leaves are cages of petite songbirds, indirect lighting, colorful artworks covering every available inch of wall space, a small office and an artist's studio that would be the envy of many. Some rooms have walls and roofs while others remain open to Havana's breezes and star-filled nights. "Bear in mind I am a *cimarrona*," she said," and I would love to live without a roof over my head." Painfully aware that *decades* passed before Mary was able to cobble together her own little garden of Eden, she emoted with passion: "Having my home was the accomplishment of my life as a fighter, as a *cimarrona*."

Mary's domain has become far more than a dwelling. Everywhere I found expressions of her artistry and passion for decor. "My shower stall is round, and the walls are embedded with colorful glass and bottles," she said with pride and a smile. Showering must be like experiencing a gentle rainfall inside a kaleidoscope! Emerging from the plaster of other walls, like mushrooms sprouting in the forest, are fragments of old wood, metal artifacts and still more colorful bottles.

While her remarkable realm is a work of art of design and architecture, of supreme importance to Mary is her creation of extraordinary artworks: large paintings in oil, subdued watercolors, bright prints and voluptuous sculptures. Her art sustains, propels and pleases her. It provides sanctuary and satisfaction. "I love to be alone, and I must be alone in order to paint, to create," she said. Mary revels in every hour in her studio, which are many each day as she sleeps only four hours nightly. "What makes me most happy is my art, and I am constantly at my easel."

Mary's studio was bathed in light, well-stocked, colorful, and in complete chaos. Canvasses were stacked and strewn about, brushes emerged from ceramic vases like so many floral arrangements, tubes of paint were everywhere, and the music of soulful Cuban ballads surrounded me. It was a snapshot of a true artist, everything it its place, and the places were *everywhere*. A painting was emerging from a large canvas on her easel: sepia and sky blue abstract human figures and faces. Could it have been a commentary on the stress pressing on people as they tried to overcome life's hurdles? Another in pale hues of green and pink portrayed two floating figures and is named *Besos* (kisses). The images are evocative and insightful, yet still playful.

To describe her as an artist of considerable renown would be an understatement. For over 30 years, "My artworks have been exhibited hundreds of times in museums and galleries in Europe, the United States, Asia, Latin and South America and, of course, throughout Cuba," said Mary with hard-earned pride. Today her home is her gallery, for in Havana there are but few art galleries. In any case, her focus has shifted to her friends, her art and her privacy. "I am no longer interested in having public exhibitions," she said. "My paintings will remain for my friends and for me. I do not want any more awards or homage. I cherish my privacy."

Among Mary's other passions is her cooking and splendid Cuban cuisine. "I love to have my friends come for dinner because my cooking is authentic Cuban and very traditional," she said. "My recipes are a heritage from my mother, and her mother and from her grandmother. Can you imagine how old they are? These Cuban recipes are from the 17th and 18th centuries, from slaves who would spend hours combining new ingredients to gain new flavors." She added ruefully, "These dishes take the time and devotion that modern women do not have."

Cuisine is an extension of Mary's artistic skills. Just as her recipes are unique in Cuba, her presentation is decorative, and it wonderfully embellishes the dining experience. Her roast honey chicken in pineapple sauce is presented on a colorful handmade ceramic plate, with condiments and spices in distinctive containers of wood and reed. Shredded beef sautéed with tomato, garlic and sweet pepper sauce is presented in a cone of green palm leaves. Some dishes are adorned with vibrant red hibiscus flowers. Says Mary, "It is my pleasure as an artist to be sure the cuisine looks attractive, and as a cook to be certain that its taste is wonderful and distinctive."

During any visit to Mary's domain, her circle of friends might include fellow artists, diplomats, foreign visitors, and simple Cuban folks. They will be bantering, laughing and enjoying her table as well as the joy that radiates in her presence. "Recently, some of my friends stopped by for lunch and lost themselves in conversation, and they finally departed at seven in the evening." Being with Mary and in her "salon" is a rich and engaging experience, total immersion.

Mary has been successful, in a uniquely Cuban way, in nourishing both body and soul. Not of necessity, but from her passion and drive to excel in these realms. Has it been a solo quest, driven by her intense desire for self-reliance? No, not entirely. At critical crossroads in her life, she has relied on the guidance and help of others. "My parents and mentors encouraged my pursuit of the arts from a very early age." A few friends helped sustain her during the awful time of her divorce and homelessness. She reflected, "I will never forget them, for maybe it was because of their friendship that I did not leave the country for good." Several arts professionals gave her encouragement and helped to promote her artworks at home and abroad. Mary is keenly aware of the importance of others in her life, and her reach is great enough to embrace them while preserving her own personal space which she so cherishes.

My cup of *café Cubano* was emptied and refilled countless times. My delicious *crème brulee* with a perfect crackly sugar glaze was consumed. Mary had grown restless and weary of my questions. But I needed to know what lies ahead for her. She said there would be no more interviews and no more public exhibitions of her art. Certainly, she will relentlessly pursue her passions: painting, cuisine, and her wide circle of friends. And what else? "There is a place that I've never been to and I would so much love to visit: it is New York. The most important work that I've painted is there, 'The Blue Boy.' I would like to see my painting once more, and I would like to visit that unique city before I die," reflected Mary. And to those who know her, this woman of strength and determination, this *cimarrona*, there can be no doubt that Mary will achieve those seemingly impossible dreams.

CHAPTER 15

U.S.–CUBA RELATIONS: A FAMILY FEUD

Talk about an odd couple. Relations between the United States and Cuba have been on a roller-coaster ride for well over a century. It has been at times friendly and hostile; mutually beneficial and predatory; balanced, and way out of whack. You have your basic elephant and mouse scenario, but for the last half-century both the mouse and the elephant have been roaring at each other.

The origins of U.S. interest in Cuba date back at least as far as Presidents Thomas Jefferson and John Quincy Adams in the early 1800s. But then Americans apparently got distracted with expanding westward to the blue Pacific Ocean. During the 1850s, a few zealous senators tried to annex Cuba as a "bonus" slave state. Later in the 19th century America seemed to have merged its concept of Manifest Destiny and the Monroe Doctrine, and the result was a resurgence of interest in Cuba.

In the grand finale of the Spanish-American War in 1898 the United States "liberated" Cuba from the centuries-long clutches of Spain and gained control of the island. It graciously relinquished that responsibility, which it had taken ever so lightly, by granting independence to Cuba in 1902. But independence is in the eye of the beholder. By that time, U.S. companies, such as United Fruit, Standard Oil and telephone giant International Telephone and Telegraph had secured not only a foothold but also a virtual economic stranglehold in Cuba. On the political side, the United States began supporting a series of compliant and corrupt dictators who assured that Cuba would continue to be an economic windfall and social playground for Americans. And the outrageous Platt Amendment guaranteed the right of the United States to intervene in "independent" Cuba virtually at will, as well as the right to maintain a military base at Guantanamo Bay.

Cuba was a key to quenching the thirst of the United States during Prohibition. Countless rumrunners were spawned and, in the process, enriched folks, such as the DuPonts and Kennedys. Cuba prospered. Sugar harvests were in huge demand as far back as the First World War, and the Second World War saw Cuba's economy grow robust. A look at Havana's cityscape today is breathtaking testimony to the vast sums that were earned and spent on the island. Mile after mile of fabulous villas overlook lush and manicured wide boulevards, nowhere more so than in the upscale modern Miramar neighborhood. Only the slightest imagination is called for to visualize mobster Meyer Lansky or crooner Frank Sinatra or aviator and industrialist Howard Hughes cruising along Havana's impressive Fifth Avenue in a lumbering Cadillac with flying tail fins. This abundance of cash, not surprisingly, drew the increasing presence of the Mafia from the United States.

Accompanying all of this extravagant self-indulgence by a few, there was a price. It was paid terribly in disease, ignorance, poverty and misery by the vast majority of all Cubans, as the government ignored basic needs of all but a few of its citizens. The practically inevitable result of grinding poverty amid a cornucopia of plenty was, in Cuba, little different from Russia in the early 20th century or South Africa later in that century. The "have-nots" got angry, and then they picked up guns and chased away the "haves."

Sometimes the bad guys (the soon-to-be former "haves") took sacks full of money and escaped in the night to obscure places that would accept them despite their character flaws and likely because of their sacks full of money. That's pretty much what happened on the night of December 31, 1958, when President Batista, barely escaping the grasp of the good guys (the soon-to-be former "have-nots") flew off to Dominica with 180 pals and an estimated $300 million in cash. Good old Fulgencio Batista must have been quite the Ebenezer Scrooge – able to amass such a fortune on the paltry salaries of an army officer and government official.

In this light one can understand why the United States, which had been propping up a series of puppet dictators in Havana for over a half-century, was not the favorite neighbor of the new government in Cuba. But it was a *big* neighbor, and life could be simpler if neighbors were friendly – especially with the proverbial fence (in this case, 90 miles of open water in the Florida Straits) between them. Keep in mind that, at this stage, Castro was the leader of a victorious popular revolution, unquestionably left wing, but also unquestionably not yet declared a *communist* revolution.

Early acts of the revolutionary government included ridding the island of the entrenched Mafia, which had been doing quite well, thank you, in the businesses of hotels, tourism, drugs, prostitution and gambling. Also sent packing were the foreign companies, mainly American, which had enjoyed such a firm and profitable grip on Cuba. Expropriation was the policy *du jour,* and what remained was to be a Cuba of the people, by the people, and for the people of Cuba. (That phrase has a familiar ring to it – now where have we heard that before?)

After taking power the new government expropriated all American-owned holdings including massive properties of

U.S. companies – and land holdings in excess of 1,000 acres that were owned by Cubans. In response, President Eisenhower directed the U.S.-owned oil refinery in Havana not to process Cuban oil. Castro was predictably annoyed and upped the ante by expropriating the property of *all* foreign companies, the great majority of which were American. The property seized from American individuals and firms was valued at about $1 billion in 1960 dollars. As the United States tightened economic pressure, most punitively by abrogating contracts to purchase Cuban sugar, Soviet Premier Nikita Khrushchev perceptively saw an emerging opportunity. "Castro will have to gravitate to us like an iron filing to a magnet," he said at the time.

The country had been purged of foreign domination by 1960 as Cuba had abruptly shredded its nearly total economic dependence on the United States. The country was in dire financial straits and sorely in need of friends, allies and angels. One promising route back to autonomy and prosperity was for President Castro to visit the United States and the United Nations to seek international recognition and legitimacy for his new government.

Instead of a cordial reception in New York City, however, the bearded hero of Cuba found himself unable even to book a suitable hotel in Manhattan. So he dispatched his entourage and himself to a tumultuous welcome in Harlem, then a poor ghetto brimming with disenfranchised black people. That's called turning a lemon into lemonade, a skill at which he excelled for almost five decades. The next debacle on the trek north was a rude jolt from President Eisenhower. Ike refused to meet with him, and in Washington conspicuously chose to play a round of golf instead. Castro was deflected to the very cordial, very conservative Vice President Richard M. Nixon.

In his September 26, 1960, speech at the United Nations, which lasted some four-and-a-half hours, Castro denounced colonialism and imperialism and was sharply critical of the United States.

An early sign of what was to follow can be gleaned from a comment by Soviet Premier Nikita Khrushchev after meeting with Castro in New York: "I don't know if Fidel Castro is a communist, but I'm a *Fidelista!*" Waiting and watching and probably chuckling in the wings was the dour but skillful foreign minister of the Soviet Union, Anastas Mikoyan. Had he choreographed a scenario for the Soviets to gain a friend and toehold just offshore of the United States at the height of the Cold War, he could not have done better than the script handed to him by the myopic U.S. government.

So Castro went home, pretty ticked off. And calls from Nikita became intense, probably something like this: "Hey, Fidel, we've got buckets of oil (and you've got about none), and you've got buckets of sugar (and we could use some). And by the way, we could sell you our oil at *really low* prices and pay you *really high* prices for your sugar. Subsidy is not a four-letter word, and you sure could use it! Oh, by the way, we have a lot of shiny military hardware that we'd like to send along with some really nice guys who would be your military advisers. An electronic listening post, by the way, would help us both to know more about the Big Bad Wolf to the north."

Along the way, having U.S. companies unceremoniously tossed out of Cuba without compensation was more than a little embarrassing to the U.S. government, whose reaction may have been: "What can we do? Aha! Let's throw an economic blockade around the island, and in no time flat they'll be begging to pay us for the expropriated property and probably inviting us right back in to the rescue. Oh, you say economic blockades are illegal under the U.N. Charter? Well, maybe they weren't really thinking of us."

The Kennedy administration, which took over in January 1961, made a concerted effort to muster international support for the economic embargo. The attempt failed, and the response of the Mexican ambassador to U.S. pressure was typical: "If we publicly declare that Cuba is a threat to our security, 40 million Mexicans will die laughing." A few months earlier, on January 3, 1961, just before the end of the Eisenhower presidency, the United States had broken diplomatic relations with Cuba and closed its Embassy in Havana. (The American economic blockade of Cuban began under Eisenhower in October 1960. With John F. Kennedy in the White House, it was increased incrementally in February 1962, February 1963 and July 1963.)

The pre-Castro Cuba years, during which the Eisenhower administration largely ignored what was happening on the island and looked inward, had given way to the renaissance of Jackie and John F. Kennedy in the White House. In the glamorous transition came some less appealing baggage, like the crazy aunt in the closet. But this one was called plans for a military invasion of Cuba, at a swampy backwater on the southern coast of the island named the Bay of Pigs. Sure, the United States used a fig leaf of foreign mercenaries so that it could plausibly deny involvement – but nobody with an IQ higher than a school zone speed limit seems to have believed that feeble explanation.

Kennedy wasn't so keen on the plan, and at the last minute he failed to provide additional support that the U.S. military assumed would be sent if needed. As it turned out, a *lot* more support would have been essential in order for the 1,500-man invasion to have succeeded. So it failed miserably. It had begun on April 16, 1961, not even three months after JFK took office, and, according to a friend who was a member of Cuba's National Assembly, "It was crushed within 66 hours, under the personal command of Fidel Castro, who had rushed to Playa Giron." Even the locals spontaneously joined the battle. A Cuban veteran explained to me in an interview, "My neighbors and I picked up our machetes and ran to repel the invaders."

The battle plan of the invading force was, to be charitable, far from perfect. Cuban intelligence was well aware of the intentions. And you don't have to be a Napoleon-level military strategist to conclude that enemy planes bombing your airports is a sure sign that something even worse is about to happen soon. Also, U.S. tactics depended on air support that never arrived, on a popular uprising that never materialized, and on capturing the only road through the swamp, which was practically a gridlock of Cuban tanks – including one with Fidel sitting proudly in the cupola – shortly after the invasion began. The invaders suffered an estimated 300 casualties, including those killed or later executed in Cuba.

Kennedy decided to tighten the embargo of Cuba several months after the Bay of Pigs fiasco. The night before doing so he dispatched his press secretary, Pierre Salinger, to buy for him at least 1,000 of his favorite cigars, Cuban-made Uppmanns, which were to be banned under the new restrictions. The next morning Salinger presented Kennedy with 1,200 of those cigars, and Kennedy immediately signed the decree. A Cuban official swore to me that a call was received in Havana from their cigar distributor in Washington reporting the huge sale to the White House. He said the Cubans connected the dots and realized the embargo was about to get worse.

The botched invasion at the Bay of Pigs was a terribly embarrassing start to the Kennedy administration. The surviving 1,2000 invaders were ransomed out of Cuba in late 1962 (for some $53 million of tractors, medicine and food), after spending a year and a half in the miserable prisons of Cuba. But the invasion had scared the willies out of Castro and drove him at a full trot into the outstretched arms of the smiling Soviets. "Hey, maybe you should have some nuclear-tipped missiles on the island to keep the big bad guy from trying any more shenanigans." "OK." "And maybe you should call this new government a *communist* one, since you are kind of left wing and we kind of need an ally in the Caribbean." "OK."

Deteriorating relations between the United States and Cuba stimulated an already remarkable exodus from Cuba, which included both the "Peter Pan" flights and the "Freedom" flights, as described earlier.

# CUBA RISING

Castro had managed a soft landing. Largesse from the Soviets flowed, protection against another U.S. attempt to invade the island seemed firm, and a good start was under way to institutionalize the goals of the Revolution. But whoops, along came a high-flying U.S. reconnaissance plane over Cuba, and it filmed what looked a whole lot like new missile sites. Big ugly missiles that could leap across the Florida Straits in seconds on their way to the population centers of the eastern United States. What followed were 13 very dangerous days in October of 1962.

With its plans well-concealed from public view, the Kennedy administration raced into crisis mode to deal with the unexpected and particularly dangerous threat from what was perceived as a Soviet client state just offshore, with nuclear missiles, at the height of the Cold War.

Military alerts lit up like Christmas trees, the airways became full of crisis, General Curtis LeMay and his Strategic Air Command were *pumped*, diplomats wrung their hands, the media raved, secret back channels were opened between Washington and Moscow, the United Nations convened special sessions, and otherwise normal folks cleared out supermarket shelves and stocked their bomb shelters. American warships and Soviet submarines were having close encounters in the Caribbean, as freighters carrying more Russian missiles approached Cuban waters. In the frenzied urgency to avoid World War III, Castro was left out of the Moscow-Washington loop – although it is claimed by some anonymous Russians that he urged the Soviets to let the missiles fly.

In the midst of the crisis, an American U-2 spy plane was shot down over Cuba by Soviet-controlled ground to air missiles, and the U.S. pilot was killed. It is alleged that Khrushchev and the Kremlin did *not* give orders for this shoot down and that Castro himself pushed the launch button. Understandably, Khrushchev was shaken by this dangerous escalation of the crisis and fear that his generals would launch a nuclear war without orders from the Kremlin.

Given the choice between a nuclear conflagration with possibly the end of life on earth, calmer heads prevailed and the crisis was defused. In the memorable words of then-Secretary of State Dean Rusk, "We're eyeball to eyeball, and I think the other fellow just blinked." An agreement provided that the Soviets would remove their missiles from Cuba, and it included a secret provision that the United States would remove its comparably threatening missiles from its ally Turkey. The Soviets soon pulled their missiles out of Cuba and, after a decent interval, the United States pulled its provocative missiles from its client state Turkey. And, significantly, America promised not to invade Cuba again, although it continued to maintain a military base at Guantanamo Bay at the eastern end of the island, which it maintains to this day.

The Soviets stayed in Cuba and the United States continued its political hostility. Diplomatic relations had been severed, and the United States had presided over the ouster of Cuba from the Organization of American States in 1962. The economic embargo was tightened periodically, including termination of aid to any country that assisted Cuba, prohibiting most U.S. citizens from traveling to Cuba, and freezing Cuban assets in the United States.

Castro focused on domestic challenges while also launching steps to promote leftist revolutions around the world. He began ascending to a leadership role among "non-aligned" nations. It's not crystal clear to me how the definition of "non-aligned" was stretched to include a country that had provided safe haven for Soviet nuclear missiles aimed at the United States. After Cuba supported the Soviet invasion of Czechoslovakia in 1968 and the subsequent occupation of Afghanistan in 1979 through 1989, her facade of non-alignment lay irreparably in tatters.

The Cuban economy showed some signs of life thanks to Soviet generosity, although Fidel still had to mobilize countless thousands of urbanites to go to the countryside to help harvest sugar cane. For sugar had become fundamental to the new economic relationship with the Union of Soviet Socialist Republics. Sending millions of tons of the sweet stuff to the Soviets served as the ostensible rationale for millions of barrels of oil to be sent to Cuba in return.

On the political side, Castro enlisted as a full-fledged cold warrior, supporting Soviet cold war goals, dispatching troops as Soviet proxies to promote revolutionary causes around the world, and welcoming airplane hijackers and other criminals from the States.

A reminder of those mischievous days, when diplomacy was driven by the concept "the enemy of my enemy is my friend," came in January of 2008, with the death of one-time U.S. master spy Philip Agee in Havana. Just a small footnote to that bygone era, Agee had fled the United States in 1975 following many years with the CIA and after authoring a book that compromised many secrets about its spy operations and misdeeds in Latin America. Pursuit by the American government forced him to leave numerous countries before he finally ended up in Cuba during the 1990s. He lived comfortably in Havana, where he ran a small travel agency promoting tourism to Cuba.

The year 1966 proved to be a turning point in several respects. Public outcry in the United States over the Vietnam War was sharply increasing. Nevertheless, President Lyndon Johnson saw fit to sign into law the Cuban Adjustment Act. It enabled Cuban émigrés to secure official U.S. residency status after two years, and it became the first big step in a continuing process of especially favorable treatment of Cubans wishing to settle there. In Cuba, Che Guevara departed for other promising revolutionary prospects in Africa and South America, including Bolivia, where he was tracked down and killed in 1967, with the not very discreet involvement of the CIA. Did this icon of the Cuban Revolution leave because the island was too small for two "alpha" males? Had Che become disillusioned by the extensive Soviet presence and influence on the island? Did he become weary of being a bureaucrat with responsibility for an economy in chaos? Did he long for new mountains, new jungles, new revolutions to foster? Maybe all of the above. It's doubtful that we will ever know for sure, but it may well be because he was a pure bottom-up revolutionary whose passion was the liberation of oppressed people.

As the 1960s rolled onward, the United States was absorbed in the domestic civil rights struggle, experienced the horror of the assassinations of the Reverend Martin Luther King, Jr. and Senator Robert F. Kennedy, "won" the space race with the Soviets by landing a man on the moon on July 20, 1969, had the fabric of its society shredded by controversy over the war in Vietnam, and saw numerous U.S. aircraft hijacked to Cuba. Meanwhile, in accord with his self-proclaimed responsibility to foster and support revolutionary causes, and with more than a little Soviet urging, Castro enlarged Cuban support for leftist revolutions around the world. This would ultimately develop into military action or mischief-making in at least 25 countries. Close to home it included support for anti-American agitators and terrorists in Puerto Rico for many years before the United States was able to confirm it. And later it resulted in a dangerous face-off with American troops on the Caribbean island of Grenada.

The early 1970s saw a tightening of the relationship between Cuba and Moscow, growing Cuban revolutionary activity abroad, and a slight thaw in Cuban-American relations that included an anti-hijacking agreement in 1973. Cuba rescinded that agreement in 1977, after only four years, but the two governments proceeded with minor agreements on fishing and offshore boundaries and, more importantly, a small step toward reestablishment of diplomatic relations was taken. Each country opened an "Interests Section" in the capital of the other, under the auspices of the Swiss embassies.

The mini-thaw continued. The Cuban government released about 3,600 political prisoners from their gulag, and steps were agreed to enable Cubans who had fled to return to visit relatives. But as evidence of Cuban adventurism abroad grew, the thaw began to freeze up once again. Modest air links between Havana and Miami were ended by President Reagan in 1982, and U.S. restrictions on travel to Cuba were tightened.

Perhaps Castro's most ambitious (and disastrous) offshore military adventure was dispatching 50,000 Cuban troops and military advisers to the west African country of Angola starting in 1975. It came at a very high price.

Angola became Cuba's Vietnam, a military quagmire. Conscripted troops grew dependent on drugs, and there was significant domestic unhappiness as thousands of young soldiers returned home in body bags. More than a few Cubans, including a woman I know, paid bribes to keep their sons out of harm's way. Sadly, Angola was merely another Cold War misadventure. The opposing antagonists were certainly funded by the United States and the Soviets, as they shed their blood while shadow boxing on the world stage for their patrons.

Castro's decision to get involved in revolutionary battles in Africa brought a quick end to secret talks about normalizing U.S.-Cuba relations. During the administration of President Gerald Ford, these promising discussions were at the hand of Henry Kissinger. His earlier success establishing a constructive dialogue with the People's Republic of China matured into a mutually beneficial relationship that was affirmed decades later by President Clinton, who said, "America has more influence in China with an outstretched hand than with a clenched fist." Kissinger naively believed that similar headway with Cuba would be easy. During 1974-1977, very discreet talks between the governments showed encouraging signs, including Castro's return of ransom funds from the hijacking of a U.S. airplane to

Cuba. Soon, however, growing Cuban adventurism in Angola derailed this dialogue.

Predictably, the United States ranted about Cuba's irresponsible military meddling overseas as a "pawn" of the Soviet Union. And it quietly held out the possibility of improved bilateral relations if Cuba were to bring the troops home, which it finally did a few years later.

During the presidency of Jimmy Carter, once again a dialogue with a view to normalization of relations took place. And once again, it was derailed by Castro's proclivity for military adventures overseas, that time (1978) because Cuban troops were being sent to Ethiopia.

A dangerous flashpoint in Cuba-U.S. relations occurred on the tiny Caribbean island of Grenada, however unlikely a place for that to happen. In 1979, a *coup d'etat* resulted in the establishment of a distinctly left-wing government there. It was followed by another coup in 1983 and the murder of the former head of state, Maurice Bishop. The United States sent a military force, ostensibly to protect and evacuate American medical students at St. George's University. U.S. officials were sharply aware that over 600 Cuban workers and military personnel were on the island engaged in the construction of a 9,000-foot runway at a new airport. Hand wringers were concerned that such a runway was far beyond the needs of a tiny tourist island but that it could easily accommodate long-range Cuban and Soviet aircraft and, potentially, a Soviet military base. In the era of President Ronald Reagan, such an outcome was considered to be intolerable.

A handful of Cuban soldiers obviously were incapable of repelling some 7,000 American troops, although 25 died trying. The United States suffered 19 deaths, and Grenada 45. Virtually all of the Cuban officers and non-coms who returned to Cuba after this dismal episode were swiftly routed to the battlefront in Angola – reportedly all with demotions to enlisted men's status.

The U.S. economic embargo of Cuba warrants a closer look. At the height of the Cold War, after the United States was unceremoniously thrown out of a nearby traditional client state, *perhaps* it could be understood in the context of the era – although economic embargoes were and remain a violation of international law. Annual votes in the United Nations have confirmed the opposition of the world community to the embargo. In October 2009, only three U.N. members supported the embargo while 187 opposed it. The three were the United States, Israel (to whom the United States has sent over $100 billion in aid during the past 50 years), and the "powerhouse" nation of Palau. Ironically, the underlying rationale for the embargo was to isolate Cuba, but the result clearly has been the isolation of the United States on this issue.

The embargo, unquestionably, has been brutally effective in disrupting the economy of Cuba, although it has completely failed in its primary goal of toppling the Castro regimes. It is comprehensive, although sometimes leaky, and it allows for the export to Cuba of only a limited number of food and medical items to the benefit of American exporters. Its enforcement has ranged from harsh criminal penalties to a lot of spankings and an occasional laugh. Since there is not much that is amusing about the blockade, I cannot resist relating the most absurd and humorous example I know, as detailed in Christopher Wren's excellent work *Cuba Handbook*.

During the mid 1990s, a piano tuner from California was determined to ship some used pianos to Cuba. The U.S. Department of Commerce, however, ruled that would be a violation of the embargo. So the enterprising fellow jokingly queried whether the pianos might have a military purpose. Believe me, I have heard some awful piano players, but none among them even remotely threatened U.S. foreign policy. When the bureaucrats, after due diligence, determined that the pianos did *not* constitute a military threat, their shipment to Cuba was approved. They were shipped, and he followed them to Cuba to tune them for the astronomical sum of $1 apiece. After all of that, another foot was to fall. Upon his return to the United States he received a notice that he was to be fined $10,000 because he had received income from Cubans! Well, be thankful that we don't always get as much government as we pay for.

So what is Cuba's beef about the embargo? She cannot import good and inexpensive products from the States, including replacement parts; she cannot export any of her products to the huge U.S. market; her import and export costs for alternatives are significantly increased due to higher shipping and insurance costs; tourism by American citizens is prohibited, costing Cuba billions in lost income; cruise ships that dock in Cuba are effectively barred from coming to the United States; investment and technology from the United States cannot be sent to Cuba, and the United States has barred Cuba from entry into various international trade and finance organizations, denying Cuba much needed low-interest funds for development purposes. You can certainly understand Cuba's objections.

Cuba's former Foreign Minister Felipe Roque estimated in 2006 that the cumulative damage resulting from the economic blockade had been $86 billion cumulatively, and increasing at a rate of about $4 billion per year. Such numbers are mind-numbing. Although the embargo does not prohibit other countries from investing and trading freely with Cuba, the reality has been a chilling (if not frigid) impact as the United States has applied major arm-twisting to foreign governments who allow its companies to engage with Cuba. In one more of the countless ironies about Cuba, the Israeli government has refused to succumb to such U.S. pressure, despite being a committed supporter of the embargo. Israeli companies have a large, growing and profitable presence in Cuba. The embargo, however, is not simply a poster child of diplomacy gone awry. It impacts real people in terrible ways.

During a tour of a hospital in Matanzas Province, I recall passing through the maternity ward, where only one of six baby incubators was in working order. I asked why. "It is not possible to buy replacement parts for those U.S.-made incubators," was the response. Do you suppose it is the intention of even the most hard-line proponent of the embargo to deny treatment to Cuban babies? I am sure it is not. I am equally sure that has been a demonstrable tragic result.

I could cite a litany of hardships the embargo has levied on the Cuban people. It has worked all too well. Perhaps one of the most powerful of its results, however, has been quite the opposite of what the U.S. government intended. It has enabled the leadership of Cuba to lay blame for *every* imaginable domestic failure and hardship at the doorstep its giant neighbor to the north. America has become the bogeyman, the root of all evil. By allowing itself to be defined in these terms and to be demonized in the eyes of the world, the United States likely has done more to strengthen the position of the Castros in Cuba and more to weaken our efforts to mobilize world opinion against them than any other path the United States might have followed.

I recall a splendid example of the Americans taking the fall for what was obviously a local Cuban mistake. While driving from Havana to the south coast through a massive citrus growing region, the Cuban guide told us with passionate conviction that some months ago the CIA had flown over and dropped obnoxious orange- and grapefruit-devouring bugs from a low-flying airplane. As this was the late 1990s and did not seem entirely plausible, we asked how she reached that bizarre conclusion.

"Just look out the window," she said as we drove past a grove of several acres where, indeed, not a bit of vegetation remained alive. Egad, it was terrible. All that had been green was now brown and withered. But it also was perfectly confined to an area bounded by dirt service roads through the orchards. "Didn't a single bug manage to crawl across the road to chow down on leaves a few yards further away?" I asked. "Was the pilot, flying at night, so darn good that not a single bug drifted across the highway on the way down?" As an act of international goodwill I didn't press the point to excess. It was patently obvious, especially to several of us who were familiar with farming and orchard sprayers, that some humble farm worker loaded the sprayer with a defoliant by mistake. And then he proceeded to perfectly spray one orchard block exactly within the boundaries of the service roads. Nonetheless, the United States and the CIA took another whack because in the battle between David and Goliath, mean ole Goliath must be responsible for any and all misdeeds.

After nearly a half-century, the embargo persists. It has been mightily effective, but not airtight. Can one find Coca-Cola in Havana? Easily. Can one buy Eveready batteries there? Everywhere. And how about the breakfast cereals Cocoa Puffs and Fruit Loops? Yours for the asking. Silly exceptions to the rule notwithstanding, the trade embargo has severely handicapped the economy of Cuba.

Although virtually unknown to most Americans, there are two small exceptions to the embargo that are worth noting. The U.S. Treasury Department issued an opinion in 1994 that American companies and individuals may invest in Cuba *indirectly*. No, I cannot waltz into Havana and set up a business. But I *can* legally invest in a company from a third country that does business in Cuba, provided that my share is not a controlling interest. So, if I wanted to buy stock in a Canadian or Dutch company, for example, which was building a telephone system or growing mangoes in Cuba, I could do so. I would not be surprised if some forward-looking American firms already have such investments on the island. As described earlier, it is also permitted for many food and medical items to be sold to Cuba by U.S. firms.

# CUBA RISING

In effect, both countries had thrown down the gauntlet with severed diplomatic relations, adversarial roles in the Cold War, and the embargo. Then it got worse.

CHAPTER 16

BRIDGING TWO MILLENNIUMS

Late in the 1970s, Cuba continued to stir the revolutionary pot around the world, with about 25,000 troops sent to be engaged in turmoil in Ethiopia starting in 1977. Perhaps in recognition of Cuba's agitation in opposition to practically any U.S. postures, Cuba was selected as the chair of the worldwide Non-Aligned Movement in 1979. Understandably, this was a great achievement for Fidel Castro, burnishing his credentials as a significant player on the world stage and collectively thumbing the nose of the Third World at Western global powers.

The domestic scene, however, continued to be restive, and in 1980 came the infamous Mariel Boatlift. Reacting to some misstatements by Peruvian officials in Havana, and a welcome offer by Jimmy Carter, an estimated 125,000 disgruntled Cubans sailed, paddled and floated their way to U.S. shores. There, under U.S. law, they were entitled to stay. Those who made it, that is. There was a tragic and huge loss of life on that perilous journey. It is said that Fidel was not entirely unhappy with this great exodus. It served to "purge" the island of disenchanted citizens

271

and it is alleged that Fidel emptied many jails and institutions of thousands of "undesirables" who had been detained

As the 1980s moved along, they were characterized by a comparatively quiet period in U.S.-Cuba relations. In Cuba, the economy was inching forward thanks largely to huge Soviet aid and subsidies. In fact, most Cubans recall that period as one of relative abundance. In the U.S. Jimmy Carter gave way to Ronald Reagan as president, and Cuba receded in the minds of most Americans, as did America in the minds of most Cubans.

Memories of the Revolution, however, continued to be sharply in the minds of Cubans both in Havana and Miami, as well as in Washington. The expatriates continued with their tirades against Castro, and more. In the "more" category, activist counter-revolutionaries, along with the CIA, did their best to destabilize the regime in Havana. Among the most notorious of their exploits was the downing of a Cubana airliner in 1976, with the deaths of all 73 people aboard. This heinous crime is widely attributed to Luis Posada Carriles, a notorious anti-Castro expatriate widely believed to have been on the payroll of the CIA. Other "terrorist" acts against Cuba included bombings, mainly at tourist hotels in Havana in 1997 that resulted in the death an Italian tourist and injuries to another dozen tourists. Tourism to Cuba plunged the following year, including a decline of more than one-third from Italy, where the attacks had extensive media coverage.

Another Cuban exile who was all but certainly involved in CIA-instigated anti-Cuban violence is Orlando Bosch. He has been accused of several bombings and attacks in Miami and elsewhere in the United States, in offices, consulates, and airlines related to tourism to Cuba and involvement with Posada in the bombing of the doomed Cubana aircraft. Bosch has served some prison time in the United States and elsewhere, but he had remained free in the States for decades.

No one has ever been tried or convicted of these crimes, although it is widely speculated that Posada and Bosch were intimately involved. To the outrage of Cuba, Posada was allowed entry into the United States in 2006, charged neither with murder nor terrorism, but merely with some document irregularities that were quickly resolved. The George W. Bush administration failed to arrest or prosecute Posada as a terrorist, despite the stark fact that the Department of Justice has described him, in official documents, as "an unrepentant criminal and admitted mastermind of terrorist plots and attacks on tourist sites." It would appear that there is merit to the Cuban claim that the United States is providing a safe haven for at least this terrorist. The lengths to which the CIA went to disrupt the government in Cuba in general, and to harm or even assassinate Fidel Castro in particular, have become legendary. Castro claims that the number of U.S.-instigated plots to assassinate him exceeds 600. More like a Three Stooges film than a spy thriller, those failed attempts including exploding cigars and a foot powder that was supposed to cause his beard to fall off. They ranged from the ridiculous to the sublime. During one of his many anti-American tirades, Castro exclaimed in 2007, "I am not the first nor will I be the last that Bush has ordered to be killed."

Despite the many real and imagined threats on his life, Castro has moved about Havana with relative ease and little fuss. I have seen him travel down beautiful Fifth Avenue in Miramar, en route to his office at Revolution Square from his compound in Siboney, with a simple police escort of a vehicle in front and behind his modest limousine. Not surprisingly, the route briefly was cleared of other traffic during his commute.

During the eight years of the Reagan presidency, there was predictably little movement in Cuba-U.S. relations. Except, that is, perhaps in reverse. In 1985, Radio Marti went on the air, broadcasting anti-Castro propaganda from Miami. Of course, the Cubans largely blocked the signal almost immediately. Are the millions of dollars spent to achieve a listenership hovering around five per cent in Cuba a good investment on behalf of American taxpayers? Does the fact that the Radio Marti board did not meet for over six years, and included a man who had been dead for 11 years, suggest a lack of oversight? Shouldn't there exist some measurable achievement after about 25 years and over $600 million expended, other than providing patronage to the exile community in Miami? Or is it a waste of money? Well, maybe not a complete waste. You see, the overseers and operators of the broadcasts were, practically to a man, anti-Cuban expatriates. In fact, Mas Canosa, founder and head of the CANF (Cuban American National Foundation), was abundantly rewarded with an appointment as chairman of the President's Advisory Board on Cuba Broadcasting, a position he occupied until his death in 1997. His son subsequently was appointed to the position.

A vast infusion of federal funds into that politically conservative community of ex-Cubans, mainly in metropolitan Miami, proved to pay significant dividends, not the least of which was George W. Bush's victory in the presidential contest of 2000. He prevailed in the controversial Florida tally by 537 votes while carrying the Cuban exile vote by a four-to-one margin.

Despite, or because of, the activities of Radio Marti and Television Marti, yet additional tens of millions of dollars were devoted to both in the following years, despite the signal having been virtually completely blocked by the government of Cuba. At best, as is the case of Radio Marti, neutral observers have described TV Marti's work as substandard, imbalanced and sometimes vulgar. And how does it impact its viewers in Cuba? Well, that may never be known. Neither I nor anyone I know has ever been able to see so much as a nanosecond of TV Marti in Cuba. Such are the results of more than $39 million invested in its broadcasting to Cuba in 2008 alone.

In addition to the vast sums spent on dubious broadcasting to Cuba, more hundreds of millions of dollars have been earmarked for funding pro-dissident groups in Cuba, administered by the U.S. Department of State and the Agency for International Development (AID). These funds appear to have followed a similar path to Miami. As they say, "Follow the money."

The road to Havana always seems to go through Miami. In reality, only a miniscule portion of the total funds actually reaches dissidents in Cuba. A critical report by the U.S. Government Accountability Office in 2006 cited expenditures on leather coats, cashmere sweaters, crabmeat, Godiva chocolates and even a mountain bike. I have difficulty picturing a dissident in Havana bumping along the Malecon on his mountain bike, wearing his leather jacket and munching chocolates.

During the Reagan administration, in the context of pandering to conservatives on Cuba policy, the United States established four preconditions to improving relations with Cuba. The island nation would have to end its support for revolutions in Central America, bring its troops home from Angola, reduce its close relations with the Soviet Union, and improve its human rights record. To the surprise of many, Cuba did all four. It was withdrawing from foreign adventures anyway, the Soviets left Cuba, and there were occasional releases of dissidents from Cuban prisons.

Then along came the presidency of George H.W. Bush, who moved the goalposts. In addition to the Reagan laundry list, Bush said Cuba also must take meaningful steps toward a market economy, reduce the size of its armed forces, and hold free elections under international supervision. Message sent from Washington. Message received clearly in Havana: These guys have no real intention of starting a dialogue.

The decade of the 1990s was both cruel and unusual for Cuba, largely and catastrophically as a result of the collapse of the Soviet empire. A simplified but defensible view is that the United States, while Reagan was president, simply outspent the Soviets on military hardware and drove them into political bankruptcy. As a consequence, I believe the successor government of Russia turned inward and swiftly ended its massive subsidies of Cuba, whose dependence on the former Soviet Union comprised about 80 percent of Cuba's international economic activity.

What followed, known as the Special Period in Cuba, lasted beyond the 1990s and was characterized by massive shifts in its domestic economy and in its global economic relations. Although Cuba had dispatched about 1,500 troops to meddle in Nicaragua, and a lesser number to prop up a left-leaning regime in Grenada, that era of global activism had come to an end. Not with a bang, not even with a whimper.

As Cuba continued to struggle, hard-liners were thriving in Miami and Washington. In 1992, Congress passed an additional punitive measure against Cuba, the Cuban Democracy Act. The legislation enacted penalties against American companies whose offshore subsidiaries might be tempted to do business with Cuba and, also of great consequence, it prohibited ships that had docked in Cuba from visiting any U.S. port during the next six months. Among its effects, cruise ships that might tap into the potentially lucrative Cuban market were effectively barred from doing so. The legislation was quickly dubbed the Torricelli Bill, invoking the name of the New Jersey congressman who led it to passage. Interestingly, Robert Torricelli had visited Cuba just four years earlier and had reacted quite favorably. Until, that is, Jorge Mas Canosa, head of the ultra-hard-line CANF in Miami, got not only Torricelli's ear but also into the habit of making generous campaign contributions to him.

A dire domestic economy gave rise to widespread discontent and even to rioting in Havana in 1994. Shortages of fuel led to numerous blackouts and the shutdown of most transportation. People went hungry as the Gross National Product (GNP) contracted by at least one-third. Castro actually took to the streets himself to try to calm the madding crowds. The government responded by tolerating the exodus of an estimated 35,000 Cuban rafters. More importantly, to stimulate an economic rebound, Castro approved the humiliating step of allowing the *Yanqui* dollar to serve as currency in Cuba, allowed the expansion of small-scale private enterprises, and adopted a huge push to promote the formerly discouraged foreign tourism to Cuba.

The exodus of this additional tsunami of rafters headed to Florida triggered a swift and positive response from the Cuban and American governments. Belatedly, as this had been the worst humanitarian crisis at least since the Mariel Boatlift in 1980, agreement was reached only a month later that provided for the legal migration of at least 20,000 Cubans to the United States annually. Perhaps this was a signal from Havana in response to positive, if subtle, overtures from the Clinton administration.

A modest foundation was developed on which meaningful progress could have been made between the two adversaries. But it was to go up, literally, in a puff of smoke fewer than 18 months later. In February of 1996, the Cuban Air Force, unquestionably with direct orders from Fidel Castro, shot down two small private planes that had been violating Cuban airspace and dropping anti-government pamphlets over Havana. Three American citizens and a Cuban resident of the United States were killed in their efforts on behalf of the anti-Cuban organization Brothers to the Rescue. Although there had been numerous prior flights and warnings to their pilots, the shoot-down shocked the American public. The resulting outcry resulted directly in Congress, only a month later, passing the Helms-Burton Act that added further restrictions to the U.S. embargo. With a sharp sense of *déjà vu*, constructive steps by the governments were derailed.

The Helms-Burton Act, despite an uproar from virtually all governments that traded with Cuba, extended parts of its application to foreign companies. Further, it codified U.S. opposition to Cuban membership in international financial institutions, which denied Cuba access to desperately needed funds from the World Bank, International Monetary Fund and others. It also contained a variety of additional disagreeable provisions, such as proscribing that the United States would not recognize any Cuban government led by Fidel or Raul Castro. Perhaps the most important provision was to lift control of the embargo from the White House and place it with the more politically volatile Congress. To understand how the conduct of U.S. foreign policy, which is assigned to the executive branch of government in the Constitution, can be blithely shifted to the legislative branch, I ask you to consult with your local constitutional scholar. Because I sure can't explain it.

Foreign policy wonks, as well as the bill's authors, were shocked that President Clinton would sign such a piece of legislation that disrupted relations with even our closest allies, simply to appease a tiny special interest group in Miami. He privately described the embargo at the time as a "foolish, pandering failure." But Clinton had received millions in campaign contributions from Florida, much of it from hard-line anti-Cubans. And the shooting down of the planes offshore of Havana provided the necessary political cover and momentum to take another whack at the Castro regime.

The political consequences of the downing of the plane were enormous, but there also were unprecedented legal and financial repercussions. The families of the victims sued Cuba, and several years later they were awarded $188 million from frozen Cuban assets in the United States, which they later collected. Looking beyond the headlines, this startling outcome resulted from an executive order from President Clinton during his last days in office. Payback time. To ingratiate himself with certain folks, he ordered that this settlement go to the front of the line of claims against Cuba, many of which dated back to the era when the claimants' property was expropriated in 1959. The government of Cuba was awfully unhappy about the outcome and took a variety of reciprocally antagonistic steps that further accelerated the downward spiral of bilateral relations.

Reaction to Helms-Burton in Havana was predictable outrage. Castro dined out on the additional U.S. restrictions for months, emphasizing that not only was the embargo itself illegal but also that extending it to apply to actions by foreign companies added insult and injury to insult and injury. Privately, it may have been another matter. This enormous flap, caused by the United States, enabled Castro to divert attention from calamitous problems at home by heaping scorn, headlines and blame for those problems, once again, on the United States.

Next came a poster child in the political barrages lobbed back and forth between Havana and Washington: Elian Gonzalez, a 6-year-old boy who was one of three survivors of a group of rafters who fled Cuba for U.S. shores in November 1999. His mother was among those who perished. Distant relatives in Miami "adopted" the boy and refused to return him to his father in Cuba. The marches and diatribe and propaganda flowed ever so freely in both Havana and Miami, greatly compounded by American politicians pandering for support in their home districts in anticipation of the upcoming presidential election. The melodrama was exploited to the point of "Elian fatigue" across the country.

After the 11th Circuit Court blocked the return of the child to Cuba, a state magistrate approved the taking of Elian, and he was picked up in an early-hours raid. There was an ugly scene of him being "liberated" by federal officers. A federal appeals court upheld a "no asylum" hearing, the U.S. Supreme Court rejected an appeal, and Elian returned to Cuba with his father, who had been flown to Florida.

An impartial observer might well conclude that this episode was a propaganda victory for Cuba, cleverly orchestrated by Fidel Castro, whose angry bearded face was, for most of seven months, supplanted by the sweet smile of young, playful Elian. The adamancy and rhetorical excesses of the Cuban-American community, in demanding that a youngster should not be returned to his father, severely undermined the credibility and support for the hard-liners in Miami. Their absolute intolerance of dissenting views, ironically, rivaled no one more than their archenemy, Fidel Castro. As a result of their excessive zeal and mindless defense of an indefensible position, their influence in U.S. political circles has diminished and never recovered.

Among the most remarkable responses of the Cuban government was to erect Dignity Plaza, a protest park next to the American Embassy building along the Malecon. It was constructed practically overnight (in a land where getting a pothole patched can take *years*), with seating for thousands, lighting and sound systems. Among its most endearing features is a bigger-than-life statue of national icon Jose Marti. He stands heroically with a baby clutched to his breast in his left arm while his right arm is pointing accusingly at the embassy building about a hundred yards away. Of course, the message is clear: "Don't mess with our kids, you rats!" But after little Elian was returned to his father, and the political flap receded, Cuban pundits began to explain that Marti is pointing to the building and saying, "That's where you get your U.S. visas."

Interestingly, a potential repeat of an Elian Gonzalez-type controversy started in 2005 but was amicably resolved in 2007. A young Cuban girl immigrated to the United States, was taken in by foster parents in Miami, and the girl's Cuban father sought (and was granted) custody. No fuss, no political rhetoric, posturing or headlines – seemingly a routine custody issue that was resolved in the courts. What a difference eight years made.

Several months after the political tremors over Elian subsided in 2000, I happened to be in Cardenas, hometown of the Gonzalez family, with a small group of visiting Americans. Not exactly inadvertently, we decided to have a meal in the restaurant where Juan Miguel Gonzalez was employed. Following our meal he graciously came out from the kitchen to greet us after we jokingly passed the word to him that we were taking full credit for the return of his son from the clutches of his Miami relatives. "I am grateful to the American people for helping me have my son returned," he recited in a way that suggested it was far from the first time that he had said so, more likely the zillionth. Juan Miguel appeared to be a pleasant and uncomplicated fellow delighted to be out of the international spotlight.

The dawn of the millennium was anything but a dawn of a new day in the persistent Cuba-U.S. melodrama. Less dependent on computers than most countries of the world, Cuba showed little concern about the predicted chaos of computer failures and breakdown of automated systems around the planet as the new millennium ticked into place. But it also had fewer programmers capable of revising defective software. While predictions of doom proved to be unfounded, a few glitches were evident briefly in Havana. I recall, for example, seeing the early January 2000 issues of the newspaper *Granma* that continued to show the year as 1999.

All too soon came the nightmare known simply as 9/11. The world's greatest bastion of liberty had come under a diabolical attack from those whose beliefs were antithetical to most of the civilized world. Of course, this horrific act was committed not by militant communists, but rather by Islamic fundamentalists. Upon learning of the magnitude of this catastrophe, of the deaths of 3,000 innocent victims, Fidel Castro led a procession of tens of thousands of Cubans to the U.S. mission to lay a wreath and express condolences. Interestingly, if not ironically, Fidel – demonstrably a past supporter of anti-U.S. terrorist acts in Puerto Rico – publicly condemned the terrorists and terrorism and offered to send medical assistance to New York. He went even further later by expressing his approval of the use of American facilities at the Guantanamo Bay military base to house accused Islamic terrorists and combatants. Unfortunately, these possibly significant gestures were met with no response from the new conservative-dominated White House of George W. Bush. After all, his presidency was made possible *only* with a victory in Florida, and that victory was attributed to overwhelming support from the anti-Castro Cuban-American community in Miami.

The year 2002 was to present another harsh blow to the Castro regime. Russia agreed, after many years of pressure from the United States, to close its electronic eavesdropping facility at Lourdes in the outskirts of Havana since 1964. Annual rental income from the Russians to the Cubans totaled an estimated $200 million dollars, which would be sorely missed. The intelligence value of the site may have been of importance to Cuba, but it had shrunk to inconsequential to the new post-Soviet Russia.

In a development that may have surprised both sides, ripe with antagonists and hard-liners, retired U.S. General Barry McCaffrey visited Havana later in 2002. His visit was ostensibly as former President Clinton's "drug czar," to evaluate posturing by some in the United States that Cuba was facilitating drug trafficking as a transshipment point for illegal drugs moving from South America to the streets of the United States. After a lengthy meeting with the Castro brothers, McCaffrey indicated that he believed Cuba was not involved in the drug trade and, in fact, was trying to interdict it. If so, it can be assumed that an agreement for cooperative efforts on drug trade interdiction would be a likely part of a thaw in relations between the two governments.

Perhaps more unexpected were McCaffrey's statements that Cuba was not providing a safe haven for terrorist organizations nor did it represent a military threat to the United States. Indeed, the Cuban military had shrunk to a mere shadow of its heydays of worldwide adventurism. I have never seen more than a handful of soldiers in Cuba's cities or countryside. Most of the active military, in fact, is engaged in farming or various commercial enterprises. McCaffrey's comments, which certainly confirmed my impressions, predictably had no impact whatsoever on the Bush administration, which was brimming with hostility toward Cuba.

Once again, in the 2005 aftermath of Hurricane Katrina, Castro extended an olive branch – or was it simply one more masterful public relations ploy? He offered to send to the disaster area as many as 1,600 Cuban physicians and medical personnel. The response of the Bush administration was negative. Moving from merely ungrateful to provocative, in the same year the Bush administration formed a "transition team" focused within the Department of State, supposedly to address issues related to a regime change in Havana. The bureaucrats instead came up with a recitation of longstanding politically driven demands that Cuba radically change its form of government, and only then would a new relationship become possible. Especially in matters of diplomacy, it seems to me rather disingenuous to establish as a pre-condition that your negotiating partner completely fold his hand before discussions even begin.

Yet another enduring controversy in the tangled mess of Cuba-U.S. relations is known in the States as the "Cuban Five" spy case and in Havana as "The Five Patriotic Heroes." The spin doctors have really earned their pay over this one. In 2001, a Miami court convicted five Cuban exiles of spying and conspiracy in Florida on behalf of the government of Cuba. They received comparatively harsh sentences to prison, ranging upwards from 15 years, including three who received life sentences. There is little disagreement that they were spying, but huge disagreement over its significance.

The five had infiltrated various militant Cuban exile groups, including Brothers to the Rescue, which had been sending aircraft to make provocative flights over Havana, and the CANF, which had been promoting mischief in Cuba for many years. They apparently also had been keeping tabs on a U.S. naval base in the Florida Keys.

While the Cuban government had been merely in a rage about the arrest and trial of the five, their convictions resulted in public and official outrage in Havana not seen since the enormous fuss over Elian Gonzalez. The National Assembly convened a special session to honor them, and Castro went ballistic and promised, "The political battle has just begun.

They will return," and the year 2002 was officially designated as "The Year of the Heroes Held Prisoner by the Empire." The five are revered in Cuba for their sacrifice in defending the motherland by learning the plans of the "terrorist" exile groups. One correspondent in Havana quoted a man on the street who seemed to have summed up the Cuban view of the U.S. position rather succinctly: "Lying bastards!"

In 2005, a working group of the U.N. Human Rights Commission issued a finding that the sentencing of the five was "arbitrary" and requested that the U.S. government "adopt the necessary steps to remedy this situation." At the time it failed to gain any response from the United States other than allegations of bias and meddling by the commission. Four years later, in 2009, one of the men sentenced to life had his sentence reduced to 22 years by a federal judge.

Havana is blanketed with posters, signs, leaflets and billboards proclaiming the five as national heroes. The United States has once again conveniently provided Castro with a cause to unify his country on a wave of patriotism and, not incidentally, to distract the natives from some of their daily woes. To the extent that past may be prologue, it is reasonable to expect that, in the course of an inevitable rapprochement between the two governments, these convicted spies might find their way back to Cuba a bit early.

The history of Cuba-U.S. relations has been pockmarked by too frequent cases of an accommodating gesture by one side being derailed by politically unacceptable antagonistic acts of the other. The collapse of deft diplomat Henry Kissinger's secret talks having been extinguished by Castro's escalating military involvement in Africa was but one example. In April of 2008 another derailment occurred. The spring of that year had been punctuated by Raul Castro's announcements of numerous small but meaningful steps to thaw the Cuban economy from its ice-bound rigidity and enlarge rights of the Cuban people. Previously prohibited consumer items were permitted, more land was disbursed to private farmers, and the apartheid policy in the tourist sector was dropped. Admittedly, these were long past due baby steps, but they conveyed an important message of change.

Then came a Miami court decision awarding $253 million to the family of a Cuban-American who died in a Cuban prison in the 1970s after being convicted in 1959 of assisting in the escape of a fellow Cuban to Miami in 1959. The relatives of the deceased man would receive little, if any, of the award because Cuban assets frozen in the United States had been previously drained by similar absurd Miami verdicts. The only significant result was likely to be yet another disincentive for the regime in Cuba to be responsive to U.S. criticism or overtures.

During these many decades of turbulent relations between the two nations, it is clear that some sort of "relations" or political dialogue actually has existed. How can this have been in the absence of diplomatic relations that were broken in 1961? Sometimes, as during the missile crisis, back channels worthy of a spy thriller were used. The absence of a direct diplomatic channel during this period gave rise to the "hot line" between Moscow and Washington, which was rather inexpensive insurance against another world war. For the most part, however, a gigantic fig leaf has been used to enable bilateral contacts when needed. Courtesy of the government of Switzerland, each country has a diplomatic presence in the other's capital known as an "Interests Section" of the Swiss Embassy. In reality, the two nations do not have diplomatic relations, but the top representative in each country has the personal rank of ambassador, although they are know simply as the "head" of their Interests Section.

The U.S. mission is in the same high-rise oceanfront building that was our embassy prior to the Revolution. It sits by the ocean, along the Malecon, with the only diversion from its "tombstone style" architecture being a small balcony that adorns the office of our ambassador. Perhaps symbolically, that small balcony looks northward to the United States that is only about 100 miles away. Also, symbolically, in the department of not-very-subtle-expressions-of-grouchiness, Castro sent a special little signal to the States by building a police station on an empty lot next door.

In the context of such "fig leaf" diplomacy, the U.S. Interests Section often provides briefings to visiting groups of Americans. Suffice it to note that our diplomatic corps in Havana has virtually no wiggle room for bilateral discussions, and briefings there are perfunctory, prolonged and predictable. Those who favor a relaxation of tensions between the countries have been, until recently, met with cold stares.

On one memorable occasion I attempted to facilitate a microscopic advance in the frozen dialogue. I was in Havana with a small group of visitors from the States and had been advised that Cuban officials and U.S. diplomats *could* be in the same room in an unofficial private setting. So I organized a modest luncheon, ostensibly for the briefing of the visitors. The day before, both sides had been informed and apparently had permission from their respective governments to attend. I was smiling broadly in anticipation.

Came the hour and came the group of U.S. officials, relaxed and enjoying a little reception before lunch. Minutes later the Cuban officials arrived, entered the room, and collectively emitted a gasp that might have been audible across the city. It did not require an expert in international relations to recognize that I was in *big* trouble! As happens all too frequently in spats among nations as well as people, apparently there was some misunderstanding or miscommunication. The Cubans arrived with the marching orders to participate *only if there were no U.S. diplomats present*. They had been under the impression that it would be a private lunch with private U.S. citizens. So, without a word, they turned on their heels, faces grim, and marched right back out the way they had come. Someone was going to get spanked and for sure it was I. Despite my good intentions, it took years for me to restore confidence and rebuild those relationships. Anyway, lunch was pretty good.

Cuban diplomats in Washington operate from a grand old mansion that was their embassy in years past. The beehive of activity within is masked by the quiet grandeur of the expansive marble reception area where visitors are greeted. And that's as far as I have ever gotten, as visitors are consigned to meetings in little rooms off to the sides of the reception area and seldom, if ever, are invited to the inner sanctums.

I've tried to learn how much of a bilateral dialogue actually takes place. It seemed promising to learn that the U.S. diplomatic corps in Havana is the largest of any country. And Cuba has more diplomats in its building in Washington than in any other capital in the world. But hardly a bilateral word is spoken.

Although there has not been much diplomacy taking place, as political relations have ebbed and flowed over the decades some agreements have been reached. For example, in 1977 and 1978, during Jimmy Carter's presidency, the two adversaries signed understandings on maritime boundaries, fishing rights, divided families, and political prisoners. Also, since the 1970s, U.S. and Cuban meteorologists have been cooperating to monitor tropical storms and hurricanes that could impact either or both countries. Bilateral talks about immigrations issues continued for years until they were suspended by the Bush administration in 2003.

Despite engaging in only a meager dialogue, both countries are sharply aware of the importance of the relationship, and each has astute diplomats who are keen observers of the other's political scene. A Cuban amigo posted to the Cuban Interests Section in Washington was knowledgeable in extraordinary detail about both congressional and executive branch players and policies related to Cuba, much more so than most Americans. Of course, for Cuba, U.S. policies remain of paramount importance, whereas in the States Cuba is barely a blip on the diplomatic radar screen.

Why is there such an enormous disparity? I think of it as "the beekeepers' syndrome." As you likely are aware, Congress allocates subsidies to producers of various agricultural products. Remarkably, this includes money for beekeepers. Why? This is presumably because a very few members of Congress have in their districts some beekeepers who are passionately interested in government handouts for themselves. And nobody else in Congress gives a hoot. To some degree, U.S. policy toward Cuba follows a similar theme. There are a few members of Congress who are responsive to the hard-liners in the Cuban expatriate community, especially from southern Florida and northern New Jersey. To say that they are passionate about policies toward Cuba would be a massive understatement. And practically nobody else gives a hoot. It is no exaggeration to say that one of this country's most peculiar, longstanding and rigid foreign policies is virtually directed by a handful Cuban exiles who comprise less than 1 percent of the population of the United States. Sort of like the beekeepers deal. I can only hope that diplomats on both sides, presumably professionals with talent and intelligence, are poised to resume a normal dialogue when the opportunity emerges as the political winds shift in both countries.

Forces are afoot that are driving the countries closer to a fruitful dialogue. In the United States, the root of hostile relations rests in the equivalent of a family feud between Cubans-Americans who have fled the island and their countrymen left behind. The early waves of émigrés suffered greatly as their lifestyles shifted from comfortable, or even lavish, to the humblest start of new lives in their adopted land. Leading professionals often found themselves working as gardeners under Miami's hot sun, or in kitchens or office buildings performing menial tasks. Predictably, their anger was vented at the Castro regime that had shown them the door.

As the 20th century moved into the 21st, however, the children and grandchildren of these émigrés transitioned to a different mindset. The early waves of emigrants have ranted for decades about returning to Cuba and recovering their assets. But what if the old family villa is now the site of a hospital? The open issues do not lend themselves to simplistic solutions or rhetorical flourishes. Not surprisingly, the younger generations are more concerned about their heritage than their grandpa's dwelling. A common attitude today embraces reconciliation and an opportunity to visit the land of their family roots. Polls of Cuban-Americans in Florida in 2009 showed they favor a constructive dialogue between Cuba and the United States by a two-to-one margin. Only a handful expressed any desire to relocate to Cuba. After decades of political activism as unalterably and dependably Republican voters, a majority of Cuban-Americans supported Bill Clinton in his presidential campaigns. This shift continued in their support of Barack Obama in the 2008 election, when two-thirds of Hispanic-Americans voted for him.

Signals that change was in the wind came shortly after the Democratic Party recaptured control of Congress in the 2006 elections. Just a month after those elections, 10 members of Congress flew to Havana and began a dialogue with Raul Castro. The visit, which earlier would have aroused the screamers in Miami, received the endorsement of an umbrella group of 12 exile organizations that also called for easing restrictions on remittances and travel to Cuba. Remarkably, the president of the formerly ultra-hard-line CANF was quoted as saying, "This is an extraordinary opportunity for Cubans of different ideologies and positions to try to come up with a peaceful solution."

Presidential candidate Obama got a positive response when he promised in May 2008 that he would immediately allow "unlimited family travel and remittances to the island" by Cuban exiles. That policy change was implemented shortly after he assumed office in January 2009. A further friendly gesture was made in June of 2009, when the United States pulled the plug on the electronic news crawler on the American embassy's facade that the Cubans correctly saw as a purposeful irritation. After the end of those slanted newscasts, down came the 126 Cuban flags that had obscured viewing them.

In some small ways, the U.S. bureaucracy may be creeping ahead of the hard-line politically driven policies that have been the cornerstone of bilateral relations. The expansion of U.S. agricultural exports to Cuba has continued, and Cuba became the third largest export market for American rice in 2006 as the United States became Cuba's fifth largest trading partner overall.

Another interesting example rests with homeland security and enforcement of the provisions of the embargo on travel to Cuba by American citizens. During recent years, a hugely disproportionate number of U.S. Customs inspections, investigations and prosecutions have been directed at travelers to Cuba. Even the process of securing a Specific License for Travel to Cuba was cumbersome, time-consuming and expensive – especially if one engaged a lawyer to handle the process. Responses from the Treasury Department, which oversees the regulations through its Office of Foreign Assets Control, often took many months or longer to be issued. Many applications were simply ignored. Arbitrariness seemed to prevail, and rejections were most common. Oversight did not end there, by any means.

On several occasions, I have identified plainclothes government agents in the departure gates of the flights from Miami to Havana, there to ensure that everyone boarding the flight had an official license. In one case, I know that a fellow was denied boarding because his license did not perfectly conform to minute requirements. And another in which a little delegation of art aficionados was turned back. Others who were unwise enough to be carrying fishing rods and chatting about their (not permitted) fishing plans in Cuba were denied boarding because tourism by U.S. citizens is not permitted by the United States. More remarkably, I have personally encountered U.S. government officials in the departure lounge in Havana presumably listening to folks who might be chatting about their tourism in Cuba (not permitted) or how many cigars they were bringing back (also not permitted).

Virtually every traveler returning from Cuba to Miami was subjected to special scrutiny, an inbound x-ray of their baggage and frequent confiscation of the occasional cigar or bottle of rum. Once when my "special inspector" clearly appeared to be of Cuban origin, he exuded hostility and told me, "We don't like Americans traveling to Cuba, and you'd better not come through here again!" In response to criticism that these practices have resulted in the neglect of potentially greater threats at U.S. borders, the number of Cuba-related penalty cases dropped from 70 percent of the total in the period 2000-2005, to "only" 26 percent during 2006. Enforcement continued to slacken in the years following.

Across the Florida Straits, it appears that Raul Castro is transmitting a more open-minded approach to bilateral relations. Early upon ascending to the position of acting head of state, he publicly noted that a dialogue would be welcome, provided no preconditions were attached. None. Don't tell us how to run our country before we even sit down at the table together, and we will extend the same courtesy to you.

Let us assume that "post-Fidel" political relations between the two nations evolve to a more mutually beneficial level. What can reasonably be expected? Among the early gestures is likely to be a further softening of the travel limits on Cuban expatriates, an easing of the travel ban for U.S. citizens, and a relaxation of the economic embargo with respect to bilateral trade and investment. Eventually, reestablishment of diplomatic relations is in the cards. All this, however, is only the beginning of a journey delayed by a half-century.

Normalization of relations will entail a host of other agenda items. A tricky one will be the handling of criminals who have found refuge in each other's country over the decades. In 2009, an estimated 100 fugitives from the U.S.

justice system, including the notorious swindler Robert Vesco and several Blank Panthers, were finding refuge in Cuba. They are justifiably nervous that they may be used as pawns when the time for rebuilding political relations finally arrives. In response to U.S. criticism that Cuba is harboring criminals and fugitives from justice, Castro has routinely cited the United States for harboring and not arresting fugitives from Cuba, such as Carlos Posada.

More customary matters, such as a postal treaty, aviation relations, an extradition treaty and normalization of complex bilateral economic relations await. Also certain to be on the agenda will be an item of paramount importance to Cuba's ability to regain economic solvency, if not prosperity. That would be a reversal of U.S. policy that has succeeded in methodically excluding Cuba from various international financial institutions, such as the World Bank, the International Monetary Fund, and the Inter-American Development Bank. As a member of those organizations, Cuba would be eligible to access low-interest loans for economic development, as well as other forms of economic assistance. Enabling Cuba to regain its seat in multilateral organizations, from which the United States has overseen its exclusion, would likely be met with less resistance than a normalization of bilateral relations.

Aviation might be a logical and easy place to start. There are currently about 80,000 aircraft overflights of Cuba each year, practically all involving planes to or from the United States or Canada. And the silly facade of having to describe the daily flights between Miami and Havana as *charters* instead of *scheduled* flights could be ended. Not that travelers really need those 90 miles for their frequent traveler programs, but because the simple realities of our bilateral relations should begin to be recognized.

In September of 2009, diplomatic trouble-shooter Governor Bill Richardson of New Mexico returned from a trade mission to Cuba and suggested moving forward on various items, such as a postal treaty and allowing the exchange of scientists and more freedom of travel for each other's diplomats. In the parlance of diplomacy, this may mean that such topics already are under discussion.

Relations between the United States and Cuba have been somewhere between a shambles and non-existent for a half-century. Disneyland had not yet been built and no Super Bowl had ever been played when the absurdity of no diplomacy and a punitive embargo began. The inevitable changes that are coming will be based on our physical proximity, the mutual benefits of economic relations, and the enduring bonds between divided families.

CHAPTER 17

## CUBA ON THE WORLD STAGE

The impact of Fidel Castro's Cuba on the word stage has been raucous and wildly disproportionate to countries of comparable size. For that we can thank the Cold War and the irrepressible energy and ambitions of Castro to leave his mark as one of the world's most famous revolutionaries of the 20th century.

Throughout Cuba's history the country has been a player in the global arena. During her earliest days, she was a link between old Europe and the New World, serving as a vital crossroads for Spanish *conquistadores*. Then came her mercantile links, ranging from tobacco to the slave trade, and centuries of subjugation to colonial Spain and the neocolonial United States and Soviet Union. After the 1959 Revolution, Cuba actively involved herself abroad, including a military presence in more than 25 countries, at least 17 in Africa alone. Her presence included over 400,000 Cuban military and medical personnel overall. She stayed in the spotlight, first with a key role in the Cold War, and then in the worldwide North-South conflicts and competitions. As a result, the Cuban people today seem sharply aware of their global context and knowledgeable about events in obscure places far from Cuba's shores.

Since the Revolution, the U.S. economic embargo and political hostility sought to isolate Cuba from the international mainstream. It was successful economically, but it may have amplified Cuba's global political role. She was elected twice to the status-rich presidency of the Non-Aligned Movement, in 1979 and again in 2006. In 1980, Cuba came close to securing one of the prestigious rotating seats on the Security Council of the United Nations. Only after being beaten back by U.S.-led fulminations during a record 154 rounds of voting was the cherished spot awarded to Mexico instead.

During the past five decades, the political pendulum has swung freely back and forth, and small Cuba brought the planet to the brink of extinction courtesy of a near miss of World War III. Now, in the twilight of the Castro era, some claim there has been a resurgence of the political Left and Castro wannabees, at least in Latin America. Or is that not so?

Hugo Chavez, president of Venezuela, appears to consider himself to be the heir apparent chief mischief-maker in Latin America. His generosity to Cuba and other regional countries has been huge and influential. Following his resounding re-election in December of 2006, Chavez continued railing against the United States: "It's another defeat for the devil, who tries to dominate the world." That hostility may have more than a little to do with the U.S. government's unsubtle support for a failed coup against Chavez in 2002. With the tenacity of a bulldog, he has barged ahead, nationalized key economic sectors, and provided Venezuelan soft loans to developing countries in the region as an alternative to the "meddling" World Bank. In a surprising and embarrassing domestic setback, however, Chavez failed to ram through provisions that would have enabled him to have an unlimited term as president of Venezuela.

The year 2006 saw leftists Rafael Correa in Ecuador, Rafael Noriega in Nicaragua, and former cocoa growers union leader Evo Morales in Bolivia come to power. The example of Bolivia may be instructive. Although Morales moved to nationalize the domestic oil and gas industries, his country lacks the abundance of resources of Venezuela and is unlikely to dissociate itself from private and foreign investment. In the words of one high-level Bolivian official. "It's a mistake to think that Morales is a copy of Chavez." As far as Noriega in Nicaragua, the former firebrand seems to have mellowed and turned away from left-wing meddling in the region.

Should we believe that Latin America reflected a rising tide of podium-pounding anti-American government leaders? Not really. In fact, moderate center-left governments came to power in Brazil, Chile and Peru, while in Columbia and Mexico moderate center-right governments were freely elected. If any Latin American political trend were to be defined, it would be the increase in democratic governments whose focus is on economic growth far more than political agendas.

In an ironic twist to the already muddled politics of Latin America, a June 2009 coup displaced the elected left-leaning president of Honduras, Manuel Zelaya. His ouster elicited predictable outrage from Cuba. And from the United States? President Obama condemned the act as "illegal," surprisingly placing Cuba and the United States on the same side of an issue that, in years past, would have been divisive and possibly incendiary.

Cuba's role in the world has evolved to take into account both obstacles and opportunities. In light of her limited tangible resources, compelling domestic needs, and growing worldwide disdain for armed insurrection, her leaders have charted new courses. What has emerged is a new role that capitalizes on Cuba's intellectual assets while still enabling her to have an active and progressive presence in the global community.

Cuba has asserted itself beyond the political realm to maintain a high profile and good relations, especially among Latin American nations, by sending aid in the form of teachers, construction workers and, above all, medical personnel. Cuba's "medical diplomacy" has been quietly winning hearts and minds since 1963, when about 60 physicians and medical workers were sent to newly independent Algeria. Education, training and direct medical assistance provided by Cuba has benefited many millions of people in an estimated 60 countries, mainly in the Third World. It has proven to be a very effective way to build helpful political relationships while providing a valuable humanitarian service. Of course, this is not comparable in scale to what, for example, the Bill and Melinda Gates Foundation is doing with its seemingly endless billions of dollars. But I find it to be impressive, if not incredible, that Cuba now has one international aid worker for each 450 Cuban citizens, while the United States has one (Peace Corps plus AID workers) for each 40,000 American citizens. That's approaching a ratio of 100-to-1, Cuba over the United States.

What may be Cuba's most remarkable example of responding to global medical needs is her "Children of Chernobyl" project. Since 1986, Cuba has hosted and treated over 18,000 young victims of radiation from the catastrophic meltdown of the Soviet nuclear power plant at Chernobyl. The cost thus far is estimated to be over $300 million, much of it diverted from pressing domestic needs. The time has long passed when Cuba marched to the drumbeat of the Soviet Union. That she continues to provide these treatments, in addition to dispatching medical personnel abroad, sends a strong message of humanitarian empathy as well as being an effective tool of her foreign policy.

Just outside of Havana I have visited the impressive Latin American School of Medical Sciences, a medical school that attracts students from throughout the region (as well as a handful from the United States). As has been elaborated earlier,

Cuba also has utilized its abundance of physicians in a mercantile way, bartering their services for goods needed in the domestic economy. It also has successfully promoted medical tourism, so foreign patients can visit Cuba for world-class surgery and other treatments at bargain basement prices.

In recent years, Cuba has expanded her provision of subsidized medical services to foreigners by providing eye surgery to working-class patients who otherwise would not be able to afford it. In just a few hours, patients have had cataracts removed and new lenses implanted with all expenses paid by the Cuban government, including air transportation, housing, food, treatment and follow-up care. The number of such treatments since 2004 likely has exceeded *one million*. This program, dubbed "Operation Miracle," has garnered huge dividends in terms of international goodwill and favorable publicity. As with most "miracles" provided by the Cuban government, there has been a cost borne by her people. Predictably, human and financial resources devoted to this project have been diverted from meeting the needs of her own citizens. As a result, medical practitioners in Cuba are stretched thin, leaving a reduced quality of care for Cubans themselves. How does that weigh in the balance with hundreds of thousands of people who otherwise would be blind today? I suppose that depends upon whether you are a cured foreign patient or a sick Cuban one.

It is apparent that Cuba's activism on the world stage has shifted from that of promoting armed insurrections and ideological revolutions to that of cheerleader. This change has been driven by financial limitations, a decline in fervor at home, and the reduction in the number of like-minded countries. Former ideological soulmates like China and Vietnam have refocused on domestic priorities. Meanwhile, Cuba has achieved more prominence in multilateral organizations, such as the United Nations and the Non-Aligned Movement. She has hosted a variety of constructive mediation efforts, including the long-standing battle between left-wing Columbian FARC guerilla fighters and the central government, and even made an effort to provide a reality check to Saddam Hussein prior to the invasion of U.S. forces in the Gulf War.

On one occasion I enjoyed lunch at a splendid little restaurant run by Fidel Castro's former personal chef and sat near a table with high-level officials of Cuba, Columbia and guerilla fighters who may or may not have been making progress on their political issues, but they certainly were having an enjoyable meal together. Laughter and free-flowing *cervezas* had replaced the stern countenance that I saw in the newspaper photographs. Another time I recall the spectacle of Cuba hosting a "road show" by the president of Iran, Mahmoud Ahmadinejad, when he was globe-hopping to mobilize support for his country's position on nuclear research and development, in the face of strong U.S. and European opposition.

Cuba's path includes both enlarging her role in multilateral organizations and strengthening bilateral ties. She can be expected to assiduously avoid dependence on any single foreign government. As the saying goes, "Once burned, twice shy." And Cuba has been badly burned *twice*. Self-reliance is an overriding goal. Political and economic links with nearby oil-rich Venezuela have been described earlier. Cuba is sharply aware that relationship, driven by political considerations, could dissolve in a moment. After all, President Hugo Chavez seems to be an anomaly in Latin America, and allies can disappear as rapidly than they emerge.

China is by far the largest growing feature on the worldwide landscape for Cuba. China has already shown a willingness to overlook the foibles of more than a few nasty dictatorships in order to advance her commercial interests. Look no farther than China's failure to use her power to diminish the calamitous conflicts in Darfur and Myanmar as affirmation. More importantly, China seems to be on an ever-growing quest for natural resources the world over. In the words of *The Economist* in March 2008, "From Canada to Indonesia to Kazakhstan, Chinese firms are gobbling up oil, gas, coal and metals, or paying for the right to explore for them, or buying up firms that produce them." It is no coincidence that China's growing presence in Cuba's mining and minerals sector coincided with several thousand wonderful new mass transit buses arriving in Cuba from China. And it has been no small benefit for Cuba that world commodity prices, including nickel, soar from time to time. So as Cuba emerges from the shadows of the world economy, I assume it will be propelled in large measure by key relationships with new commercial allies.

Cuba's historic position as a crossroads in global commerce and an activist in world politics has considerably sensitized the Cuban people to the community of nations. A senior Cuban Foreign Ministry official said to me with a smile, "If you talk to someone on the street he could talk about Pakistan as if he were there last week. We are that kind of people." Her leaders amplify this awareness. Paraphrasing the words of former U.S. Secretary of State Henry Kissinger, "Cuba is a small country with big country policies."

It is clear that Cuba will choose to maintain its momentum and carry forward an active role on the world stage. She has made a run for a rotating seat on the U.N. Security Council and will do so again; she is very anxious to regain her membership in the Organization of American States, and she has demonstrated her presence in a diversity of issues, including biotechnology, health care, battling the scourges of AIDS and cancer, climate change and global warming, alternative fuels, terrorism, drug trafficking, and more that are bold in the headlines today and certainly will continue to be so tomorrow. Logically, Cuba seeks to do so on a level playing field, as a fully respected member of the family of nations. She asks no favors; she accepts no discrimination.

An interesting signal of Cuba's international role in a post-Fidel era may have been transmitted in the spring of 2008. A potentially dangerous confrontation occurred on Columbia's borders with Venezuela to the north, and with Ecuador to the south. Columbia, whose president, Alvaro Uribe, has been a close ally of the United Sates, was sandwiched between two leftist governments closely allied with Cuba. As military forces gathered at the borders, Raul Castro remained silent. And sometimes silence tells more than hours of ranting. Perhaps the half-century of inflammatory Cuban rhetoric and "the enemy of my friend is my enemy" diplomacy has passed.

CHAPTER 18

LOOKING OVER THE HORIZON

Looking in the rearview mirror is far from the best way to size up the road ahead. It may reveal where you have been, but it does precious little to indicate where you are going. Yet this is the mindset of most pundits and observers of Cuba. It presumes that Cuba is a prisoner of its past. But who would say that has been the case with China or Vietnam, both communist countries that have propelled themselves onto the world stage and into the global economy with remarkable skill and speed during recent years?

After rigid adherence to the status quo for decades, Cuba has begun to draw a road map to the future. Possibilities are at last being openly discussed in official offices and on the streets of Havana as well as in the watering holes of Miami and the marbled halls of Washington. Even the most seasoned observers, however, hesitate to predict the future, which is a euphemism for "after Fidel." Their crystal balls are only slightly less cloudy than yours and mine.

Among the most strident of pessimists (or optimists, depending on your viewpoint) there is the school of thought that after Fidel's demise, the "long-suffering masses" will rise up in a tsunami of outrage, will expel the hard-liners, and will sweep into power a democratic form of government. Berlin Wall *redux*. Countering that wistful prospect is the reality that most political and economic dissidents have long since fled the island. Those comparatively few remaining have been rendered ineffective by decades of limitations and harassment, even jail, as described earlier. Also realize that more than 500 years of feudalism, colonialism, corruption and Marxist-Leninism have not created fertile ground for democracy (or the organizations, communications and infrastructure necessary for it to take root and flourish).

What is surprising is not the absence of popular demands for democracy by Cubans, but rather that there are any such impulses at all. Is there an undercurrent, at least, to replace guys named Castro as head of state? For two-thirds of all Cubans, a Castro is the only ruler they've ever had. While some are grouchy about that, most people feeling strongly so have voted with their feet and left the country. The vast majority of those still on the island will happily recite a litany of progress from the Revolution until now. But the path to Cuba's future will be drawn not only in Havana but also in Washington.

During the years of the George W. Bush administration there was a lot of flagrant pandering to the Cuban exile community, especially in Florida. A pre-condition to even opening a dialogue with Cuba was its installation of a democratic form of government. While this position may be effective in garnering votes in Dade County, as a foreign policy position it has been far less than uniformly applied around the globe. It is evident that the United States is well-engaged with governments such as China, Vietnam and even North Korea – none of which could even remotely be described as a democracy. As a member of the Cuban National Assembly pointedly reminded me, "The

United States lost 50,000 dead in Vietnam and only one in Cuba (the pilot of a U-2 spy plane, in October of 1962), yet you have good relations with Vietnam. Explain to me how that makes sense." Of course, it makes no sense at all. But we were both aware that there have not been a million strident Vietnamese expatriates in Miami clamoring for restrictions against their homeland.

Attempts to export democracy to Iraq, even after a hostile government was erased, fail to inspire anyone to apply that model elsewhere. In reality, if democratic values are to prevail in Cuba, which barely exist now, then proponents will need to gird themselves for a long and arduous effort to collaborate with Cuban government officials, courts, legislatures, journalists, political parties and organizations, all of which themselves will be responsible to implement a transition. Democracy is not like a sack of beans that you can just strap on a parachute and drop on Havana, or Baghdad.

And how does it look for a measurable change of attitude emerging from the United States? Since the 1990s, the pivotal Cuban-American voting bloc, especially in southern Florida, swung back and forth between Republican and Democrat based largely on which presidential candidate was tougher on Castro's Cuba. "The bloc" recently seems to have lost much of its political clout as hard-liners fade from the scene, their children and grandchildren are less strident, and other Hispanics, such as Mexicans and Puerto Ricans, diluted the voice of the Cubans. My bet is that the era of U.S. policy toward Cuba being dictated by a handful of Cuban expatriates in Miami is past. For those who favor a more rational and less emotional approach, that's good. New realities have set in, and the shift in focus on the transition in relations likely will move across the Florida Straits to Havana and up the coast to Washington.

Another troubling scenario anticipates a civil war between the entrenched military/bureaucracy/Communist Party and the supposedly great frustrated and repressed masses. First, this assumes a roaring but suppressed level of political activism and discontent, and that is certainly not apparent. Second, there are probably more light weapons in the average donut shop in Wichita than in all the civilian hands in Cuba. The outcome would be predictably bloody and brief. The horrifying notion of a civil war in Cuba seems to be confined to a tiny group of hopelessly vindictive "nostalgistas" in Miami.

Of real importance to the outcome will be the battle-ground of ideas, in which those conservatives devoted to preserving the legacy and the reality of Fidel Castro's path will be pitted against progressives who favor a more pragmatic course. Cuba is a land of subtle signals, especially when it comes to looking over the horizon, so let me illuminate several.

From early on, Fidel himself ordered a taboo on his image being promoted on the island. Not on billboards, posters or T-shirts. No Mao-style cult of personality ever existed. Although he is a continuing presence on Cuban television and in the Communist Party windbag *Granma*, it is *not* as a cult figure, *not* with the reverence of the billions of Chinese decades ago who paid homage to Mao Tse-Tung, or the millions of Vietnamese who so honored Ho Chi Minh. Until *recently*, perhaps. Starting in 2005, pictures of the smiling bearded father of the country were popping up on walls and streetscapes like dandelions magically appearing in the spring. Not with his co-revolutionary Che, not with national hero Jose Marti, and not with Raul. Just smiling Fidel offering various platitudes from posters adorning crumbling walls. Who do you suppose had the authority to reverse an almost five-decade long prohibition of such a promotion? Of course, *only* Fidel.

Among the consequences of Fidel's focus on his legacy is the dynamic tension between what is best for Cuba and what is best for the history books. In the remarkably bold (but private) words of a Cuban official who described the push at the time, "Politics increasingly overrides economic decisions." And some of the Cuban people grow restless. With the Cuban economy chronically on the verge of collapse, Fidel had precious little room to maneuver his personal agenda ahead of the well being of his countrymen. In the cautionary words of John Steinbeck in *The Grapes of Wrath,* "The line between hunger and anger is a thin line."

Also, until recently, it was taboo to even raise the subject of "after Fidel." No longer. Top government officials have been speaking about it on Cuban television, among themselves, and in public. And who do you suppose has allowed for this to happen?

Perhaps Fidel has had a reality check. Certainly, he seeks the preservation of his historic legacy – maybe not an unreasonable goal for one of the revolutionary giants of the 20th century. Yet, with Raul ostensibly in power, Fidel cannot ignore the inevitability of change.

For many years Fidel stacked the deck. He inserted his sycophants into key positions in many government ministries. Nowhere was this more evident than in the Ministry of Foreign Affairs, where Felipe Perez was appointed foreign minister at the age of 34, after serving as Fidel's chief of staff for a decade. He was a capable fellow who ranted well at the United Nations and who could have been a "poster child" of unalterable devotion to Fidel and the ideals of the Revolution. But I keenly recall a scene that may have illustrated Fidel's priorities. During the May 2002 visit of former President Jimmy Carter to Cuba, Fidel and Carter attended a baseball game. Before the game, and to the delight of the crowd, Carter and Castro were tossing a baseball around the infield. And who do you suppose was scurrying around behind Fidel and picking up the muffed throws? No one other than his young foreign minister. Somehow I have difficulty picturing Henry Kissinger shagging errant tosses behind Richard Nixon!

Indeed, loyalty appears to be a trait both strongly admired and abundantly rewarded by Fidel. While there are countless examples, one in particular stands out. Little known is the existence of a huge farm named Rancho Azucarero – about an hour outside of Havana. Rumors abound about what happens there. Are there really specialty foods grown there for Fidel's table? Is there really a herd of yaks to provide yak yogurt for *El Jefé's* breakfast? One item there for sure is an old thoroughbred racetrack, complete with grandstands and amenities. Also to be found on the farm is a stable with the vestiges of Cuba's thoroughbred stock – a handful of fine racehorses. During a visit there, my friends and I actually were allowed to gallop some of the horses for a lap around the oval. Our host injected a politically sensitive comment. "If the U.S. blockade had not prevented us, our thoroughbred breeding program would have been much more successful."

And more to the point, who do you suppose is in charge of this fine farm? Answer: retired Generals Lorenzo and Guillermo Garcia, now over 50 years past the day when these two then-illiterate peasant boys were among the first to help Fidel and his fellow invaders from the yacht Granma find their way to the safety of the mountains. The Garcia brothers served loyally in Cuba's armed forces for over 40 years and have been rewarded with a wonderful homestead and light responsibilities in their retirement.

Unquestioning devotion to the Revolution and personal loyalty to Fidel have been passports to success and future opportunities in Cuba. As mentioned previously, Castro ordered the execution of his close friend General Arnaldo Ochoa possibly because of his fostering the use of illegal drugs in the armed forces. Insiders have maintained, however, that the actual reason was Ochoa's not sufficiently private questioning of some of Fidel's decisions and authority. In Castro's mind that was treasonous. Closer to home, and illustrating the all-encompassing nature of Fidel's demands for loyalty, those who should know claim that Fidel's temporary "exile" of his older brother Ramon into obscurity in the western boondocks of Cuba in 1960 was the direct result of a newspaper article that quoted Ramon making a critical comment about his brother.

Prior to Raul Castro's formal accession to the presidency, there were frequent reminders of the succession plan of the government. Under the Constitution, the president of the Council of State is the head of state, and second to him is the vice president of the Council of State. Conveniently, this was Fidel's younger (by five years) brother Raul, whose day job was minister of Defense. Raul also served as second secretary of Cuba's Communist Party, where he again played second fiddle to his older brother. In the event of incapacity of the president, not surprisingly, the vice president was to assume the top post, and indeed he did. Maybe the deck was stacked with fellows named Castro, but it came as no surprise to anyone that Raul constitutionally succeeded to the presidency of Cuba in early 2008.

Raul was born in 1931 and, like Fidel, he studied at Belen, then Dolores and then at the University of Havana. His classmates remember him as quieter, lower-profile, and less keen-minded than Fidel. In fact, Raul was expelled from Belen by its Jesuit faculty because of his disinterest in studies. While his attention span was short, Raul's memory proved to be long. When he came to power some 30 years after being tossed from Belen, he ordered the school to be closed, and it was converted into a military academy.

From his youth until today, Raul always has been a dim shadow in comparison to the bright beacon of his larger-than-life brother Fidel. He always seemed to follow quietly, with deference and unquestioned loyalty: from home to various schools, to Havana, to Moncada, to jail, to Mexico, to the Granma, to the Revolution, and finally to victory. He only rarely diverged from Fidel's path. Raul was the first of the brothers to meet Che Guevara in Mexico, he embraced communism earlier than Fidel, and he became a capable, even clinical, hands-on executioner of opponents along the way.

Raul led one of the three main military fronts that prevailed during the Revolution, with Che and Fidel in charge of the others. Although he became a communist believer in 1953, when he attended a communist youth congress in Vienna, he is reputed to be more moderate and pragmatic than Fidel, especially when it comes to reforming the Cuban economy. During the depths of the Special Period, when the Cuban economy was in the dumpster, Raul was the leading promoter of independent markets, where hungry Cubans could find food, even if it was more expensive than normal. "Beans have as much importance as cannons, if not more," he said at the time. On another infamous occasion, Raul was on a rural inspection trip in 1994, when he suffered through a speech by a local Communist Party official reciting the many splendid achievements in the area. Raul fidgeted and then lost it. He slammed his fist on the table and hollered, "How come, if we are doing so well, the people complain of hunger?" He then fired the guy on the spot.

Raul headed the military establishment, which, among its other responsibilities, operates many business enterprises, especially in the important tourism sector. It is estimated that the military is responsible for as much as 60 percent of tourist revenues, with virtual invisibility. Countless times I have ridden on the modern tourist coaches with the name *Gaviota* prominently painted on the side. Those beautiful buses have comfortable seats, air conditioning, refrigerators for refreshments, television screens, and even restrooms. They are state of the art, and they certainly display no indication whatsoever that the operator of this company was founded to be in battle, not business. Another time I toured a huge citrus plantation only to learn later that the army of fruit pickers was, *literally*, the army.

Although Raul was devoted, active and passionate about the Revolution, the decades have seen him transition into more of a technocrat and administrator. He had led the military establishment not only in war but also in managing enterprises. As Cuba's best-organized and administered organization, it has performed effectively and is playing a growing role in the domestic economy in running businesses, such as ground transportation, hotel management and airline operations.

Consider the transition of leadership that has been under way, in reality, since Fidel stepped aside in August of 2006. Raul formally took over in February 2008. It is true that Raul seems to have muzzled some of Fidel's more vocal true believers. He has tweaked some government policies more toward pragmatism and away from constant hyperbole about anti-imperialism. He has made it clear that he does not suffer the bureaucracy well. In a statement interpreted as a shot across the bow of the entrenched paper-pushers, Raul warned that his goal is "to reduce the enormous quantity of meetings, co-ordinations, permissions, conciliations, dispositions, regulations, circulars, etc." In others words, let's get some traction because the future rests with well-managed institutions, not with the political legacy of any individual.

Although Raul has not spent even a full day in the United States, he seems to be well-aware that Cuba's future is inextricably linked to rapprochement with its neighbor to the north. His encouragement of public discussion of issues facing Cuba has resulted in some modest critical results, including from artists, intellectuals and students of the University of Havana who, in early 2008, voiced criticism of government limitations on Internet use and stifling foreign and domestic travel restrictions.

Another development to which pundits attach real importance was Raul's indefinite postponement of the Communist Party Congress, scheduled for late 2009 and again delayed after several prior postponements. Raul heads the party that traditionally has played a pivotal role in defining Cuban government policies. It appears that no one, and no organization, is yet ready to articulate the new course for Cuba.

The transition in Cuba, let there be no doubt about it, will be challenging and painful – especially to the entrenched bureaucrats and members of the Communist Party who have enjoyed a somewhat better lifestyle than the average working stiff. One pessimistic senior official said to me, "If you look at history, no country has changed significantly because of the death of a powerful leader," as he cited the examples of Mao, Tito and Ho Chi Minh. "On the other hand," I responded, "changes in leadership sometimes have been followed by remarkable transformations, such as in Eastern Europe, Russia and South Africa."

Once greater personal freedom can reasonably be expected without reprisal, once the free market genie gets out of the bottle, then the momentum for change could become a cascade. How long would that take? It could flow rapidly, as happened in Eastern Europe and Russia. It could unfold incrementally, as in China and Vietnam. Or there might be a delayed reaction, as it could imitate nature, where a pine tree once struck by lightning can take many days to explode into fire. More likely, Cuba will find its own path. Not a clone of other transitions but likely with focus on the economy. Fidel Castro's official biographer, Ignacio Ramonet, has predicted, "The new regime will initiate changes at the economic level, but there will be no Cuban *perestroika* – no opening up of politics, no multiparty elections." Ramonet is clearly in a position to have credible insights. But he failed to specify whether "new regime" was a reference to Raul or to Raul's successor.

Once the conditions that nourish free markets become established, then a liberalized economy can emerge in a remarkably short period of time. You can be certain that American companies are poised to enter the Cuban market. Many such as hotel, marina and golf course developers are said to have negotiated and agreed upon non-binding letters of intent that already are sitting on shelves at the Ministry of Foreign Investment in Havana, awaiting only relaxation of the embargo and signatures. Oil companies are enthusiastic to secure plots for exploration in Cuba's potentially rich offshore fields. Certainly, the United States has great interest in Cuba's estimated 20 billion barrels of oil (more than half of the amount estimated to be from Alaska's North Slope) and 10 trillion cubic feet of natural gas, some as close as 50 miles from the Florida Keys. And American lawyers, as surely as night follows day, are looking forward to mining a mother lode of past legal entanglements and future possibilities. A growing economy will provide not only more and better jobs and higher incomes but also will enable the government to tax such economic growth in order to sustain its commitment to funding social welfare programs.

A preview of anticipation in Cuba was offered late in 2007. The government (read: Raul) responded to the widely held view of workers who were employed by foreign companies in Cuba that they should be allowed to be paid in hard currency. Given the choice between the fluff of a Cuban peso (valued at less than 5 percent of a convertible peso) and the enormous buying power of a U.S. dollar, a Euro or a Cuban convertible peso, not a Cuban on the entire island would opt for the national currency. In all likelihood, the feeble local peso will fade into oblivion after the Cuban economy emerges from its long sleep.

While it is common knowledge that foreign firms do, in fact, slip some hard currency under the table to their workers, legalizing that practice would be a bold step toward a rational system of wages, yet it will tend to undermine the egalitarian nature of wages in Cuba that has prevailed since the Revolution. Such a change risks antagonizing millions of Cubans who would have no such opportunity to secure hard currency. Nevertheless, doling out some desirable currency in this way became legal in 2008, rather a nice concession to the workers, most thought. And then, in a splendid example of the silliness of the Cuban government, it was announced that a substantial tax on such earnings was to be installed. This, mind you, in a country that has had no tax on wages for generations.

So, picture yourself as one of these "lucky" guys laying concrete for a new tourist hotel. Each month you get 20 bucks under the table. Wow, suddenly that becomes legal. Very good! And a minute later the government tells you that new taxes on your legal foreign currency earnings will reduce them by almost half. Very bad! You whip out your new Chinese calculator and start punching buttons. "Let's see, before I was making 20 bucks, and now I'm making 10 bucks. Perhaps this is not such a good thing after all, perhaps this is not progress at all. In fact, I'm moving in reverse at high speed." So the workers gave Raul an earful early in 2008, and the jury is still out as the necessity for change bumps up against the harsh realities that accompany it.

What would be the prospects for the economy of Cuba, assuming the political will and reforms and an end to the economic embargo enable it to progress? All of that is necessary but perhaps still not sufficient. After all, Cuba has a history of nationalizing foreign property, and it has tens of billions in foreign debt that likely will never be repaid. It's a little country with rather few natural resources, but then again so is Switzerland, which thrives. Cuba spends a great amount of money providing free education and free universal health care, but then again so does Denmark, which is prospering and has a very contented population. Cuba has virtually no experience with a free market economy, but neither did China, whose economy is booming. Cuban officials are sharply aware that China's transition to a market driven economy has resulted in a fourfold increase in its GNP in fewer than 15 years. And how about Vietnam, whose economy has surged at a remarkable average annual rate of 7.5 percent during the past decade? In the words of *The Economist*, "Vietnam began to be a success only after its ruling Communists accepted that capitalism, free markets and free trade were the surest route to riches."

How can Cuba's economy rationalize and grow? Like any developing country, its priorities must be to simulate exports, substitute domestic production for imports, advance technologically, and secure an infusion of foreign capital in the form of loans and investments.

What would be the incentive for foreign governments and companies to seek out economic opportunities in Cuba? With the acquiescence of the U.S. government, other governments, firms and international trade and financial institutions may rush to get aboard.

Private companies will be enticed by a variety of factors: Cuba is a market of some 11 million folks, not an insignificant opportunity for most firms; some will be drawn to preempt the presence of a competitor, and many will be attracted by the highly educated work force in Cuba. No, it is not likely to be a destination for those needing cheap labor to perform low-tech repetitive piecework. More likely will be the appeal of a labor force that is now low paid and brimming with underutilized engineers, scientists and technology people. More likely a call center for a computer company than a shoe factory; more likely a research and development complex than a garment assembly plant.

Of further importance is the reality that the Cuban economy has weathered the worst of the storm, and it has been rebounding in recent years. Many factors have come into play, including the intermittent soaring price of her nickel exports, hefty growth in her export of biotechnology and pharmaceutical products, an increase in tourism revenues, and significant growth in her export of medical services. By 2006, more than half of Cuba's GNP was attributed to the services sector, which is an auspicious sign for a developing economy. Assuming official government statistics have some bearing on reality, Cuba claims that its GNP growth was in the range of 12 percent in 2005 and again in 2006. In recent years, that rate has slowed because of declining commodity prices, global economic malaise, and the terrible impact of hurricane damage on the island in 2008. Estimates for 2009 were for one percent growth, and projections for 2010 are only slightly better.

In reality, one cannot expect momentous changes while Fidel's presence is still strong. In August of 2009, he was lively and chatty in a television appearance. Although he has emitted signals that he recognizes his mortality and the need for new people to assume leadership, he also has cited the example of a famous Brazilian architect who remained active and productive at the age of 100. It is clear that Fidel remains very much in charge. As if that needed any clarification or amplification, Fidel sent a subtle signal in January of 2008 by continuing to stand for re-election in his home district, which is a prerequisite for remaining as head of state. The contrary signal, not given, would have been for him to *not* stand for re-election, which would have resulted in Raul being regarded as the new guy fully in charge. At risk of reading too much into the election results, it seems significant that the results showed Fidel garnering *merely* 98.4 percent, while Raul's victory came with 99.4 percent of the votes in his district. Not that either seems to have been at much risk of losing, but that Raul's percentage of victory was slightly higher than that of his older brother could be one of those miniscule but huge political signals that cause Cuba wonks to salivate.

The newly elected National Assembly met on February 24, 2008, and elected a new Council of State, the selected president of which holds the position of head of state in Cuba. Four days earlier Fidel Castro announced that he did not wish to hold that position any longer, effectively resigning as president and commander in chief after 49 years in power. Significantly, for a transitional period he maintained his position as head of the Communist Party of Cuba.

How did Fidel plan to spend his retirement? "My only wish is to fight as a soldier in the battle of ideas," he said. No, not likely that this guy will spend his days exercising his dog in the park or mall-walking. While Fidel's resignation came as a mild surprise, the real melodrama was to unfold a few days later, when the National Assembly formally anointed Raul as president. As weeks turned to months, the errors of the Miami exile community's predictions became clear. Words such as those of the father of hard-line Florida Congressman Mario Diaz-Balart, who said, "When Fidel Castro goes, this regime will disintegrate like a sugar cube dropped in a glass of water," could only be described as delusional wishful thinking.

At the same time as Raul's election, and much more importantly, the Council of State had to reveal Raul's replacement as first vice president. For that would indicate a great deal about the future course of Cuba.

To the surprise of many, the selected vice president to Raul was Jose Ramon Machado, then age 77, known mainly as a Communist Party ideologue of the old school. He is a member of the Politburo and unquestionably cast in the same mold as Fidel. To most he appears to be another recycled revolutionary, chosen at a time when the need for a signal of forward-looking pragmatism seemed urgent to many. The reaction in Cuba as well as abroad was shock and dismay, characterized by the choreographer Fidel a few days later as "the howls of the wolves."

Machado's selection may not be an indication, however, of a retro outlook by the next generation of leaders. More likely it can be interpreted to mean that the "powers that be" are not yet ready – and may not be ready while Fidel is alive – to embrace a future with leaders showing less revolutionary zeal. Significantly, some other vice presidents elected included reform-minded officials who are only in their 50s or 60s.

A more significant appointment, this one by Raul in early 2008, was Jorge Bolanos as Cuba's top diplomat in Washington. Bolanos was a top official in the Foreign Ministry who has served as ambassador to England and Mexico, two of Cuba's most important relationships.

Another revelation of particular interest, and one that speaks to the future direction of the country, was the selection of a new minister of Defense to replace Raul Castro. Instead of a distinguished military leader, the choice was General Julio Casas, whose forte clearly has been established in management of commercial enterprises. "He's more a businessman than a soldier," said one observer. Most of Cuba's modest 55,000-person military establishment already is involved in the civilian economy, from picking grapefruit to running airlines. In 2009, it was estimated that the Defense Ministry employed one out of five government workers, is responsible for almost two-thirds of tourism revenues, and manages as much as 90 percent of Cuba's exports. Casas' selection was a clear signal of priorities, of business over battle.

The reaction to Fidel's relinquishing his formal office to Raul was a gigantic yawn. No one believed that his role would diminish. No one believed that Raul would initiate or tolerate any meaningful degree of change at home or abroad while Fidel was still looking over his shoulder. Brother Fidel attempted to dispel such well-founded notions by denying that he would continue to run the show, stating in one of his periodic essays published in *Granma* that Raul, as the newly-elected president, would have "all legal and constitutional faculties and prerogatives" of the office. Sure, and I also believe in the tooth fairy. It was interesting to see, however, that in the worldwide media coverage of Raul's formal election to the presidency, he was dressed in a dark business suit, not in his usual military uniform. Yes, he seemed to be taking a page from Fidel's playbook and was sending a subtle signal to those who are mindful of them.

Even in Miami, where mere rumors of Castro's death had launched huge raucous street parties, no one seemed to care. The typical reaction there, as well as in Washington, was, "A transition makes sense because he is sick, but nothing will change." Indeed, the Bush administration once again failed to seize a moment that was ripe for an overture of goodwill, and it responded with the customary demand for free elections.

Nonetheless, the event will be long heralded in the history books. Just a year shy of a half-century as the ruler of Cuba, no head of state in the world had ever served longer, nor likely ever will, than Fidel Castro.

While some speculate that Raul will not be inclined to relinquish his succession to the presidency of Cuba, others believe he will serve only transitionally. He could be, in reality, the last of the revolutionaries, and he is a distant second to his brother in the departments of charisma, leadership and renown. However, he who controls the tanks is someone to be reckoned with in any country. For a variety of reasons, in the words of Cuba expert Ann Louise Bardach, "It was very foolish of the Bush administration to refer to Raul as 'Fidel lite.' But never underestimate the stupidity of anyone in Washington vis-à-vis Cuba."

Let us suppose that Raul decides to opt for early retirement a year or so after Fidel passes, when a "next generation" leader emerges, almost certainly from the Council of State. Rumor has it that he doesn't hanker for the top job, that approaching 80 years old he has in mind a mellow retirement rather than running a struggling country. It is said that he savors time with his family and dotes on his four children and eight grandchildren. In 2007, his wife of 48 years, Vilma Espin, passed away. She had been the most prominent and powerful woman in Cuba since the Revolution, where she had fought alongside the rebels in the Sierra Maestra mountains. Understandably, that loss seems to have further trimmed some of Raul's energy and enthusiasm. Add to that the daunting task of following in the gigantic footsteps of brother Fidel, who no doubt will leave a turbulent wake behind him, and you can easily imagine the temptations of a simpler life.

So perhaps Raul will opt for life without a security detail always underfoot, without a cell phone always in his ear, and without starting a sixth decade of playing Sisyphus, the character in Greek mythology who was destined to spend eternity rolling a boulder uphill, only for it to always roll back down when it reached the top of the hill. Sounds pretty good.

What can we expect? Well, the good news is that those 31 members of the Council of State include a high percentage of well-educated, street-smart veteran bureaucrats. Not revolutionaries. Just a few of them lugged rifles around the Sierra Maestra mountains. Most of them know administration better than armaments, bureaucracy better than ballistics. They spend their days shuffling papers, not returning phone calls, and being way too busy – just like other senior government officials around the world. Most of them have been posted in foreign countries for years and are attuned to the great rhythms of history. It is true and understandable that none of them has been known to murmur so much as a syllable of dissent from the policies of *El Jefé*. But then again, how often do you recall a U.S. Cabinet member slamming the president whom they are serving?

It is clear that, after Fidel, change will be in the wind. A senior government official confided to me, "Our political system depends very much on Fidel Castro, and when he's gone things will have to change and the system must work differently. Fidel and Raul realize that their style of leadership is passing. It is necessary to have adjustments in our economic and social policies." No longer heresy; reality is afoot in Havana.

And who might be among the possible successors to the Castros? Ricardo Alarcon, the president of the National Assembly, has been close to Castro for decades, served as foreign minister and as Cuba's ambassador to the United Nations, and certainly is among the contenders. His penetrating understanding of the Cuba-U.S. dynamic was illustrated by his humorous quip in 2006, shortly after Fidel Castro stepped aside in favor of Raul. When asked about the whereabouts of Raul, who had not immediately appeared in public, Alarcon responded. "He's in Havana. Where is Mr. Cheney now?" alluding to the American vice president's periodic disappearances to "undisclosed locations."

Carlos Lage, a recent vice president and executive secretary of the Council of Ministers, who oversaw some unprecedented economic reforms during the 1990s, is another insider who has the poise, savvy and experience necessary for the top job. Although he fell from political grace in Havana when Raul cleaned house, I wouldn't rule out his resurrection. Lage has a keen understanding of modern economies and recently stated, "Cuba has a mixed economy . . . with space for foreign investment and self-employed people." Predictably, there are numerous other long shots and dark horses among the contenders.

Consider some of the paths that communist governments have followed in recent times. After the demise of the Soviet Union in 1990, Russia and the former provinces and satellites were overwhelmed by the transition to new forms of governance and economic systems. Russia chose to liberalize the political system, and one of the results was that the wheels came off, both in the political realm and in the economy. Chaos reigned, and it had not entirely subsided more than a decade later.

On the other hand, consider the Chinese model. Transition away from the original revolutionaries; maintain tight (even brutal) central political control, and allow the economy to liberalize and it surges and flourishes. Oversimplified perhaps, but which of the two alternative models would seem to be more appealing to a successor government in Cuba? A senior Foreign Ministry official commented to me, "I wouldn't dismiss the possibility of changes similar to those that happened in China, including a possibility of economic interdependence with the United States." As Cuba has shown its willingness to cozy up to China for a variety of economic and geopolitical reasons, it is even more logical for Cuba to strive for a balanced and mutually beneficial relationship with the colossus of the nearby north. Dependence on a single foreign power is, in Cuba, the moral equivalent of a four-letter word.

Cuban officials are finding no shortage of models for economic growth in the context of a strong central government. Even Singapore's experience may be instructive, with a booming economy and a government that few would confuse with a democracy. An array of possibilities awaits and, it likely that Cuba will find a hybrid path to follow.

Although Cuban officialdom could, by no means, be described as a group of "closet capitalists," it is true that for many years students have been sent to universities in the West to learn about market economics. Even the University of Havana has courses in capitalism. Does this mean Cuba is getting to "know thine enemy" better or preparing for change in its socialist economy? I bet on the latter.

A key element of a more progressive economy, one that could dependably raise the standard of living of many Cubans, would be to relax restrictions on small-scale private enterprises without crippling them with confiscatory taxes. To some degree, this would merely recognize an existing reality. While there were perhaps 130,000 licensed, legal little private enterprises in 2008, at the same time there were an estimated *double* that amount of illegal businesses. Thus, an initial step would be to simply grasp reality and gently tax it! Score one for the government! To the extent liberalization allowed for additional such enterprises, it would enable hundreds of thousands of Cubans who struggle on miserable government salaries to increase their income by tenfold or even many times more. One fellow who formerly sold handicrafts in a government store said to me, "After I quit and began making and selling handicrafts on my own, my income rose by 20 times." Score one for the people!

Does such change mean that Havana's splendid Capitolio will again function as a legislature instead of a museum and ministry offices? No, don't hold your breath till that happens. I expect to see continuing tight political controls, a dominant Communist Party, and highly centralized management of the social systems. While speeches about the need for democratic government in Cuba continue to fan the political flames in the United States, that outcome is unlikely and maybe even undesirable. In the words of one Cuban official, "It is much easier to have a democracy when you are in the developed world than when you are in the Third World." Sadly, democracy is seen by many as a luxury item that most poor countries simply cannot afford to place ahead of improving standards of living of their people.

For the aspirations of the Cuban people to be realized, it is essential to have a major overhaul of the economy. That calls for serious organized efforts to facilitate an orderly transition. Would you want even the U.S. Congress, with its countless committees, lobbyists, earmarks, parochial interests, insufferable delays and pork barrel spending to be responsible for such a sweeping sort of change in the United States? Don't misunderstand me, I am a true believer in democracy. Winston Churchill said it best: "Democracy is the worst form of government, except for all those other forms that have been tried." Let the public debate grow. Allow for some flexibility and free choice. Unleash those with entrepreneurial drive to prosper. More importantly, if the marketplace is unshackled, if entrepreneurs can seek out opportunities beyond the current bicycle tire repair shops and a handful of tiny restaurants, then the Cuban government will be taking its first real steps toward prosperity and meeting the needs of its people.

Let us assume the next government actually assumed control in July of 2006, when Fidel relinquished the hot seat to brother Raul. Surprising changes started to be visible after only weeks. When asked about his plans, in an enticing hint about his outlook, Raul responded, "He who imitates, fails."

Consistent with Raul's empathy for the Cuban people, public works projects began to be more common. Road repairs were noticeably increased; planting along highways gained pace; some public buildings were sporting new coats of paint, and water began to flow in public fountains that had been dry for years. Raul verbally spanked inefficient managers of state enterprises and bureaucracies, and he suggested that many of Cuba's problems were self-inflicted and not always to be blamed on foreign bogeymen.

Other steps planned by Raul included distributing idle land to farmers, permitting the import of parts for Cuba's antiquated automobile inventory, and allowing Cubans to own consumer items, such as microwave ovens, DVD players, cellular phones and even energy-gulping air conditioners. He also publicly acknowledged that the salaries of Cuban workers are inadequate and should be increased, noting the important distinction between egalitarianism and exact equality. While all of the tweaking of government policies was welcome news to the Cuban people, many remained skeptical. "All Raul is doing is giving back a few of the rights that they took away from us in the 80s,"one hotel executive told me. And changes, such as allowing Cubans to enter and use tourist hotels, were greeted more with disdain than with welcome, as people whose average monthly wage is under $20 are not likely to be able to book hotel rooms that commonly cost $100 to $200 per night. How many among us would chose to spend five to 10 months of wages for a single night in a local hotel?

Cuba is a land where such subtle changes and encouraging comments have significant meaning. More importantly, some of the zealous young officials who Fidel had inserted into high-level government positions began to fade from view. Some were fired and many were muzzled. It remains to be seen if Raul's rumored inclination toward small-scale free enterprise will come to pass. It will be a conspicuous surprise and disappointment if the trend to stamp out the few vestiges of individual economic freedom will continue as it has since 2002, when the government began a campaign to reduce permitted independent businesses.

Choices will have to be made, and the entrenched bureaucrats in Havana are abundantly smart to see the alternative paths and choose ones that most likely would lead to stability and a rising standard of living for their people. Does "staying the course" and seeing Cuba become a clone of North Korea really have wide appeal, even in Havana? Not. Should one anticipate a surge toward democracy and a free market economy? Not. There will have to be trade-offs between liberalization of the economy and continuing political controls. Cuban officials are keenly aware of the sharp contrast between the country's increasingly efficient and modern international business sector and the inefficiencies, shortages and deprivation that characterize the domestic economy.

Let us hope and assume that neither the American nor the Cuban people would find chaos in Cuba after Fidel to be an appealing option. It need not be, nor does it seem likely. In March of 2007 the U.S. Coast Guard conducted a highly publicized exercise off Miami and in the Florida Straits. It was designed to practice interdiction of at least 95 percent of any mischief-makers in boats headed north or south. In a splendid irony of the day, two boatloads of Cuban illegal émigrés landed safely in Miami smack dab in the middle of the interdiction exercise.

I conclude that U.S.-Cuba relations are likely to take a turn for the better in the post-Fidel era, amplified by the new policies of the Obama administration. Not a headlong rush into each other's arms, but a step-by-step rapprochement may be in the wind. It will be tempered by a half-century of mistrust, powerful anti-Cuban politicians and lobbies in the States, and some hard-liners with clout in Havana. Also of growing consequence will be the reality of Cuba's improving relations with China and Venezuela. Both have the cash and the political inclination to be allied with Cuba. Both enable Cuba to enjoy a broader range of possibilities with less dependence on the politically charged policies of the United States. With Venezuela's subsidized oil (allowing Cuba 100,000 barrels per day at deeply concessional prices and terms), and China's investment in key economic sectors (most notably in nickel mining and refining), and Brazil's growing investments, Cuba will be able to afford the luxury of making careful decisions rooted in her national interests and goals.

And how has Cuba defined her goals, in the critically important area of normalizing relations with the United States? A top Foreign Ministry official summed them up for me this way: "We are ready to start a dialogue at any time, but there must be no preconditions. Cuba will not demand that you change your system of government before talks begin, and you should not demand that we do that either. We have three simple goals: first, respect our sovereignty and recognize that our national self-determination must be preserved – we reject demands that anyone but Cuba alone will decide its type of government or economy; second, Cuba should be able to participate in an open world economy, without discrimination of any sort, and third, we wish to participate in a truly multilateral global system, without preferences or penalties to any country." In other words, big boy, lose the embargo and quit isolating us. While the political dynamics certainly are evolving to allow for an easing of the embargo, there will be other factors coming into play.

Consider, for example, the huge adverse impact that an end to travel restrictions would have on tourism to Florida, Puerto Rico and the Caribbean. At least in the early years of permitted tourism to Cuba, how many millions of Americans will choose to sample Cuba's mystique and low prices? Cuba's Ministry of Tourism projects two million in the first year alone. Another business sector that cannot be ignored and stands to be profoundly disrupted could be the Florida citrus industry. Cuba overflows with oranges and grapefruit now mainly destined for Europe and the Far East. But the temptation to ship them just across the Florida Straits, instead of across the width of the Atlantic or Pacific Ocean, will be great.

Cuba has a long tradition of participating in the community of nations, going all the way back to its role as a rendezvous point for the Spanish fleets that carried gold from the New World back to Spain. Cuba was an original member of the United Nations and the World Trade Organization. Of course, this tradition was radically disrupted by the U.S. economic embargo. A Cuban economist said to me, "Our national identity has always included involvement with other countries and we cannot live without fair relations with the outside world."

Implicit in these goals is an end to the economic embargo of Cuba. That will give her long-troubled economy traction in critical areas, such as imports and exports with the United States, access to capital and technology, more foreign investment and accelerating exploration for oil. Moving in these directions would not be solely to the benefit of Cuba. Trade and investment flows are premised on mutual benefit. It is estimated that the U.S. embargo of Cuba costs American manufacturers and farmers in excess of $20 billion per year, along with the loss of hundreds of thousands of jobs. So when the embargo ends it can be expected that the American economy also will be a beneficiary.

The future outlook for Cuba is, for the most part, in the hands of the Cubans. But by no means entirely. During 2005, the Bush administration made a fuss over its establishment of a transition team in the State Department, tasked with defining a path toward normalization of relations with Cuba. In reaction to this presumptuousness, the president of the Organization of the American States, Jose Miguel Insulza, scolded, "There is no transition, and it's not your country." To no one's surprise, the policy review was merely some window dressing, the real purpose of which was to articulate, once again, the failed policies of the conservatives that have defined American policy toward Cuba for a half-century.

As the past 500 years have abundantly shown, Cuba's future rests, to a large degree, in the hands of other nations, none more than the United States. The lament of a 19th century Mexican dictator comes to mind when he described his country as "so far from God and so close to the United States." But this lemon can be turned in to lemonade. The conditions that shape U.S. policy toward Cuba are evolving, albeit slowly. The tiny but passionate group of Cuban exiles who have traditionally driven hostile American policies has been mellowing. American business interests have experienced a taste of the opportunities on the island, and enthusiasm is growing. The political dynamic in Washington has changed enormously. Democrats have secured not only a stronger position in the Congress, which must act to change many of the limiting measures targeted against Cuba, but they also have the executive powers and the bully pulpit of the White House.

I foresee a softening of the positions on both sides of the Florida Straits. In the words of Wayne Smith, formerly our top diplomat in Havana, "Our present policy is an impediment to Cuba moving in the direction we'd like to see it take. Cautious engagement would work far better." Such engagement likely will be in incremental steps toward normalization. It has begun with relaxing the restrictions on travel and remittances to Cuba by Cuban-Americans. Clamor for an end to all travel limits, an objectionable feature that most Americans want removed, dates at least as far back as 1963, when then-Attorney General Robert F. Kennedy wrote, "Removing present restrictions on travel to Cuba is more consistent with our views of a free society." The beginning of the end to those limits likely will take the form of permission for cruise ships with Americans on board to visit Havana and the resumption of scheduled direct air service between the countries. Assuming this test drive is successful, a series of minor agreements likely will be negotiated between the governments, and U.S. companies will see fewer restrictions from Washington as they press forward in Cuba. Looking further over the horizon, I expect elimination of U.S. travel restrictions for tourism in Cuba. If this scenario does indeed unfold, momentum and inertia will drive normalization even further.

Among the thornier and politically sensitive issues will be the resolution of claims by individuals and companies whose property was nationalized in the early years following the Revolution. Interestingly, Cuba has long since resolved all other such claims from around the world. In the case of the United States, however, Cuba maintains that the cost of the economic blockade during the past half-century is now approaching $100 billion, which should be counted to offset U.S. claims. I do not predict a quick or easy resolution of this conundrum.

Primitive tribes apparently believed the crowing of the rooster caused the sun to rise. In a modern parallel, some politically active "tribes" in Washington, Miami and Havana have believed their crowing will cause the rise of various new regimes in Cuba. All of them have it backwards. Fundamental global political and economic forces are in play. With a new administration in Washington, mellowing of the stridency from Miami, and the passing of Fidel in Cuba, the sun will rise on Cuba rejoining the community of nations. And one of the most bizarre and tragic episodes in American and Cuban diplomatic history will give way to progress and the renewal of dreams that have been lost.

The End

# CUBA RISING

# ABOUT THE AUTHOR

Jonathan Showe has traveled to Cuba more than 70 times during the past 12 years, ranking him among America's most frequent visitors to the "forbidden" island. One of her cabinet ministers was recently overhead exclaiming, "How the hell does this guy Showe keep getting to Cuba?" Persistence, tenacity, curiosity – and some modest irreverence for U.S. travel restrictions would be the answer.

Showe's awakening to international geopolitics emerged during his Grinnell College years, when he served as a foreign stringer for his hometown suburban Pittsburgh newspaper and earned membership in the Society of Professional Journalists. His skills as an observer took shape while earning a master's in international relations from the Johns Hopkins University School of Advanced International Studies, located in Washington. That two-year program was interrupted by military service, including a tour of duty with the U.S. Army in Vietnam, where he was awarded the Bronze Star.

After he received his master's, Showe joined the Nixon, then Ford White House, where he was involved in the nation's foreign economic policy and its international trade negotiations.

His skills both as an analyst and writer were sharply honed as materials emerging from his desk found their way to foreign and domestic leaders. These included position papers, speeches and other writings. Subsequent years of work at a leading U.S. multinational corporation involved further analysis and presentations to international businesspeople and shapers of foreign policy.

Showe transitioned from big government and big business into heading a smaller firm and membership in the global Young Presidents' Organization. During those years, his travels grew to include more than 60 countries, and his skills as an international observer, commentator and cross-cultural ambassador continued to grow. Periodic guest lectures at various colleges and universities have been greeted as insightful.

Since 1998 Showe's principal activity has involved Cuba – trying to understand that enigmatic place by visiting there *frequently*. Enigmatic because it is much more than a place; indeed, it is a state of mind. With the skills of observation accumulated and sharpened during a career of 40 years in the international realm, Showe has a keen ability to weave disparate threads into a fabric of clarity and understanding.

# TIMELINE OF CUBAN HISTORY

## Colonial Cuba

1492 – Christopher Columbus claims Cuba for Spain
1511 – Spanish settlement in Baracoa
1514 – Havana founded
1527 – African slaves arrive in Cuba
1597 – El Morro Castle built at entrance to Havana harbor
1728 – University of Havana is founded
1762 – Havana is captured by British troops.
1763 – British return Cuba to Spain in exchange for Florida
1868-1878 – First war for Cuban independence
1886 – Slavery abolished in Cuba
1895-1898 – War of independence, led by Jose Marti, who is
    killed in battle in 1895
1898 – U.S. wins Spanish-American War and gains
    sovereignty over Cuba from Spain

## Republican Cuba

1902 – Cuba granted independence from U.S., but Platt
    Amendment preserves U.S. right to intervene; U.S.
    also secures military base at Guantanamo Bay

1926 – Fidel Castro Ruz is born
1928 – Ernesto (Che) Guevara is born in Argentina
1931 – Raul Castro is born
1933 – Elected President Machado is overthrown in coup by Fulgencio Batista
1944 – Batista retires from presidency
1952 – Batista retakes presidency in a *coup d'etat*
1953 – Castro leads failed military attack on Moncada barracks, is captured and jailed
1955 – Castro and his brother Raul are released from prison and go to Mexico, where they meet Guevara
1956 – Castro leads 82 revolutionaries and returns to Cuba
1958 – U.S. halts military aid to Batista government; revolutionaries continue victories in countryside and provincial capitals

Revolutionary Cuba

1959 – Batista flees (December 31, 1958), and Castro's revolution is victorious; radical agrarian reform is launched
1960 – U.S. companies in Cuba are nationalized; U.S. breaks diplomatic relations and starts economic embargo of Cuba
1961 – U.S.-sponsored invasion of Cuba at Bay of Pigs is defeated
1962 – (October) U.S. discovers Soviet missiles in Cuba, leading to Cuban Missile Crisis
1965 – Cuban Communist Party becomes sole political party in Cuba
1967 – Guevara is captured and executed in Bolivia
1972 – Cuba joins Comecon (Soviet economic bloc)
1976 – Cuba sends troops to Angola
1980 – 125,000 Cubans flee to U.S. (Mariel Boatlift)
1983 – U.S. and Cuban troops clash in Grenada

# CUBA RISING

1988 – Cuba withdraws troops from Angola, followed soon by its withdrawal from Ethiopia

1991 – Cuban economy collapses as Soviets end economic assistance and leave Cuba

1993 – Cuba allows some foreign investment

1994 – U.S. agrees to admit 20,000 Cubans per year

1996 – Cuba shoots down two U.S. civilian aircraft; U.S. tightens embargo

1998 – Pope John Paul II visits Cuba, which eases restrictions on religion in Cuba

1999 – Elian Gonzalez is rescued in Straits of Florida

2000 – U.S. allows sale of food and medicine to Cuba

2002 – Former President Jimmy Carter visits Cuba

2003 – Cuba continues crackdown on dissidents and writers

2004 – U.S. restricts visits to Cuba by Cuban-Americans and bans transactions in U.S. dollars

2006 (July) – Castro undergoes gastric surgery and Raul Castro assumes presidential duties

2007 – Castro fails to appear at May Day and Revolution Day celebrations

2008 (February) – Raul Castro assumes presidency after Fidel announces his retirement

2008 (summer) – Cuban government announces various economic reforms

2008 (November) – Barack Obama elected president of U.S., shocking Cuban government; presidents of Russia and China visit Havana

2009 (March) – Top Fidel-selected leaders are shuffled out of power; U.S. relaxes restrictions on Cuban-American visits and remittances to Cuba

2009 (July) – U.S. mission in Havana shuts down controversial electronic news crawler on facade of its building; dialogue between U.S. and Cuba grows

2009 (October) – United Nations opposes U.S. embargo in vote of 187 to 3.